NEW TESTAMENT ESCHATOLOGY
IN AN AFRICAN BACKGROUND

NEW TESTAMENT ESCHATOLOGY IN AN AFRICAN BACKGROUND

A Study of the Encounter between New Testament Theology and African Traditional Concepts

BY

JOHN S. MBITI

PROFESSOR OF THEOLOGY AND COMPARATIVE RELIGION,
MAKERERE UNIVERSITY COLLEGE, UGANDA

OXFORD UNIVERSITY PRESS

1971

Oxford University Press, Ely House, London W.1

GLASGOW NEW YORK TORONTO MELBOURNE WELLINGTON
CAPE TOWN SALISBURY IBADAN NAIROBI DAR ES SALAAM LUSAKA ADDIS ABABA
BOMBAY CALCUTTA MADRAS KARACHI LAHORE DACCA
KUALA LUMPUR SINGAPORE HONG KONG TOKYO

PRINTED IN GREAT BRITAIN BY
WILLIAM CLOWES AND SONS LIMITED
LONDON, COLCHESTER AND BECCLES

PREFACE

THE substance of this book was submitted as a Ph.D. dissertation in the University of Cambridge in 1963. For publication purposes, I have made changes and modifications; for example, I have broadened the scope of the work, though omitting here what was originally included as the practical aspects of evangelization arising from this study.

I wish to acknowledge my deep gratitude to the following: the members of the Saratoga Federated Church, Saratoga, California, who generously made it financially possible for me to undertake the research; the Reverend Canon Dr. C. F. D. Moule, the Lady Margaret's Professor of Divinity at Cambridge University, for his scholarly guidance and supervision and for the warm friendship which he lavished upon me then and long after I left Cambridge; Mr. G. I. Jones, then Lecturer in the Faculty of Archaeology and Anthropology at Cambridge, for his advice on the anthropological aspects of my study; the Right Reverend Dr. Lesslie Newbigin who originally established the contact between the Saratoga Federated Church and myself, and followed my endeavours with great interest; my parents for their love and home where as a child, I learnt and 'began to call upon the Lord' and read the Kikamba New Testament; Mrs. M. Nicol, my secretary who, with great care and efficiency, typed the MS for the press, often bringing to my attention important items which in the draft were either not clear or in error; and finally, missionaries of the Africa Inland Mission, and Akamba evangelists who, through their sacrifice and labours, have made it possible for a thriving Church to exist in Ukambani which, among other things, forms part of the subject of this study. All these duly deserve my affectionate appreciation, but they are in no way responsible for any errors, omissions, heresies and deficiencies which may be present in this work.

In *African Religions and Philosophy* (Heinemann Educational Books, London 1969), I have discussed the African concept of time in the context of traditional religions. Since the study of Eschatology in the present work involves a consideration of time, there is a certain amount of overlapping in the two books concerning the basic thesis about time. The purposes are, however, completely different; and while the views do not contradict each other, they are developed differently. Time is discussed here in its bearing on a Christian understanding of Eschatology. I am grateful to both publishers for allowing me to discuss the notion of time in both books. In another separate work, *Concepts of God in Africa* (S.P.C.K., London 1970), I have given full information about God, spirits, and man according to traditional African beliefs. That book too serves quite a different purpose from the present one, but it is inevitable that a small proportion of the basic material is repeated and I am grateful to the Society for Promoting Christian Knowledge for their permission to use this material.

JOHN MBITI

CONTENTS

CONTENTS

ABBREVIATIONS

Adver. Haer.	Irenaeus' Adversus omnes Haereses
AFER	*African Ecclesiastical Review*
A.I.C.	Africa Inland Church
A.I.M.	Africa Inland Mission
Am.	Amos
Apol.	Justin's Apology
Aram.	Aramaic
Bar.	Baruch (II Bar.: Syriac Baruch; III Bar.: Greek Baruch)
Barn.	Barnabas (Epistle of)
BDB	Brown, F., Driver, S. R., Briggs, C. A., *Hebrew and English Lexicon of the Old Testament.*
Bel	Bel and the Dragon
BJRL	*Bulletin of John Rylands Library*
Cant.	Canticles
CD	the Damascus Document or Zadokite Fragment
cf.	confer (compare)
Chron.	Chronicles
Clem.	Clement
C.M.S.	Church Missionary Society
Col.	Colossians
col.	column
Cor.	Corinthians
Dan.	Daniel
Deut.	Deuteronomy
Dial. Try.	Justin's Dialogue with Trypho
Did.	Didache
Eccl.	Ecclesiastes
Ecclus.	Ecclesiasticus
En.	Enoch (I: Ethiopic; II: Slavonic)
Eph.	Ephesians
Esd.	Esdras
esp.	especially
Est.	Esther
ET	English Translation
Ex.	Exodus
Ex T	*Expository Times*
Ezek.	Ezekiel
Gal.	Galatians
Gen.	Genesis

Germ.	German
Gk.	Greek
Gk. Bar.	Greek Baruch (or III Bar.)
Gk.-Eng. Lex.	*A Greek-English Lexicon of the New Testament* . . . by W. Bauer, ET by W. F. Arndt and F. W. Gingrich (1957)
Hab.	Habakkuk
Hag.	Haggai
Heb.	Hebrew, Hebrews
Hos.	Hosea
ICC	*International Critical Commentary*
Is.	Isaiah
Jas.	James
JBL	*Journal of Biblical Literature*
Jdt.	Judith
J.E.	*The Jewish Encyclopaedia* (1901–6)
Jer.	Jeremiah
Jn.	John
Jon.	Jonah
Jos.	Joshua
JR	*Journal of Religion*
JRAI	*The Journal of the Royal Anthropological Institute*
JTS	*Journal of Theological Studies*
Jub.	Book of Jubilees
Jud.	Judges
Kik.	Kikamba
Kin.	Kings
km.	kilometres
Lev.	Leviticus
Lk.	Luke
LQHR	*London Quarterly and Holborn Review*
LXX	Septuagint
Macc.	Maccabees
Mal.	Malachi
Mart. Is.	Martyrdom of Isaiah
Mic.	Micah
Mk.	Mark
MS, MSS	Manuscript(s)
Mt.	Matthew
Nah.	Nahum
n.d.	no date
NEB	*New English Bible*
Neh.	Nehemiah
No.	Number
N.T.	New Testament
NTS	*New Testament Studies*

Num.	Numbers
Obad.	Obadiah
ODCC	*The Oxford Dictionary of the Christian Church*, ed. F. L. Cross
op. cit.	opere citato (in the work already quoted)
O.T.	Old Testament
p., pp.	page(s)
par., pars.	parallel(s)
Pet.	Peter
Phil.	Philippians
Philem.	Philemon
pl.	plural
Prov.	Proverbs
Ps., Pss.	Psalm(s)
Pss. Sol.	Psalms of Solomon
I QH	Qumran Psalms of Thanksgiving
I QM	The War between the Children of Darkness and the Children of Light
I Qp Hab.	The Habakkuk Commentary
I QS	The Manual of Discipline
I QSa	The Two-column Document (Serek ha-edah)
q.v.	quod vide (which see)
Rev.	Revelation
Rom.	Romans
RSV	Revised Standard Version
Rt.	Ruth
Sam.	Samuel
SJT	*Scottish Journal of Theology*
Sus.	Susanna
Syr. Bar.	Syriac Baruch (II Bar.)
Test. Sim.	Testament of Simeon
Test. XII	Testaments of the Twelve Patriarchs
Test. Zeb.	Testament of Zebulun
Tex. Rec.	Textus Receptus
Thes.	Thessalonians
Tim.	Timothy
Tit.	Titus
Tob.	Tobit
TWzNT	*Theologisches Wörterbuch zum Neuen Testament*, ed. G. Kittel (1933–, continued under G. Friedrich)
Zad. Work	Zadokite Work
Zech.	Zechariah
Zeph.	Zephaniah

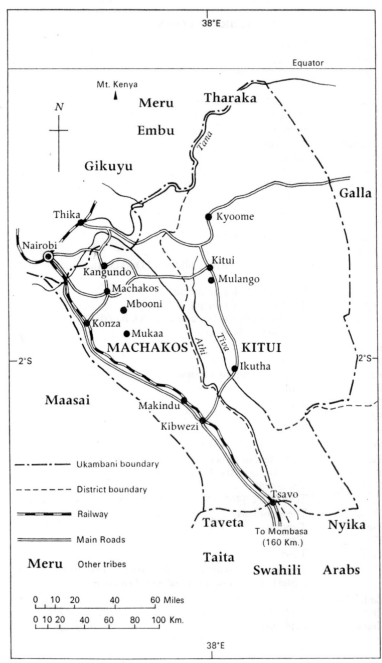

MAP OF UKAMBANI

CHAPTER I

Christianity Comes to an African Society

(a) The Scope and Necessity of Our Enquiry

THE Gospel is a revolution in which Jesus Christ is at the centre as the Lord of Faith. It contains powerful demands and challenges, as well as promises and fulfilment. This study investigates the process of proclaiming the Gospel and establishing the Church in an African tribal setting. It is an attempt to look at the encounter between Christianity and African traditional concepts, paying attention especially to the practical and theological consequences of that encounter.

But it is a selective investigation in that it focuses upon the Akamba people on the one hand, and certain aspects of New Testament Eschatology on the other. This makes it possible for us to examine the situation in some depth. Where relevant, reference is made to other African societies by way of comparison in order to draw some conclusions which are both specific (for the Akamba situation) and general (for other areas in Africa).

One feels that this is a pioneer piece of work in a field of study which has hardly been touched by scholars.[1] What little literature there is looks at the problem in very broad geographical and thematic terms, without taking up a specific issue and analysing it at length. Over the last one hundred years the Church has been established in tribal Africa, and yet we do not know much about the theological issues precipitated by the presence of the Christian Faith in the African setting. A great deal has, however, been written on African Independent Churches and there are endless reports of missionary work, all of which, no doubt, add to our understanding of some aspects of

[1] A few of the recent works include: J. V. Taylor, *The Primal Vision* (1963); S. G. Williamson, *Akan Religion and the Christian Faith* (1965); J. Mullin, *The Catholic Church in Modern Africa* (1965); A. Hastings, *Church and Mission in Modern Africa* (1967); C. G. Baëta, ed. *Christianity in Tropical Africa* (1968); H. Bürkle, ed. *Theologie und Kirche in Afrika* (1968); D. B. Barrett, ed., *African Initiatives in Religion* (1969); H. Sawyerr, *Creative Evangelism*, (1968); and articles in journals like *African Ecclesiastical Review* (Masaka, Uganda), *Africa Journal of Theology* (Usa River, Tanzania), *Flambeau* (Yaounde, Cameroon), and *Ministry* (Morija, Lesotho).

Christianity in Africa. But weighty issues remain to be investigated. We shall face some of these, which may be stated in the form of questions such as: to what extent can we find theological meaning in the traditional religious life of African peoples? In what language or vocabulary is the Christian Gospel being propagated in traditional societies, and to what extent can their languages and dialects sustain biblical concepts? What theological issues derive from the encounter between Christianity and traditional life? What are the possibilities and limitations of an African theology—or better, African systems of theology, and what may be the unique content and direction of such a theology—and hence its contribution to Christian theology at large?

These are but some of the questions and issues which I attempt to discuss here. Obviously they are too vast to be adequately covered in a single study, and we must set limits to the field of our investigation. It is for this reason that we shall concentrate on the Akamba people and the theme of Eschatology.

I have chosen the Akamba people because I belong to them, I know them better than other African societies, and they are a sizeable part of Kenya's population (in the proportion of 1:9 according to the 1962 census). In addition to personal interest in the subject of Eschatology, there are other reasons why I have chosen it.

(a) The Christian faith is intensely eschatological, and wherever the Church expands it brings and displays its eschatological presence, manifested in activities and experiences like the kerygma, repentance, conversion, salvation, sacraments, mission and Christian hope.

(b) Missionary work or evangelization is an eschatological transaction—in content (proclaiming an eschatological message), in obedience (to the eschatological Adam, I Cor. 15: 45) and in expectation (of the 'end' ($\tau\grave{o}$ $\tau\acute{\epsilon}\lambda os$) (Mt. 24: 14, cf. Acts 1: 8, Mt. 28: 19)).[1] Whenever the Church is conquering new fields in individual or community lives, it is making a deeply eschatological progress.

(c) Akamba religious ideas and practices, like those of many other African societies, are directed primarily to 'eschatological' aspects of life, concerning death, the departed, the spirits and the hereafter.

(d) As will emerge in this study, Akamba Christians show great interest in eschatological themes like the parousia, death and destiny of Christians, heaven and the hereafter. This means that, *inter alia*,

---

[1] Cf. O. Cullmann, 'Eschatology and Missions in the New Testament', essay contributed to *The Background of the New Testament and its Eschatology*, ed. W. D. Davies and D. Daube (1956, cited here as the Dodd Festschrift), 409–21.

Christianity is embraced and pictured primarily as an eschatological Faith.

Yet, while Eschatology may be regarded as being at the centre of the New Testament, it is to be borne in mind that the Christian Faith is more complex than that and has many other dimensions all of which are interrelated. It needs no emphasis to warn that an examination of Christian Eschatology and its encounter with African concepts does not exhaust the field. One hopes, however, that some light might be thrown upon the New Testament by this African background and vice versa. Eschatology seems to be one of the items presenting us with the largest area of encounter between Christianity and African religiosity, but obviously with similarities and differences.

(b) *The Methodology and Sources of the Study*

Without being too mechanical about it, the material is examined and presented in five steps. The first gives an account and analysis of Akamba traditional concepts related to Eschatology, drawing examples also from other African societies, to illustrate how far the Akamba may, or may not, be typical of African societies in general. This, however, is done only in passing, as the purpose here is not to indulge in generalizations, but to concentrate on a particular area. On the Akamba there is little literature, but a great deal of written information is available on African religious concepts and life in general.[1]

Secondly, the aspect of the New Testament under discussion is presented in a theological manner, without wading too far afield in any given school of thought. As Eschatology is saturated with literature I draw from a vast number of sources without, however, yielding to the temptation of scrutinizing in detail theories and propositions that scholars are constantly putting forward. The temptation here is indeed great, but to yield to it would seriously distract attention from the scope of the study, and one must reserve such investigation to others or to another study.

Thirdly, I present the teaching of the main evangelizing agent among the Akamba, which is the Africa Inland Mission (founded in 1895). This is an 'interdenominational' society which, however, draws its missionaries and doctrines mainly from evangelical and Funda-

[1] In addition to the works cited in footnotes, there is a select bibliography at the end of the book.

mentalist denominations like the Baptists, Mennonites and 'independents'. Their written sources are almost non-existent apart from the Kikamba Bible (1956), hymnbook (with some 210 hymns translated from English, n.d.), the Catechism (n.d.) and Constitution of the Africa Inland Church (1954 revised 1962). An early periodical *Hearing and Doing*, now no longer published, contains some relevant historical data.

Arising from these three main parts comes the fourth stage of examining how Akamba Christians may have understood (or misunderstood) the Christian teaching, and with what results or consequences.

Finally I draw conclusions and deductions, some of which are purely theological while others tend in the direction of practical issues of evangelization.[1]

We may now start with background information about the people and the Church in the area of our investigation.

(c) *The Akamba People*

The people are *Akamba*, one of them is a *Mukamba*, their land is *Ukambani* and their language is *Kikamba*. They number just over one million (out of $10\frac{1}{2}$ million people in Kenya), and live mainly in the east and south-central part of Kenya. Ukambani has an area about one-fifth of Britain, or twice the size of Holland. Two rainy seasons (March–July, October–December) and two dry seasons a year are the norm, and temperatures range between 10 °C. in the cool months in the highlands and 27 °C. in the hot months. When it is dry, water is scarce and people and animals may have to go long distances to find water. During the British occupation of Kenya, Ukambani was divided up into two districts, Machakos (on the west) and Kitui (on the east). These were then subdivided into locations, for administrative purposes. This structure has been retained since Kenya's independence in 1963. There are large settlements of Akamba in other parts of Kenya, notably around Mombasa on the east coat, in addition to Akamba who live in other towns and cities outside Ukambani.

---

[1] I shall here minimize the treatment of this side of the study, as I have published elsewhere some reflections on the practical issues of evangelizing Africa in an essay: 'The ways and means of communicating the Gospel', contributed to C. G. Baëta, ed., *Christianity in Tropical Africa* (1968), 329–50.

Kikamba is spoken throughout the country with only local varia-
tions. It is closely allied to Swahili and belongs to the Bantu family
of African languages. It was first reduced to writing by Krapf (see
infra) in 1850.[1]

There is no written history of the Akamba before the middle of the
nineteenth century.[2] Traditions say that they came from around Mt.
Kilimanjaro, or from the coast. I am more inclined to favour the
latter. Akamba trade was already a flourishing occupation in the
nineteenth century, the traders penetrating into the interior of Kenya
and Tanzania as far as Lake Victoria, particularly in search of ivory
which they traded with the Arabs and oriental peoples at Mombasa
and elsewhere on the coast.[3]

When the missionary J. L. Krapf arrived at Mombasa in 1844,
he not only heard much about the Akamba but met a number of
them, from whom he learnt Kikamba. It was probably because of
their important or leading position that he felt it imperative to evangelize them. Ukambani was to be the starting point of his proposed
'Equatorial Mission-chain', which was intended to be 'a line of
missions' stretching from the east coast of Africa to the west coast.
But this brilliant plan never materialized in the period of '10 to 12
years' which he contemplated.[4]

Later in the nineteenth century the British arrived in what is now
Kenya, and established their rule there. They opened police stations
at Machakos in 1892 and Kitui in 1893. The railway from Mombasa
to the shores of Lake Victoria passed through Ukambani between
1896 and 1900. With only a little resistance, the Akamba succumbed,
probably for the first time, to foreign rule. Part of their land was
taken by the British Government and allotted to European settlers
in 1903. During the First and Second World Wars, Akamba men
served in the forces, through their own choice, and by pressure and
conscription.

During the period of British rule for over sixty years, many trading

[1] J. L. Krapf, *Vocabulary of Six East African Languages* (1850), and his
translation of St. Mark's Gospel into Kikamba (1850).

[2] See J. L. Krapf, *Travels, Researches and Missionary Labours* (1860), *passim*,
but especially 283–366.

[3] Krapf, in *Travels*, 144; and *Vocabulary*, vi. It is interesting to observe that B.
Davidson in *Black Mother* (1961) speaks of African trade with the peoples
of Arabia, the Persian Gulf, India, Ceylon and China, as having continued on
the east coast of Africa for over two thousand years (157 f.). If this is correct the
Akamba were very much at the centre of that trade, at least in later centuries.

[4] Krapf, *Vocabulary*, vii; *Travels*, 144, 204, 212, 283.

centres sprang up all over the country, through mainly Indian, and, later, Akamba traders. Missionary work proceeded simultaneously, with the establishment of schools in or around mission stations and urban centres. There is today an increasing trend for Akamba to move from rural peasant life to life in towns all over Kenya.

Akamba social life is organized along clan and kinship systems. The tribe is divided into thirty to forty clans which are patrilineal and exogamous. They are dispersed throughout the country, but each Mukamba knows his own clan—it is his 'birth-certificate' by which he identifies himself when he meets another Mukamba. Clans are divided into 'gates' (*mivia*), which in turn are sub-divided into 'houses' (*nyumba*), and subsequently into smaller units of 'households' or 'families' (*misyi*). The household centres around the oldest male member in the family—something not unlike the ancient Hebrew households, as described by Pedersen.[1] The clans, mivia, nyumba and households are of no fixed sizes. This social structure is reported among many other African societies, as any sociological or anthropological account will bear witness.

The family, like in early Hebrew society, is not simply a horizontal extension of tribal solidarity, it is also a vertical link between departed members of the tribe and those who are still alive.[2] Kinship ties extend like a giant network uniting with one another those who are alive, and joining them to the kinsmen who have departed. The household is the smallest and most intimate nucleus of Akamba life, and each household is bound to others through kinship so that the families are also bound together into 'houses', 'houses' into 'gates', and 'gates' into clans which compose the entire people. One Kikamba word, *mbai*, means clan, tribe, nation, race, species, type and kind, all of which are meanings similar to those covered by the Hebrew term מִשְׁפָּחָה.[3] The people have a long and elaborate form of kinship terms, which shows the supreme importance of these ties in their whole life. One early British administrator noticing this, remarked that 'family and clannish feeling are extraordinarily strong in him

---

[1] J. Pedersen, *Israel—Its Life and Culture*, I–II (1926), 30 ff.

[2] Cf. Pedersen, op. cit., 53 f.

[3] F. Brown, S. R. Driver, and C. A. Briggs in their *Hebrew and English Lexicon of the Old Testament* (1907 rep. 1959), define מִשְׁפָּחָה as: '1. clan . . . a. family connection of individual . . . b. popular, loose sense = tribe; . . . e. late, div. of other peoples . . . f. in wider sense = people, nation . . . 3. = species, kind . . .' (1046 f.). Pedersen discusses it along similar lines, op. cit., 46 ff.

(Mukamba)'.[1] This could be said of many other traditional societies in Africa.

In the past the Akamba had neither regional nor national rulers. Writing his short 'History of Kitui', Dundas commented that 'they never could submit to a common chief, or join to oppose a common enemy. Above all the Mkamba prizes his independence, to be subject to anyone or bound to anything beyond mere family ties is hateful to him.'[2] Political power resided in the hands of family *atumia* (elders), and the 'age-grade system' governed and influenced the social and political life of the people at every phase, with power and responsibility increasing according to seniority. The functions and composition of the council (*nzama*) of elders, were like those of the Hebrew 'elders at the gate' (Deut. 22: 15–18; 25: 7–9, etc.).[3] This situation has been obviously changing in many places in recent years, but the older people still play an important role in the life of their communities.

The *atumia* (elders) are married men (who have beards), and are 'heads' of their individual or extended families. The *atumia* of a neighbourhood deal with legal and political matters, such as imposing fines, hearing and judging disputes, witnessing transactions, planning trade undertakings, and 'war' matters in the past, etc. They sit together at an open courtyard, *thome*, belonging either to individual homesteads or communally to several households. Some matters are, however, dealt with by clan, rather than neighbourhood, *atumia*, although the latter may attend and listen at such meetings.

From time to time in the past, there have been men and women with outstanding talents of leadership, who led or organized sizeable groups in commercial, 'war', or other corporate undertakings. It was probably such leaders that founded clans and subclans.

Individual life follows a regular cycle from birth, through initiation, marriage, procreation, to death and entry into the community of the departed.[4] Initiation is an extremely important stage of life, because

[1] C. Dundas, 'History of Kitui' in *The Journal of the Royal Anthropological Institute*, Vol. 43, No. 16 (1913), p. 488. A summary of Akamba kinship system is found in J. Middleton and G. Kershaw, *The Kikuyu and Kamba of Kenya* (1965). For African societies in general see, in addition to individual anthropological accounts, A. R. Radcliffe-Brown and D. Forde, eds., *African Systems of Kinship and Marriages* (1948, reissued many times since).

[2] Dundas, op. cit., 487.   [3] Pedersen, op. cit., 35 f.

[4] Most of the long articles, booklets and books on the Akamba, cover these stages adequately. For a full bibliography to date, see: J. Middleton and G. Kershaw, *The Kikuyu and Kamba of Kenya* (1965).

it is through it that a person becomes fully incorporated into the community of the nation and learns to participate in all its duties, responsibilities, privileges and activities. The first stage of the initiation is *nzaiko ila nini* (the small circumcision) at which boys of about five to eight undergo circumcision and girls of the same age undergo clitoridectomy. This is followed, several years later, by *nzaiko ila nene* (the great circumcision), which is a ceremonial initiation lasting seven to ten days. During that period the boys and girls are separated from other people, and are instructed by specialists in matters pertaining to the whole life of the people. Some of the men, at a much later age, undergo a third stage known as *mbavani*. This is so secret that only a very little information is known about it by those who have never gone through the initiation.

Marriage is crucially important, as it is through this that a person's name and line of kinship are propagated. There are no bachelors or spinsters among able-bodied adults.[1] Where possible, a man would normally have more than one wife; and polygamy (polygyny) is an accepted and respectable institution of traditional life. The Akamba also practise 'levirate marriage' (cf. Deut. 25: 5 ff.), so that a man takes the wife of his deceased brother and raises (more) children for him. If a person dies before getting married, his parents arrange his 'marriage' in absentia, and through a close relative (cf. Rt. 2: 20), children are born to him and his name is perpetuated. A woman who has no male children can arrange a similar marriage on behalf of her 'imaginary son', but this is seldom done.

Divorce is still very rare.[2] As part of the engagement and marriage transaction, the man's family gives *mali ya waasya* ('fiancée-bride wealth', 'bride-gift') to the girl's family. This consists of labour (cf. Gen. 29: 18 ff.), cattle, sheep and goats, money and foods, etc. It is a symbol of solemn gratitude to the parents and relatives of the girl, and also the seal and symbol of the marriage covenant. If the

---

[1] This statement applies to life in the traditional setting, which is now rapidly changing. So also Dundas, who reports (1913) that 'spinsters are . . . non-existent', and that in his long stay in Ukambani he heard of only 'one or two' bachelors (p. 521). Lindblom (1920), speaking about one area, Ikutha and around, mentions that for economic reasons some men remain unmarried for a long time, but that 'there seems to be none who die as bachelors' (p. 81).

[2] Middleton and Kershaw say that 'divorce is said to be uncommon', op. cit., 82; but G. Lindblom takes the opposite view, viz., that 'divorce often occurs among them', in *The Akamba* (1920), 82 ff. Judging from the Akamba conception of 'marriage' and 'divorce', my impression is that divorce is very rare, and almost totally absent after about five years of married life (in traditional background).

engagement or marriage is broken, the *mali ya waasya* (except labour and food), is returned to the giver.

Infant mortality is very high. At least one out of every four children born alive dies before the age of ten, which is a disturbingly high rate of 'infant wastage' in spite of the correspondingly high birth rate.[1]

Magic, witchcraft and sorcery play a prominent role in Akamba life. The people are saturated with beliefs, fears and superstitions connected with these practices. Every Mukamba, whether Christian or otherwise, has a dormant or active share of these beliefs. The people have not been sufficiently armed to fight against witchcraft and sorcery, in spite of many years of contact with Christian teaching and western education. It will take many more years to eradicate beliefs in witchcraft, sorcery and magic from the lives of the Akamba. The picture is very similar to that of other societies in Africa, as borne out by the vast literature on the subject.[2]

Since in this study we shall be dealing with religious concepts and practices, little needs to be said about them at this stage. The Akamba recognize *Mulungu* as God, the Creator and Preserver of all things. He gives them children, rain and food, but nobody knows where and how He lives, or what He looks like. Other names for Him are *Mumbi* (Creator), *Mwatuangi* (Cleaver), and *Ngai*. The last term is probably connected with the Maasai word for God, *Engai* (or *En-kai*), and I have not found it in any accounts of Akamba life and language prior to this century. But it is the word used in the Kikamba Bible and in Christian circles.[3]

The first men were husband and wife (or two couples according to another version of the tradition), whom Mulungu created and brought out of a hole in the ground, or from the sky, leaving them to bear

[1] 'Infant mortality rate' is, strictly speaking, the number of 'deaths under one year per 1000 live births'. According to the census of 1948, Kenya's 'infant mortality rate' was 184, or approximately 'one out of every five children born' . . . Goldthorpe, *infra*, p. 9. It is clear therefore that at least one out of every four children born would die before reaching the age of ten years.

See J. E. Goldthorpe's discussion of the question of birth and death rates in East African population in his *Outlines of East African Society* (1958), 9 ff.

[2] See, e.g.: E. E. Evans-Pritchard, *Witchcraft, Oracles and Magic among the Azande* (1937); J. Middleton and E. H. Winter, eds., *Witchcraft and Sorcery in East Africa* (1963); H. Debrunner, *Witchcraft in Ghana* (1959); G. Bloomhill, *Witchcraft in Africa* (1962), and anthropological accounts, most of which include something on this subject.

[3] For a comprehensive record and study of traditional African notions of God, see: J. S. Mbiti, *Concepts of God in Africa* (1970).

children and propagate. It is not known where the hole is. They were originally created to live forever, but when God sent the chameleon to convey this news to the people, it lingered along the way and stammered in delivering the message. Mulungu then sent the swift-flying weaver bird with a message that they were to die and disappear like the roots of the aloe tree. Before the chameleon finished delivering the message, in a stammering slow speech, the weaver arrived and promptly announced the terrible news of Man's loss of immortality. Then Man began to die.

Apart from this, the bulk of Akamba religious ideas and practices is to be found in connection with the 'spirits' of the departed, or *Aimu* (sing, *Iimu*). Concepts regarding Aimu are more fully developed than those regarding God or the universe in general. There are two types of Aimu. Firstly, there are the 'spirits' of people who have died recently, up to three or four generations back. These we shall call the *Living-dead*, to distinguish them from the other Aimu. Secondly, there are the 'spirits' of those who died many generations back, or whom people do not recognize or remember by name, and for these alone we shall retain the term Aimu. The Akamba believe firmly that both the living-dead and the Aimu are real 'people' living in a land very much like their own. Beliefs and practices connected with these 'people', pervade the whole of Akamba religious and secular life.[1] It is relevant, therefore, that a study of Christian Eschatology be undertaken in relation to evangelizing the Akamba, since this takes us into the heart of their religious concepts and life.

(d) The Coming of Christianity to Ukambani

Such then are the people and country of Ukambani which the missionary J. L. Krapf visited on two occasions, in 1849 and 1851. He made the second journey with a view to establishing the first link of his visionary 'Equatorial Mission-chain' across the continent. He was given instructions and full support for this project by the Anglican Church Missionary Society (C.M.S.) under which he served, although he himself was German. Accordingly, he was to take the Gospel to the Akamba, to enquire for the route to Unyamwesi (further inland by Lake Victoria), and to search for the route to the source of

---

[1] I want to avoid terms like 'ancestral worship', 'animism', 'animatism', 'spiritism', 'ancestor cult', etc., none of which would fit precisely the Akamba type of religious ideas and practices.

the Nile, and to 'those still surviving Christian remnants at the equator of whom I had heard in Shoa'.[1]

On arrival at Mombasa, in 1844, Krapf made an early acquaintance with Akamba in and around that ancient city, learnt Kikamba, and translated the first two Gospels, publishing St. Mark's in 1850. He also included Kikamba in his *Vocabulary of Six East African Languages* (1850).[2] In his contacts with the Akamba both on the coast and in Ukambani, Krapf told them the Christian Gospel. From his account in *Travels, Researches and Missionary Labours* (1860), it is clear that he would have had great success in founding a station in Ukambani had he not, for various reasons, temporarily abandoned the idea. He had the support of several Akamba men of power and influence. One of these men was Kivoi of Kitui, of whom he wrote that he 'was well acquainted with Europeans, Swahili, and Arabs (and) possessed great influence, too, on the coast and in the interior.'[3]

The unfortunate assassination of Kivoi on 27 August 1851, by a band of robbers from other tribes, while he was taking Krapf to Gikuyu country and the foot of Mt. Kenya, and the subsequent sufferings that Krapf endured after his narrow escape, were some of the depressing experiences that led him to the idea of quitting Yata, the spot in the central Ukambani where he intended to found the mission station. He records the decision with moving words: 'it grieved me not to have been privileged to make a longer missionary experiment in Ukambani, as I could not feel satisfied that a mission in this country would not succeed, as the people of Yata had behaved with friendliness towards me; yet, situated as I was, my further stay was impossible.'[4] Leaving some of his belongings at Yata, he went back to Rabai near Mombasa, intending to return shortly to Ukambani. But he never saw Ukambani again, for he had to return 'to Europe broken in health in 1853'.

Apart from showing interest in the Gospel story, there were no Akamba converts, apparently, from this early phase of evangelization. Up to 1864, twenty years after the arrival of Krapf on the east

---

[1] Krapf, *Travels*, 212, 284, 300. Shoa is in Ethiopia where he worked unsuccessfully as a Missionary from 1837 to 1844, before moving to Mombasa (Kenya) in 1844.

[2] The six languages are: 'Kisuáheli, Kiníka, Kikámba, Kipokómo, Kihiáu, Kigálla'.

[3] Krapf, *Travels*, 307 ff. Others were Muilu wa Kiwui (p. 306), and Mtangi wa Nsuki of whom Krapf says that he 'gave us a friendly reception'.

[4] Krapf, op. cit., 344.

coast, there were only six baptized converts and six catechists at Rabai,[1] and presumably there was no Mukamba among them. Although other missionaries had joined and succeeded Krapf on the coast, for forty years none of them went to Ukambani, to carry on from where Krapf had stopped in 1851.

Towards the end of the century, the colonial scramble reached its peak and the British acquired 'British East Africa'. The railway which they constructed from Mombasa to Lake Victoria, went through Ukambani and was opened in 1901. Oliver says that this event 'provoked a hurly-burly race among missions new and old into the hitherto unoccupied territory.'[2] In the closing decade, missionaries of different backgrounds invaded Ukambani. The East African Scottish Industrial Mission led by the directors of the Imperial British East Africa Company, bought land and opened a station at Kibwezi in 1891, only to abandon the enterprise and 'transfer it to Kikuyu in 1898'.

The Leipzig Evangelical Lutheran Society opened mission stations at Ikutha in 1892, and at Mulango in 1895. The latter date also saw the founding in the United States of America, of the Africa Inland Mission (A.I.M.), by a certain Peter Cameron Scott. The Society was 'supposedly undenominational, but with a strong flavouring of Baptists and Adventists.'[3] This was the Mission destined to do, at least for a long period, most of the work of evangelizing Ukambani. Its first station, Nzaui, was opened in 1895 but had to be abandoned after the death of the founder of the Mission. It opened other stations at Kangundo in 1896, at Mumbuni (Machakos) in 1902, and at Mbooni in 1908. Mukaa station which was briefly occupied by the C.M.S., was given to the A.I.M. in 1910. (See the map on page xii for these and other places.) The Mission expanded its work in other parts of Kenya, and eventually entered Tanzania, Uganda, the Congo, the Sudan and the Central African Republic. In 1902, however, the Adventist group broke away and formed the Gospel Missionary Society, which never gained a strong foothold in Ukambani.

At the beginning of this fresh start of evangelization in Ukambani, the Akamba do not seem to have responded enthusiastically. In

---

[1] R. Oliver, *The Missionary Factor in East Africa* (1952), 6. The first was apparently a cripple named Mringe, about whose interest in and enquiry concerning the Gospel truth, Krapf reports in his *Travels*, 193, 195, 199.

[2] Oliver, op. cit., 168.   [3] Oliver, op. cit., 171.

spite of the joint efforts of German, American and British missionaries
—many of whom died in the country—Akamba hearers remained
'unresponsive', as Oliver describes them.[1] One of the German missionaries, Kanig, complained about this indifference of the Akamba
even after they had gone through the dire experience of the great
famine and smallpox epidemic, both of 1898–9. He wrote in 1902
that 'die Wakamba nicht williger gemacht haben, durch die enge
Pforte in das Himmelreich einzugehen', because of their 'grossen
Unstetigkeit . . . mit ihrer Vergangenheit zusammenhängen mag.'[2]

Yet this lack of interest and response must not be attributed entirely
to Akamba character or life. There were factors also from the missionaries' end of the story. For example, they beat some of the Akamba, exploited their labour force, exhibited a superiority complex
and showed racial discrimination towards them, kept themselves as
far apart from the 'heathen' as possible, and described the people in
the most unpalatable language.[3] Such factors could not effectively
add to the execution of the Gospel imperative which had called them
to Ukambani. The situation in the missionary–Akamba relationship
seems to have changed only slightly in the course of these years,
worsening in certain aspects but generally improving.

Yet, with the turn of the century, the Akamba began to respond
to Christian teaching with all its cultural-social appendages from the
countries of the evangelizing missionaries. The A.I.M. reported its
first Baptismal service of three Akamba converts, in the Mission's
official organ, *Hearing and Doing*, October 1905. The report said:
'it was an impressive sight as Brother Hurlburt led these men into
the water and baptized them. The banks were crowded with men,
women and children.'[4] This was at Kangundo, and one of the 'two
young' men (who were baptized together with an old man), is still
alive today (June 1968).

The German missionaries similarly began to witness conversions
on and around their stations. By the time of the outbreak of the

[1] Oliver, ibid.

[2] G. Kanig, *Dornige Pfade eines jungen Missionars in Ukamba* (1902), 13.

[3] For example, Kanig says concerning the Akamba whom he failed to impress,
'dass der Charakter dieses Volkes aussergewöhnlich niedrig steht', op. cit., 16.
A missionary of the Africa Inland Mission was reported as being asked in his
home country why they went to evangelize Africa where ' "the natives are un-
attractive, their hovels unsanitary, their customs revolting and their society
depressing" '—in the official organ of the A.I.M.: *Hearing and Doing*, Vol. XXI
No. 2 (April–June 1916), p. 5.

[4] *Hearing and Doing*, Vol. X, No. 4 (July 1905), p. 7.

First World War when they were interned by Britain, there were small nuclei of Akamba Christians at Ikutha, Mulango and Miambani—all in Kitui where the Lutherans had been working. In 1915 the A.I.M. took over these three stations, but abandoned both Ikutha and Miambani afterwards. The newly arrived A.I.M. missionaries reported the situation at Mulango in January 1916, as follows:

Several of the converts give evidence of living lives of victory and joy and are giving themselves to prayer and testimony; the effect of this is seen on those who are not Christians. . . . The people from the surrounding villages are coming in large numbers, some meetings having from 100 to 160 in attendance . . . The school has increased in attendance and we are gaining confidence of many who formerly forbade their children to come. I have just finished translating the book of Hebrews and several hymns . . . Mulango is a fine place.[1]

This was indeed a note of encouragement, so different from the earlier note of despair when in 1905, some of the missionaries were being greeted by Akamba cynics on entering their villages, in the words: ' "Here comes the white man to tell us more lies" '.[2]

The Mission split in 1902; the outbreak of the War in 1914, and the death of missionaries, were other drawbacks and discouraging events in the work, and some stations had to be abandoned. But progress was, nevertheless, being made even through these difficult years. In the Annual Report for 1919, Charles Hurlburt, the A.I.M. General Director, reported the conditions in Ukambani as follows:

The AKAMBA tribe, in which the Mission first started its work in 1895, now has six stations: Kangundo, Machakos, Mboni, Mukaa, Mulango and Kinoi. These report 107 communicants, 160 enquirers being taught, and 23 native helpers in teaching and evangelism. This tribe, which has been considered the most difficult one in British East Africa for missionary work, is showing some results of the long years of sowing in a marked spiritual interest at nearly every station. Practically the whole of the New Testament has been translated within the last few years, but the translations are necessarily imperfect and changes are constantly being made . . . The tribe is one of the brightest and keenest in which we work . . . and we should have here the very best schools and the most aggressive evangelism.[3]

[1] *Hearing and Doing*, Vol. XXI, No. 2 (April–June 1916), p. 14. My interviews with Akamba Christians who survive from this early period at Mulango, confirm these observations.

[2] *Hearing and Doing*, Vol. X, No. 4 (July 1905), p. 4.

[3] *Hearing and Doing* (August 1919), p. 3. The Mission was at that time, 'working in twenty different tribes, on forty different stations, and attempting work in twenty different languages . . . with . . . 157 missionaries on the field.'

The Roman Catholic Church started a mission agency at Mombasa in 1890, and by 1906 there were two societies well established in the interior of the then British East Africa. These were the Holy Ghost Fathers and the Consolata Fathers. In 1912 the Catholics began to work in Ukambani, but for several years their work was confined to the Machakos District, and only moved into Kitui in 1945. But by mutual agreement among the non-Roman Missions, Ukambani remained as the 'field' for the Africa Inland Mission for nearly the whole first half of the twentieth century.

By 1934, the A.I.M. had a following of 3,675 church members and adherents in Ukambani, with 5 stations but only 10 missionaries. It also had 22 schools under its supervision, with 1,185 pupils, and there were 37 'native workers'. In the same year nearly 9,000 patients were treated at its hospital at Mulango. The only other Society was the Seventh Day Adventists, working in Machakos at the border between Ukambani and Gikuyu, which had 83 Church members and adherents, 2 missionaries, 4 'native workers', 1 school with 85 pupils and 1 dispensary through which 300 patients were treated.[1] So the Church in Ukambani began to take shape and to grow, under the strong influence of the Africa Inland Mission (except for that branch which the Roman Catholics started).

The methods of evangelization which different Mission Societies followed in Kenya are described by H. R. A. Philp in his book, *A New Day in Kenya* (1936)[2] as follows:

A. The 'Agricultural Approach': a method which 'has always exercised an extraordinary attraction for missions and missionaries in Kenya'. This meant the use of the plough and 'better' (new) methods of farming, etc., through setting up 'mission estates' which became, *inter alia*, 'asylums' for Christian refugees, practical 'schools' for teaching Africans in hand and heart, and centres for setting the example of growing crops for export and home consumption. This is what the East African Scottish Industrial Mission tried without success in Ukambani from 1891 to 1898.

B. The 'Industrial Approach', by which it was attempted to teach industrial arts to Africans, but this never gained any success, except for the secular 'Native Industrial Training Depot' at Kabete near Nairobi.

[1] H. R. A. Philp, *A New Day in Kenya* (1936), 154 (appendix III).
[2] Philp, op. cit., 69–103.

C. The 'Medical Approach' became by far the most successful and impressive from the very beginning, especially in a country with many and great medical needs. The A.I.M. tried to have dispensaries at its Ukambani stations, whenever it was possible. The Government also established dispensaries in various parts of the country, but medical needs can never be exhausted nor can the supplies become superfluous. Philp points out that Christian medical work was not simply 'to alleviate suffering . . . but to follow the great example of the Master . . .' Treatment was given for a small fee. Though proportionate to their little amount of money, for many patients it was not so small.

D. The 'Educational Approach' made a slow start, but in due time it proved to be the most effective and revolutionary method in bringing people into contact with the Christian Gospel. Schools and Churches went side by side, in spite of the indifference which Akamba people showed towards education at the beginning of the century. At first the schools were nothing more than simply a gathering of big and small boys together with a missionary sitting under the trees on the mission station. Most of the early conversions came from these schools, and Christianity was closely associated with western forms of education, so closely that Christians came to be known as 'Readers' (*Asomi*), a name which is still in use today. Nearly all those who attended mission schools were certain to become Christian since they were in constant contact with missionaries,[1] and were more likely to grasp the Christian teaching faster than the people who only heard it occasionally. This principle still operates today, on a much wider scale.

In the twenties, the Kenya Government took greater interest in educational work than before, and began to increase its otherwise meagre financial aid to mission schools. The 'Protestant' Missions in Kenya jointly started the 'Alliance High School' near Nairobi in 1926, where junior secondary education was given to successful African students from primary schools all over the country. They received moral and financial assistance from the Government. A few of the brilliant Akamba youth gradually began to come to that School.

The Roman Catholics established a parallel school at Kabaa in

---

[1] Cf. *Hearing and Doing*, Vol. X, No. 4 (July 1905), p. 4. The Catholic Mission at Machakos counts as 'Catechumens' the 18,250 children in its schools (according to a letter from T. Timmins, the missionary in charge, dated 19 April, 1963).

Machakos in 1927, under the leadership of the Consolata Mission of Turin which had arrived in Kenya in 1902. But partly because of insufficient enthusiasm from the Akamba, the school was transferred afterwards to Mang'u in the Gikuyu country, although Akamba students, whether Roman Catholics or otherwise, were allowed to study there.

(e) The Church in Ukambani

From about 1935 onwards, the rate of conversion to Christianity increased tremendously among the Akamba. Several factors seem to have contributed to this rapid growth of the Church in Ukambani. Briefly these were that:

(i) During the Second World War, many Akamba soldiers served in the forces and came under Christian teaching and the pastoral care of the Chaplains. A great proportion of them returned to Ukambani, on leave or at the end of the War, already baptized. Their families immediately followed the example, embraced the Christian Faith, and sought Baptism, if they had not already become Christian.

(ii) The number of missionaries working in Ukambani increased, particularly after the War. In the decade preceding the War, some of the missionaries used to visit many villages and homes, and taught or proclaimed the Gospel to Akamba people. This method of 'personal evangelism' has, however, been abandoned by missionaries who, instead, remain on their stations or move only in cars along the highways!

(iii) The number of schools increased at an astronomical rate. Although these are now all financed by the local and central governments, most of them are still under 'mission supervision', for which the A.I.M. and the Roman Catholic missionaries in education work, receive a fat stipend from the Kenya government. Thousands of children are now in these and government schools, where they come under Christian teaching and influence (for the Scriptures are taught in all schools, according to government regulations). Nearly all of them become Christian while they are in school if not before. Through some of the children, the parents are also reached with the Christian teaching.

(iv) Akamba Christians, both the few ordained men and the large host of laymen, increasingly began to go out to the homes and villages, telling non-believers the Gospel, and 'reviving' believers who might have turned back to non-Christian living. I many cases, Christians still make it a point to tell non-believers, especially their relatives, something about Jesus Christ, Salvation, Heaven and the Fire of Gehenna. Many of the hearers show interest, and not a few embrace the Faith as a result.

(v) 'Out-churches' have been, and continue to be, established wherever new schools are started. In recent years one has seen efforts by the A.I.M. 'to get a new school before the Catholics get it'. The ethics and motives behind such spirit of competition may be questionable, but at least new schools and new churches are started perhaps sooner than would otherwise be the case (cf. Phil. 1: 15–18).

(vi) With increasing literacy it is now possible to give Christian teaching and influence to many people, for the purposes of conversion or widening their understanding of the Faith. Literature of any kind is, however, very scanty compared to the great demand for reading material.

(vii) The Kikamba New Testament which was published in 1920, followed by portions of the Old Testament in the course of the years, played an important role in the work of the Church. In 1956 the whole Bible was published, and Akamba Christians received it with great enthusiasm, as they had waited for it for many years. The hymnal which contains hymns, songs and choruses translated from English and American hymnals, is another favourite possession of the Christians. The Bible or the New Testament together with the hymnal, are often the only two books in the 'library' of a Mukamba Christian.

(viii) Material prosperity has, perhaps by accident, been associated with Christians, the people who have had closest contact with western culture and education. This draws some of the unbelieving people to a kind of full or loose association with the Church. Many children evidently also get 'converted' in order to remain in Christian schools and receive education, but afterwards they 'shuffle off' their temporary 'conversion'.

(ix) This is the period when the seeds which had been sown over the years have now begun to germinate, and the plants which had sprung up during the years of sowing likewise have begun to flower and bear fruit. So we are able to see both growth and harvest, and the Church is in its most prosperous period.

But it is not without problems. In 1945 a group of Akamba Christians severed themselves and formed the African Brotherhood Church. They were not satisfied with the leadership of the A.I.M., and the way in which the missionaries were treating the people and handling the infant Church. About the same time, there was another split in the Mission, and some missionaries formed a new Society known as the Gospel Furthering Fellowship. These two groups have gained a considerable following, and the African Brotherhood Church has a remarkable influence under the strong and able leadership of N. K. Ngala. The teaching methods and contents of the two separate bodies are, however, very much like those of the A.I.M., and there is an amount of co-operation as well as some friction between the three organizations.

Many members of the Church in Ukambani frequently lapse into tribal ways and life which are denounced as being non-Christian. These are mainly disciplinary matters connected with marriage customs, beliefs in and practices of magic, sorcery and witchcraft, quarrels, and tribal methods of dealing with troubles and problems like sickness, barrenness and misfortunes.

Another noticeable feature is that in spite of the numerical and geographical expansion of the Church under the Africa Inland Mission, missionaries have kept themselves 'aloof' from the local Church. In the 1930s they constituted the Africa Inland Church (A.I.C.), composed of African followers of the Mission. This is *just* a Church, without theological, doctrinal, historical, liturgical or ministerial connections with other bodies of the Church universal. In the eyes of the public, the A.I.C. is made up of 'black or brown' Christians only, while the Africa Inland Mission is made up of 'white' or 'pink' Christians only. Currently there are discussions of missionaries becoming 'members' of the A.I.C., but I am not aware of African Christians joining the A.I.M. In practice and theory the A.I.C. is 'presbyterian', with an incorporation of 'Baptist' principles like adult baptism by immersion. The missionaries who are recruited from the United States, Canada, Britain, Australia and the Republic of South Africa, come from different denominational backgrounds. In doctrine they are 'evangelical' or 'fundamentalist'. The A.I.M. has six main centres or stations in Ukambani at Kangundo, Mumbuni, Mbooni and Mukaa in Machakos district, and Mulango and Kyoome in Kitui district. Each station has between two and ten adult missionaries.

The Africa Inland Church is organized under congregational (or local), district and regional councils. Ukambani forms one of the 'regions' of the A.I.C. in Kenya, all of which are linked at the top through the Central Church Council (*Baraza Kuu*). The A.I.M. has councils at parallel levels. According to the 1954 *Constitution, Rules and Regulations* of the Africa Inland Church, district, regional and central Church councils must all have missionary representatives (pp. 8 ff.). In the same document it is also laid down that 'the Church shall not be deemed to have any legal right to any properties belonging to the Africa Inland Mission unless and until such properties be transferred . . .' (p. 17). Membership of A.I.M. missionaries to the three councils was made rather optional in the 1962 revised Constitution, making them 'eligible' to be appointed or co-opted, but property arrangements remained relatively the same (pp. 5 ff.). This revised constitution thus gives the Church a certain amount of paper autonomy. But the dichotomy between the Mission and the Church still remains, even if there is co-operation and full fellowship between the two bodies, both of which date back to 1895 when the Mission was founded.

For training Akamba catechists and pastors, a Bible School was started in Machakos in 1928–9 which has since gone through various phases of growth. At present there are three Church institutions: Scott Theological College and a Bible School at Machakos, and a Bible School at Kitui. The Mission pioneered school education in Ukambani, and there are innumerable schools all over the country which have come into being as a result of the Mission's efforts. All of these, except the theological college and the two Bible schools, are financed by the Kenya government, and missionaries engaged in educational work are paid by the government, the remuneration going into the Mission Funds and not into their personal pockets. Ordained pastors in active service number about a dozen, but there is a host of licentiates, catechists, evangelists, school teachers and other lay workers who serve the congregations. A number of the congregations, however, have no regular leaders, apart from elders and conductors of singing.

There are other Churches, denominations and missionary societies at work in Ukambani, though the Africa Inland Mission and the Africa Inland Church are numerically by far the largest. The total outward appearance of the Church in the country is as follows, though the statistical data should not be interpreted as an accurate representation of the picture, but only as a guide to the overall situation.

The *Anglican Church* of the Province of East Africa through non-resident missionaries of the Church Missionary Society (C.M.S.) and local African Christians, has about twenty-five congregations but no mission station. The C.M.S. has never established a firm footing in Ukambani, leaving, until recently, the evangelization of the country to the A.I.M., under the 'agreement' among missionary societies by which different areas of Kenya were assigned or left almost exclusively to one or two missionary groups.

The *Salvation Army* has about forty congregations or 'prayer houses'. The *Seventh Day Adventists* have about ten local congregations, mainly in the Machakos District. The *Independent Board of the Presbyterian Foreign Mission* (U.S.A.) has about twenty congregations, including two stations, mainly in the Kitui area.

The *Roman Catholic Church* has at least forty congregations, including five main mission stations. Its work was for a long time confined to the Machakos district, and it was only in the mid 1940s that it began to establish itself seriously in the Kitui district. As with the A.I.M., the main strength of the Roman Catholic Church has been in education work, through which it has started schools and churches and won many converts or followers.

The *Africa Inland Mission* and *Africa Inland Church* have about 400 congregations (and six mission stations) throughout Ukambani.[1]

Independent Churches are increasingly active in the country, drawing their followers mainly from the mission Churches and the non-Christians. Of these the biggest is the *African Brotherhood Church*, which has about 100 congregations and one headquarters (at Mitaboni, Machakos). This broke off from the Africa Inland Mission/Church in 1945; and under the leadership of pastor (now 'bishop') N. K. Ngala, has grown enormously in membership, congregations and expansion to other parts of Kenya. The *Gospel Furthering Fellowship* (G.F.F.) also broke off originally from the A.I.M. under missionary leadership, in the 1940s. This has recently branched off into the Gospel Furthering Church (G.F.C.), part of which is currently reported to be on the verge of splintering from its mission counterpart. The G.F.F. and the G.F.C. have about seventy congregations and one station. The *Friends of the Holy Spirit* started originally among the Gikuyu people (neighbours and traditional

---

[1] The statistics here are estimated, since accurate figures either do not exist or are not available (to me). When I approached the A.I.C. for their figures, they said that the matter would first be put before their councils to decide whether or not they would divulge them to me! I am still waiting for their reply. The A.I.M. does not seem to have reliable figures either. I have gathered my information from government offices and individual informants through conversation or correspondence.

friends of the Akamba to the north and north-west of Ukambani) in the 1940s, reaching Kitui around 1948. It was registered with the government in 1960, and the Akamba members of the sect broke off from the Gikuyu section the same year. It is a minority but very active group, with bands of followers all over Ukambani, and reportedly reaching to other areas of Kenya, Tanzania and Congo (Kinshasa). The Friends of the Holy Spirit come primarily from the Africa Inland Mission background, and a few from the other Churches as well as the non-Christian population. It is not possible to estimate their numerical strength since they do not erect buildings for their meetings, but generally congregate under trees or in people's houses, unless the numbers are so large that it becomes necessary to erect 'a meeting place'.[1] There is also the *Kenya African Church* whose headquarters have been in Machakos since 1961, with a present membership of about 2,000 individuals. Its exact origin is unknown to me. *The African Independent Church of Kenya* broke off from the A.I.M. in 1961. The *Maria Legio* is an independent group which broke off from the Roman Catholic Church in Kenya in 1963, and has drawn some following from Akamba people, but its exact state in Ukambani is not clear; one has the impression that it is not strong there, though it is an active group elsewhere in Kenya.[2]

Going through Ukambani one often sees Church buildings of every size and description, and on Sundays there are streams of Christians on the roads going to or from services. Some of the Christians gather for worship in school buildings, people's homes, or under the trees. It is not uncommon for Christians to cycle or walk up to 8 k. to attend Church services on Sundays. The total number of congregations in Ukambani would range between 700 and 800, each with from a few dozen people to two or more thousand believers. It would seem that an estimate of about 300,000 Akamba Christians, catechumens, 'adherents', and 'enquirers', gives a fair picture of the numerical impact of evangelization in Ukambani. This means that about 30 per cent of the population may be considered 'Christian', in the

[1] For the only available and comprehensive account of the *Friends of the Holy Spirit* in Ukambani, see D. N. Kimilu 'The Separatist Churches', article in *Dini na Mila* (Revealed Religion and Traditional Custom), Vol. 2, Nos. 2 & 3 (Kampala, December 1967), pp. 17–61 (giving also, *inter alia*, the English version of their hymns, to which I will refer later in this book).

[2] A full account and assessment of independent Churches in Africa is: D. B. Barrett, *Schism and Renewal in Africa* (1968), with many bibliographical and statistical data.

broad sense of that term. The remainder of the people are still non-Christian (or 'pagan', to use a rather derogatory word), some are lapsed Christians, and the number of Muslims is almost negligible. The majority of these have, however, been exposed to Christian teaching, through contact with Christians, schools and evangelization methods. To my knowledge, there are no areas in Ukambani where the Gospel has not been proclaimed in one way or another.

Such then is the outward picture of the Church and Christianity in Ukambani. The Church is obviously 'struggling' between infancy and full maturity, between being under foreign missionary control and becoming independent of such control. For nearly 120 years, Christianity has been proclaimed in Ukambani, except for the 'silent' period of forty years between 1851 and 1891. Nearly the whole population of one million Akamba has heard the Christian Gospel, even if only one third has positively embraced and kept the Faith. Nearly the whole country has come under Christian influence, both directly and indirectly. No one today can grow up in Ukambani and reach the age of twenty without being exposed to Christianity in one way or another. Christianity, divided and subdivided as it is, has been the cause or instrument of the greatest influence in Ukambani this century, and probably throughout the history of the country.

The time is ripe, and one has every reason, for examining the inner, more profound, question of what Christianity has meant in this African situation. It is necessary, therefore, to analyse and evaluate one aspect of the Christian Faith in this tribal setting:

(a) to see what the conceptual background of the Akamba is;
(b) to find out what has been taught and received as the Christian Faith, and the methods employed in its propagation;
(c) to assess the impact of such teaching upon the people's total understanding;
(d) by bringing together both traditional concepts and the New Testament, to see what light is thrown by each upon the other; and
(e) to draw some theological implications of the whole picture.

This enquiry is no doubt very relevant to other areas of Africa, since in general the situation is similar. By taking the Akamba as the basis of our study, it is hoped that the picture which emerges will contribute something to an understanding of the present state of Christianity in Africa. Conclusions on a continental scale will obviously have to await more studies from elsewhere in Africa.

CHAPTER II

Time, History and Eschatology

TIME and History are essential elements of Eschatology. Any consideration or understanding of Eschatology must presuppose a certain attitude towards Time and History. We need, therefore, to start with a discussion of both Time and History and their relationship with Eschatology in Akamba thought and in the New Testament.

(a) *Akamba Concepts of Time and History*

For the Akamba, Time is not an academic concern; it is simply a composition of events that have occurred, those which are taking place now and those which will immediately occur. What has not taken place, or what is unlikely to occur in the immediate future, has no temporal meaning—it belongs to the reality of 'no-Time'. My researches from other East African peoples, like the Gikuyu, Baganda, Acholi, Bakiga and Luo, indicate the same approach to the understanding of the meaning of Time.

From this basic attitude to Time, other important points emerge. The most significant factor is that Time is considered as a two-dimensional phenomenon; with a long 'past', and a dynamic 'present'. The 'future' as we know it in the linear conception of Time is virtually non-existent in Akamba thinking. My findings from other African peoples have not yielded any radical difference. The future is virtually absent because events which lie in the future have not been realized and cannot, therefore, constitute Time which otherwise must be experienced. Time as a separate reality does not 'move'; only events come and go, often in a rhythmic succession. It is, therefore, what has taken place or will shortly occur that matters much more than what is yet to be. What has taken place is an elongation of the 'present': it simply adds to the events that constitute Time.

Thirdly, for the Akamba and, one would add, many other African peoples, Time as a succession or simultaneity of events 'moves' not forward but backwards. People look more to the 'past' for the orientation of their being than to anything that might yet come into human History. For them History does not move towards any goal yet in the future: rather, it points to the roots of their existence, such as the origin of the world, the creation of man, the formation of their customs and traditions, and the coming into being of their whole structure of society. The 'present' must conform to the 'past' in the sense that it is the 'past', rather than any distant future, by means of which people orientate their living and thinking.

Arising from the last point, Akamba and other African peoples have innumerable myths which are the most dominant feature of both History and Prehistory. It is these myths that help them to explain or understand their present state and that of the universe. It is by looking towards the 'past' that they give or find satisfactory explanations about the world and man's experience of it.

Consequently, since man's orientation is towards the 'past' dimension of Time, the Akamba have no conception that this universe will ever change radically or come to an end, and the same seems to be the case with other African peoples. Man looks back whence he came, and man is certain that nothing will bring this world to a conclusion. The universe is endless. There is nothing to suggest that the rhythm of days, months, seasons and years will ever come to a halt, just as there is no end to the rhythm of birth, marriage, procreation and death.

These findings concerning Akamba and other African peoples' understanding of Time and History, are based on analyses of myths and language. We shall take myths first and deal with them briefly.

Every African society has its own myths, and there are many books that give accounts of such myths. All of these myths deal with the 'past', and cover themes like the creation of the world, explanation of natural phenomena, the origin of man and his various customs and traditions, the coming of death into the world, and the evolution of different societies. Myths are a basic part of oral traditions and education. Some of them are pure imagination, while others are based on historical events which, in non-literate societies, have to be handed down orally. In the course of this oral journey down the generations, such events acquire mythological colour. But myth and History belong together in the corpus of Akamba (and African) thinking and interpretation of the world. The significant point for our purpose here is that there are no myths about the future, as far as I have been able to gather from all the available sources that record African myths and stories.[1] This means, if one may so conclude, that the future dimension of Time has not been formulated and assimilated into the mythology of African thinking and conception of the universe. It leaves us with a two-dimension concept of Time. But we must test the hypothesis also on linguistic grounds.

I have analysed the tense pattern of a number of East African languages, including Kikamba, Gikuyu, Luganda, Lukiga, Acholi, Lusoga, Gisu and Rutoro. The same pattern emerges from these languages, but we shall take only Kikamba as an illustration. One of these languages, Acholi, belongs to the Nilotic language family, the remainder to the Bantu languages. I have not observed any significant difference on account of the language families, though it is perhaps necessary to take a larger sample of Nilotic languages.

Broadly speaking there are nine verb tenses in Kikamba.[2] Using the verb 'kuka' (to come), in the first person singular, we can tabulate its time range in the following manner:

Tense	Verb	English	Approximate Time
1. Far Future or Remote Future	Ningauka	I will come	About two to six months from NOW
2. Immediate or Near Future	Ninguka	I will come	Within a short while
3. Indefinite Future or Indefinite near Future	Ngooka (Ngauka)	I will come	Within a foreseeable while, after such and such an event

[1] One slight exception might be cited from the Sonjo in Tanzania. According to them, the world will one day shrink and come to an end, this event being preceded by a darkening of the sun as a result of a storm of dust, a flock of birds and a swarm of bees. I do not consider this as a serious myth about the future: rather, it is more of a 'possibility' against which the Sonjo have to be on guard. Their small country is dominated by a volcanic mountain which is still active and which, quite certainly, erupted several times in the past and brought their 'world' to the verge of an end (through the volcanic dust which 'darkened' the sun). This past event (or events) has now been transposed mythologically to the unknown future, as a 'possible' repetition with even greater dangers. See the account in: R. F. Gray, *The Sonjo of Tanganyika* (1963), especially 107 f. I have given the myth my own interpretation.

[2] These verb tenses, except number 9, are employed in Kikamba grammar books, viz.: E. M. Farnsworth, *A Kamba Grammar* (1954); W. H. Whiteley and M. G. Muli, *Practical Introduction to Kamba* (1962). Grammarians writing on the other languages employ different terminologies, but the ground covered is the same. I have included the ninth tense here as it plays an important role, especially in narratives, stories and myths.

Tense	Verb	English	Approximate Time
4. Present or Present Progressive	Ninukite	I am coming	In the process of action, NOW
5. Immediate Past or Immediate Perfect	Ninauka (Ninooka)	I came (I have just come)	in the last hour or so
6. Today's Past	Ninukie	I came	From the time of rising up to about two hours ago
7. Recent Past or Yesterday's Past	Nininaukie (Nininookie)	I came	Yesterday
8. Far Past or Remote Past	Ninookie (Ninaukie)	I came	Any day before yesterday
9. Unspecified TENE	Tene ninookie (Nookie tene)	I came	No specific time in the distant 'past'

In speaking or thinking about events, it is necessary to fit them into this tense-pattern. Nothing can be conceived of except within this framework, which falls clearly into two main categories. The first comprises the tenses around NOW, within the range of the 'present', or tenses 1 to 7. To avoid the associations with the English words 'Present' and 'Past', I will substitute Kikamba words, *Mituki* and *Tene*, respectively. *Mituki* concerns all that can be described or contemplated within the scope of tenses 1 to 7; *Tene* is everything else that falls within tenses 8 and 9. It is within the *mituki* period that we have what in a linear concept of Time amounts to the future, as represented by tenses 1 to 3. But we notice that these verb tenses carry the thought into an extremely limited range of the future stretching to about six months, and in any case not beyond two years from NOW. Similarly the 'past' part of *mituki* period is brief, up to about yesterday (tense 7).

For the Akamba then, *mituki* is the time period of greatest intensity, immediacy and nearness. It is the period of immediate concern; the point when Time is experienced in terms of 'now-ness', 'immediate-ness' and near 'pastness'. If an event is two or more years ahead, it falls outside the horizon of people's experience and it is hardly possible to conceive it. People cannot articulate what is in the distant future; they cannot speak about it and cannot, therefore, form myths about it. The Kikamba language is incapable of sustaining such a reality. Only what is in the rhythm of natural phenomena (day and night, rain and dry seasons, birth, marriage and death, etc.) can be thought about and expected to take place as it has always done. If anything else in the future is to be comprehended, it must be so near and certain that people have practically experienced it in their time consciousness (around tense 4). So, events which constitute Time in the *mituki* period must be either about to occur, or in the process of realization, or recently experienced. *Mituki* is the most meaningful Time period of the individual (and the community), because he has a personal recollection of the events or phenomena that constitute Time for this period, or he is about to experience them—they are within reach in both directions. *Mituki* is not mathematically constant: it is simply an experiential extension of the NOW moment into the (short) future and past. Individuals and communities, therefore, have different lengths of the *mituki* period. It is in this Time dimension that a person (or community) is most conscious of his existence; and it is within the same range of Time that he projects most meaningfully his being into the different strains of Time. One individual has a longer or bigger *mituki* period than another, depending partly on actual age and partly on the nature and intensity of his experiences.

The *tene* period is technically an extension of the *mituki*, but in the 'backward' direction. Both of these overlap; and when something disappears from the *mituki* period it enters the *tene* dimension of Time. Before anything has been absorbed into the *tene* period, it must go through the *mituki* dimension. *Tene* becomes the final storehouse, the point beyond which a phenomenon cannot go, the ultimate destiny of all things that may be caught up in the rhythm of motion.

Because *tene* is the dimension into which all phenomena sink, History according to Akamba (or African?) conception, is a movement from the *mituki* dimension, from the now period to the *tene* period. History moves 'backward' from the now moment to that period beyond which nothing can go. So the *tene* period is the centre of gravity in the Akamba conception of History: people's thinking and understanding of the world are orientated towards this finality—not in the future but in the past, in the *tene* dimension of Time. It is not a period of inactivity or extinction; it is not only *when*, but *where*, an explanation of the major cosmological problems and national experiences is to be sought—such as the creation of the universe, the origin of man, or the coming of death. In other words, here we meet once more the process of mythologizing the universe and national affairs.

Time reckoning according to the Akamba (and other African societies) is governed by phenomena rather than mathematics. People reckon Time for a concrete and specific purpose: one event in relation to another. There are no numerical calendars among the Akamba, nor have I encountered them in other African traditional societies. Time (the constitution of events) is reckoned according to the relation of its various events. The day, for example, is reckoned according to the major events: rising up, milking cattle, herding, working in the fields, driving cattle to the watering places, returning home for the night, preparing and eating the evening meal and going to sleep. It does not matter exactly *when* the event of rising up takes place; the important point of reckoning time is the fact of rising up in the morning. The Akamba recognize lunar months, but these are named according to the major events or phenomena taking place in the country, such as the 'hot' month (about October), 'the month of early rains' (about March), 'the month of millet' (about July), etc. The year is also reckoned according to its major phenomena, chiefly the seasons of rain and dry weather together with all the events that go with them. It does not matter whether the month is 25 or 35 days long, nor whether the year is 330 or 380 days long. So long as the events that constitute a complete month or year take place, then the month or year is complete, since it is the events and not the mathematics which constitute Time and hence determine its reckoning. There is nothing to indicate that this rhythm of nature will ever change radically or come to a complete halt.

Human life follows also another rhythm which knows neither end nor radical alteration. This is the rhythm of birth, initiation, marriage, procreation, old age, death and entry into the company of the departed. Each rhythm gives way to the next and hence appears to be moving forward, but the whole momentum as a one-piece drama, is in reality, according to Akamba conception, moving from the *mituki* period to the *tene*, from the 'present' to the 'past', and not forwards to some far off event or goal. As the individual gets older, he is in effect moving gradually from his *mituki* period to the *tene*, he is sinking from the *now* to the distant oblivion. Death is, therefore, a process of removing a person from the *mituki* of his being and that of his contemporaries, until he eventually disappears into the remote *tene.* We shall return to this concept for further discussion when we consider the meaning of death and the spirit world. We need only observe here that physical death starts the long process of removing the individual from the NOW period, until, after four or five generations, he disappears completely when the last person who knew him also dies physically. It is here that we must appreciate the importance of 'remembering' the departed, which is one of the most dominant features of African religious concepts and activities. By remembering the departed, his relatives retain him in their *mituki* period, in what may be called '*personal immortality*' since he is remembered personally and by name, and is addressed as such during the act of pouring out libation and giving of food—which constitute acts of 'remembrance', fellowship and renewal of relationship between the living and the living-dead. For that reason, the departed of up to four or five generations are best described as the 'living-dead' for they are dead in body, but alive in spirit and in the memories of their surviving relatives. When five generations or so are over, then the living-dead is remembered no longer by name: he now *dies* relative to human beings, but survives in spirit form, in the state of *collective immortality* (where his spirit is one of myriads of unknown spirits of those who once were human beings and those created by God as the species of spirits).

Time and Space are closely linked in Akamba thinking as evidenced by the use of many common words, thus:

TIME: Ivinda, Vandu, Uthei, Mwanya, Kilungu

SPACE: Kundu, Vandu, Uthei, Mwanya, Kilungu

We can now draw some conclusions arising out of this discussion of the Akamba (African?) concept of Time and History.

(i) We have seen that the Akamba (and probably most other African societies) have a two-dimension concept of Time. This constitutes an indefinite 'past' which is the terminus of all phenomena and events, and which is dominated by the myth; and an intensely active 'present' in which the individual or community is most conscious of his (its) existence and being.

(ii) There is virtually no future dimension of Time, beyond a few years at most. What is certain to occur in the future must either take place shortly, or be embedded in the rhythm of natural phenomena like birth, procreation and death, or day, night and seasons.

(iii) We arrive at these two conclusions through an analysis of African myths and the verb tenses of several languages. Accordingly, there are no myths about the future; and the languages examined cannot sustain or express the concept of the future outside the rhythmic phenomena.

(iv) Since there is no indefinite future in Akamba thinking, there is also no concept of the end of the world. To Akamba and other African peoples, history moves 'backwards', and cannot therefore head towards a goal, a climax or termination. There is nothing to suggest that the otherwise constant two-dimension Time will ever be altered or terminated. People have nothing to fear and nothing to set their mind upon, as far as the future is concerned. The momentum of History is a gradual process of moving from the 'present' to the 'past'. The centre of gravity in History lies in the past and not in the present or the otherwise very short future. Any sense of historical depth is in what has happened rather than what will yet happen. The whole thinking and expectation of the people is directed towards the 'past' dimension of Time which, consequently, is rich in mythology, shines with a brightness of explaining what otherwise puzzles man today, and takes pride in its national pillars and heroes.

(v) Technically speaking, Akamba (or African) eschatological concepts are not 'eschatological' in the strict sense, since they are directed towards 'the end' of the opposite direction, the 'end' which has been rather than will be, in the context of a two-dimension concept of Time and History. They lack τὸ τέλος—they are eschatological but not teleological. Paradoxically, in Akamba concepts, these events or phenomena come to an end because they are swept from the now (*mituki*) period to the *tene* period in an endless rhythm which knows neither interruption nor termination. By removal from the *mituki* to the *tene*, events come to an 'end', to a terminus. There is, therefore, both an 'endness' and an 'endlessness' about them: they have a finality and a repeatability, a constant and a rhythm. There is no room in this scheme of thought for teleology and fulfilment.

(vi) In passing we need to observe, however, that a future dimension of Time is being born in Akamba thinking and life. This is partly due to the Christian concept of Eschatology, and partly to a western type education with its emphasis on individualism and planning for, or thinking about, the future. I have the impression that for people who speak only Kikamba, this future orientation is still very short and without any serious impact upon their whole life; but the case is different for those who constantly use English and have assimilated a three-dimensional concept of Time into their perception and living.

At this point we shall turn to the picture in the New Testament.

(b) Time and Eschatology in the New Testament

Of the literature on New Testament Eschatology there is no end. In a brief survey such as is offered here, one pretends to do no more than give a summary of familiar ground rather than propose any new formulations.[1]

The New Testament and the Christian Faith evolved against a background of Jewish Eschatology and apocalyptic. Much of the extant Jewish literature produced between 200 B.C. and A.D. 100 shows great interest in this direction. This is clear from the contents of later chapters of Daniel, the O.T. Apocrypha, the Pseudepigrapha and the Dead Sea Scrolls. Every writer of the New Testament has something to say on the subject of Eschatology.

But whilst primitive Christianity was thus influenced by Jewish ideas, there is a turning point which makes Christian Eschatology radically different from Jewish. This is the Incarnation. In Jewish thought there were two Ages: הָעוֹלָם הַזֶּה (This Age) and הָעוֹלָם הַבָּא (The Age to Come).[2] The former was evil, sorrowful, etc., but the latter would be the opposite, and with God's reign fully established. This is precisely the point at which the Christian differentia comes into the picture. Through the Incarnation, the Age to Come has intercepted This Age. Christian Eschatology becomes, therefore, fundamentally a Christological phenomenon. As Bornkamm points out in his *Jesus of Nazareth* (ET 1960), the future and the present are interwoven; the present reveals the future, and the future unlocks and lights up the present.[3] All this happens in the Life,

---

[1] Some of the familiar names on the subject of Eschatology include: J. Weiss, R. H. Charles, A. Schweitzer, A. F. Loisy, E. von Dobschütz, R. Otto, E. F. Scott, J. Héring, C. H. Dodd, T. W. Manson, C. J. Cadoux, E. Grässer, T. F. Glasson, O. Cullmann, W. G. Kümmel, J. Jeremias, R. Bultmann, K. Barth, J. A. T. Robinson, J. Moltmann, H. Conzelmann, etc.

[2] I En. 71: 15 (II En. 65: 8), II Bar. 14: 13; 15: 8, IV Ezra 4: 27; 7: 12 f., 47; 8: 1, Mt. 12: 32, Mk. 10: 30 par. See a recent consideration of the two Ages in terms of their temporal and spatial dimensions by T. L. Wilkinson, 'Doctrine of the Two Ages', in *Vox Reformata*, No. 8 (1967), pp. 1–13.

[3] G. Bornkamm, *Jesus of Nazareth* (ET 1960), 92 ff. The importance of the present as the day of Salvation is also stressed by J. Jeremias in his *The Parables of Jesus* (ET 1954), especially 93–9, (Jeremias' book is cited here as *Parables*.)

Ministry, Death and Resurrection of Jesus Christ. That is the general understanding of New Testament writers, even if they work it out with different emphases.

The Incarnation precipitates 'the last event', the event which, as Barrett rightly observes, 'is not merely one member of the series: it is the determinative member, which reveals the meaning of the whole.'[1] It is Jesus who sets in motion the great eschatological wheel.

But this is not the wheel in terms of Albert Schweitzer's contention. According to him, at the time of sending out the Twelve (Mk. 6: 6b–13 pars.), Jesus is expecting the Kingdom of God to come speedily, but He waits in vain. Consequently He decides to force the issue. So, Schweitzer writes, 'the Son of Man lays hold of the wheel of the world to set it moving on that last revolution which is to bring all ordinary history to a close. It refuses to turn, and He throws Himself upon it. Then it does turn; and crushes Him . . . .'[2] By his death, Jesus sets in motion the eschatological development of History, letting loose the final woes, and thus introduces the supra-mundane phase of the eschatological drama, according to Schweitzer's 'Konsequente Eschatologie', expounded in *Das Messianitäts und Leidensgeheimnis* (1901) and *Von Reimarus zu Wrede* (1906).[3]

But 'Konsequente Eschatologie' ('Thoroughgoing Eschatology' or 'Consistent Eschatology') does not adequately interpret the teaching and work of Jesus. This is partly because of the wrong basis for Schweitzer's thesis, and partly because it attempts to explain too much.[4] Schweitzer ignores altogether the Fourth Gospel, and much of the Synoptic material, which otherwise is relevant in such a study. In

[1] C. K. Barrett, 'New Testament Eschatology', article in the *SJT*, Vol. VI, No. 2 (June 1953), p. 136.

[2] A. Schweitzer, *The Quest of the Historical Jesus* (ET 1910), 396 (cited here as *Quest*); cf. his *The Mystery of the Kingdom* (ET 1925), especially chapter 1 (cited here as *Mystery*).

[3] The English titles are: *The Mystery of the Kingdom* (1925), and *The Quest of the Historical Jesus* (1910), respectively.

[4] Schweitzer started from the thesis of Johannes Weiss in the latter's *Die Predigt Jesu vom Reiche Gottes* (1893), in assuming that the Life and Teaching of Jesus have to be explained on either eschatological or non-eschatological lines only. But these are not necessarily the alternatives by which we have to intepret our Lord's life and Ministry, and, by taking the eschatological alternative, Schweitzer omits items which fall outside these alternatives. It is impossible to accept the assertion that by going to Jerusalem to be crucified, Jesus was thereby forcing God's hand to bring about the Kingdom. Schweitzer does not convincingly explain why the 'Messianic Secret' was supposed to be so vital in the Life of Jesus. Neither does he explain the basis on which he assumes that Jesus expected the Kingdom

effect, 'Konsequente Eschatologie' makes the Kingdom of God a still future event, even though the Messiah has come but only 'as the Messiah that is to be . . . .' This Messiah remains two personalities —terrestrial and celestial figures, one for the present, the other for the Age to come.[1] Such interpretation seems to do injustice to the New Testament, and deprives the ministry and life of our Lord of their present impact except in terms of an 'Interimsethik'.[2] Using the same principles, Schweitzer attempts to interpret Paul's writings in *Die Geschichte der paulinischen Forschung* (1911).[3] But, in spite of its weaknesses, Schweitzer's study of the Gospels marked a turning point from the liberal studies of the life of our Lord in the nineteenth century. The debate opened by his 'Konsequente Eschatologie' was centred more in England and America than on the Continent.[4]

In reaction to Schweitzer's 'Konsequente Eschatologie', E. von Dobschütz put forth the idea of 'Transmuted Eschatology', in his *The Eschatology of the Gospels* (1910). He argued and pointed out that 'Jesus Himself by His complete union with God brings in this domination of God: it is where He is; it is present among men; it is to be found in men's hearts . . . He is actually bringing it in . . .' (Mt. 11: 9–10, Lk. 7: 26–8; 16: 16). After the Resurrection, the disciples have 'actual possession of a present benefit' of that which had hitherto been a matter of anticipation. In Jesus Christ 'the Kingdom is at hand, it is present in His person, in His casting out devils, in His bringing sinners to repentance—but it has still to come in glory.'[5] It is mainly in the third lecture of this book that von

to appear so precisely at the time of the sending of the Twelve (*Quest*, p. 357; Mt. 10: 23). Some of his exegesis and rearrangement of historical data is dubious and subjective.

Among the many critics of Schweitzer's approach and theory, see: N. Perrin, *The Kingdom of God in the Teaching of Jesus* (1963, cited here as *Kingdom*), 32–57; J. Moltmann, *Theologie der Hoffnung* (1965), 31 ff.; R. H. Hiers, 'Eschatology and Methodology' in JBL, Vol. 85, No. 2 (1966), 170–84; and R. Clark 'Matthew 10: 23 and Eschatology', in *Restoration Quarterly*, Vol. 7, Nos. 1–2 (1963), pp. 73–81 and Vol. 8, No. 1 (1965), pp. 53–68.

[1] *Mystery*, 190 ff.

[2] *Mystery*, 84–155—he concludes that the Lord transformed eschatological ethics into ethical eschatology (p. 115); *Quest*, 328–95. Cf. A. N. Wilder, *Eschatology and Ethics in the Teaching of Jesus* (rev. 1950, cited here as *Eschatology*).

[3] ET: *Paul and His Interpreters* (1912).

[4] See Perrin's comments about this, op. cit., 35 f.; and for a summary of the subsequent discussion, see 37–57. Note, however, the support of Schweitzer's views in Germany by, among others, M. Werner in *Die Entstehung des Christlichen Dogmas* (1941).

[5] Op. cit., 21 ff.

Dobschütz propounds at length his concept of 'Transmuted Eschatology'. Of this he says that it is 'transmuted in the sense that what was spoken of in Jewish eschatology as to come in the last days is taken here as already at hand in the lifetime of Jesus; transmuted at the same time in the other sense that what was expected as an external change is taken inwardly: not all people seeing it, but Jesus' disciples becoming aware of it.'[1] Von Dobschütz thinks that 'Transmuted Eschatology' is most evidently represented in the Fourth Gospel, where it is also individualized.[2] Thus, according to von Dobschütz, the 'last days' have dawned, and the Kingdom of God has come and is coming in glory. This is clearly a different emphasis from that of Schweitzer's.

The idea was carried much further by C. H. Dodd, the chief exponent of 'Realized Eschatology'. He made the first statement of his 'Realized Eschatology' in a brief paper in 1927, and developed it much further in *The Parables of the Kingdom* (1935), *The Apostolic Preaching and its Developments* (1936), and *The Mind of Paul* (1936). In reacting strongly against Schweitzer's 'Konsequente Eschatologie', Dodd goes almost to the extreme view of emphasizing the 'realization' of the Kingdom of God at the expense of its future reality. This tends to minimize the tension between the present and the future aspects of the Kingdom. 'Realized Eschatology' as such falls into the danger of ignoring the fruition of the Kingdom at the consummation of all things. But not all scholars accepted Dodd's exposition, and J. Y. Campbell made an outright rejection of Dodd's interpretation of ἐγγίζειν and φθάνειν.[3] The same decade saw also the views of T. W. Manson who emphasized that the present realization of the Kingdom pointed towards the future consummation.[4] At a later date, Dodd modified his views in *The Coming of Christ* (1951).[5]

---

[1] Op. cit., 150.

[2] Op. cit., 187–207; cf. C. F. D. Moule on the individualistic Eschatology in John's Gospel, in *Novum Testamentum*, Vol. V, Fasc. 2/3 (1962), pp. 171–90, entitled 'The Individualism of St. John's Gospel'; and echoed in his *The Birth of the New Testament* (1962), 98.

[3] J. Y. Campbell, 'The Kingdom of God has Come', in the *Ex T*, Vol. XLVIII, No. 2 (November 1936), pp. 91–4.

[4] T. W. Manson, *The Sayings of Jesus* (in *The Mission and Message of Jesus*, together with H. D. A. Major and C. J. Wright, 1937), and his earlier work, *The Teaching of Jesus* (1931). See N. Perrin, *Kingdom* (1936), 68, 90 ff.

[5] See Perrin, op. cit., 57–78, for further discussion and criticism on Dodd's 'Realized Eschatology'. Dodd's later position recognized the Coming of the Kingdom in the Ministry and Resurrection of Jesus, as well as at Pentecost, and fuller manifestation 'beyond History' (so Perrin, op. cit., 67 ff.).

A balance seemed necessary between Schweitzer's and Dodd's approaches. Some scholars have attempted to provide this, such as C. J. Cadoux, H. A. Guy, R. H. Fuller and others.[1] A summary and review of the discussion are given by N. Perrin in *The Kingdom of God in the Teaching of Jesus* (1963), and we need not enter more fully into this debate. There are, however, a few other interpretations put forward, which we ought to mention, although these have not received great publicity or support.

R. Bultmann's 'Reinterpreted Eschatology'[2] tries to interpret History from the point of view of Eschatology, whereby the latter swallows up the former. Accordingly, 'the Christian community understands itself as the goal and consummation of the history of salvation,' so he writes in his *History and Eschatology* (1957). As such, 'the new people of God has no real history, for it is the community of the end-time, an eschatological phenomenon. . . .'[3] Yet Bultmann recognizes the tension, that Christian existence is between 'no longer' and 'not yet', and the importance of the Sacraments in this interim period. But it does not seem adequate to eliminate the element of time from the teaching and attitude of Jesus, as this existentialist approach tries to do.

There is also T. F. Glasson's contention in *The Second Advent* (1945) that the doctrine of the Parousia is foreign to the Old Testament, to the Apocrypha, and to the teaching of Jesus. He goes on to say that it is difficult to find support for the 'axiom' that the early Church believed in an imminent Parousia; and that 'the Parousia clearly did not form a part of the original Gospel.'[4] He asserts that the idea of 'coming again' came from O.T. passages about God which were applied to Jesus as coming for judgement, even though 'we could find no solid foundation in His own teaching' for such doctrine.[5]

[1] See Perrin, op. cit., 79 ff.

[2] R. Bultmann, 'History and Eschatology in the N.T.', an article in *NTS*, Vol. I, No. 1 (Sept. 1954), pp. 5–16; and *History and Eschatology* (1957). It is impossible to do full justice to Bultmann's views here, but for a summary and criticism of his interpretation, see N. Q. Hamilton, *The Holy Spirit and Eschatology in Paul* (1957), S.J.T. Occasional Papers No. 6, pp. 71–82; and Perrin, op. cit. 112–19. Bultmann has updated this material in *Geschichte und Eschatologie* (1964).

[3] R. Bultmann, *History and Eschatology*, 34 ff.

[4] T. F. Glasson, *The Second Advent* (1945), 151–6. In reconstructing what he calls the essential skeleton of the Kerygma (154 f.), Glasson omits the item of the Lord's 'coming again'.

[5] Op. cit., 176. Glasson speaks about 'transmuted eschatology' (though his usage is different from that of von Dobschütz), which is especially 'at home'

The same conclusion is reached by J. A. T. Robinson in *Jesus and His Coming* (1957), though by a different argument. He sees the future as belonging to Christ, 'till the final consummation of this age and the reduction of its powers to the authority he has been given . . .'. But, 'of another advent of Christ after an interval—of this we saw no evidence in the teaching of Jesus; of it too we found no signs in the earliest preaching and creeds of the Church . . .'.[1] In this book Robinson advocates what he calls 'Inaugurated Eschatology'. Such Eschatology 'looked, that is to say, not for another coming of Christ, but to the certain reduction of all things to the Christ who had come, and whose "coming to his own", alike in victory and in visitation, was from now on the ultimate and most pressing reality with which men must reckon.'[2]

But there are other scholars who have asserted the future consummation in form of the Parousia or the Second Advent.[3]

Another interpretation of Eschatology which is very relevant to our discussion of Time and Eschatology, is the one put forth by O. Cullmann, in *Christus und die Zeit* (1945, ET: *Christ and Time*, 1951). This interpretation is in terms of a 'Heilsgeschichte' built around the notion that in Christianity the 'mid-point' in a linear conception of Time, has been reached on the Cross.[4] The D-Day is over, and only the final victory is yet to come. This is an interesting approach, but we cannot draw such a sharp distinction between words like καιρός and χρόνος, as Cullmann does. The analogy of war and victory is likewise overdone. It is false to suggest only a single biblical

---

in the Fourth Gospel, 210. Cf. the résumé and criticism of Glasson's views by Perrin, op. cit., 136 ff.

[1] J. A. T. Robinson, *Jesus and His Coming* (1957, cited here as *Coming*), 137, and especially chapter six, 118–39.

[2] Op. cit., 161. Robinson admits that Jesus saw a future consummation—a point denied by Glasson. See Perrin, op. cit., 143 f. Cf. N. Clark, in *An Approach to the Theology of the Sacraments* (1956), 27 *et passim*, where he uses the same term, 'Inaugurated Eschatology'.

[3] E.g., G. R. Beasley-Murray, *Jesus and the Future* (1954)—a conservative approach to the discussion of Mk. 13 (cf. Perrin's comments, op. cit., 130–4); and O. Cullmann in *The Early Church* (1956, ed. A. J. B. Higgins), 141–62, following a similar approach to his *Christ and Time*. Cf. also E. Grässer, *Das Problem der Perusieverzögerung in den synoptischen Evangelien und der Apostelgeschichte* (1957), arguing that Jesus taught only a futuristic Eschatology.

[4] O. Cullmann, *Christ and Time*, 81–93, 119–74; cf. his *The Early Church* (1956), 141 ff., 150 ff. He gives a further discussion and some modification of these ideas in his *Heil als Geschichte* (1965), bringing together the past and future as a cultic event on the horizontal dimension of Time.

conception of Time, and this false basis must undermine the whole theory and interpretation.

The question of Time is not a major concern of the Bible. Consequently there is no single or consistent view of Time in the Bible. Instead we find several views of Time, of which we might cite a few examples below. It seems as if the characteristically western notion of Time with a threefold linear dimension has so deeply and subconsciously governed our understanding of New Testament Eschatology that we presumably have a distorted or exaggerated picture of the whole subject. Outside the linear concept of Time, there are, to my knowledge, no studies of biblical views of Time. J. Barr's *Biblical Words for Time* (1962) attempts, *inter alia*, to undermine this linear interpretation of Time; but modern studies hardly depart from what has now come to be taken for granted.[1] The three-dimensional linear concept of Time is clearly one of the biblical views, but why has it been allowed to dominate our thinking and understanding of Eschatology to the exclusion of other views? It appears, too, that in relation to New Testament Eschatology, Time is an intensely christological phenomenon. Any departure from that is bound to do much injustice to the subject of Eschatology. Jesus is the Christ of Time as well as of ultra-Time; He is the Jesus of History as well as of ultra-History; He is simultaneously the Alpha and the Omega, in Time and beyond Time.

In the Lucan writings there is a clear chronological account of the Life, Ministry, Death, Resurrection and departure of Jesus, followed by the geographical and temporal expansion of the Church from Jerusalem to the uttermost parts of the earth. As a historical portrait, this could be regarded as a linear concept of Time, and a number of scholars have considered Luke's Eschatology along these lines.[2] Yet, a closer examination of Luke's use of Time in eschatological utterances seems to make room for a modification (or complication)

---

[1] See, for example, in addition to Cullmann's book cited above, H. Conzelmann, *Die Mitte der Zeit* (2nd edn. 1957); J. Moltmann *Theologie der Hoffnung* (1965); E. E. Ellis, 'Present and Future Eschatology in Luke', in *NTS*, Vol. 12, No. 1 (1965), pp. 27–41; J. Kingsbury, 'The "Jesus of History" and the "Christ of Faith"; in Relation to Matthew's view of Time—Reactions to a new Approach', in *Concordia Theological Monthly*, Vol. 37, No. 8 (1966), pp. 500–10; J. E. Bruns, 'The Use of Time in the Fourth Gospel', in *NTS*, Vol. 13, No. 3 (1967), pp. 285–90; J. Mánek, 'The Biblical Concept of Time and Our Gospels', in *NTS*, Vol. 6, No. 1 (1959), pp. 45–51; and others.

[2] See note 1 (*supra*), for contributions by H. Conzelmann, E. E. Ellis and J. Mánek.

of what on the surface appears to be a straight linear concept of Time.[1] Could we continue to be content with an assumption of only a linear concept of Time even in Luke?

The Fourth Gospel clearly confronts us with an entirely different understanding of Time. Here, Time is almost suppressed for the sake of Eternity which lends new dimensions to the characteristic themes of Life, Light, Knowledge, Belief, Judgement and the like. It is almost ridiculous to discuss Time in the Fourth Gospel, and in any case it cannot be done in terms of a linear concept.[2] It is here, more than elsewhere in the Gospels, that we find Eschatology most personalized[3] and, if one may so coin the phrase, most christologized.

If we may digress to the Old Testament, we find a 'cyclic' view of Time in the book of Ecclesiastes (e.g. 1: 4–11, 3: 1–8, 15, etc.) where we hear that 'what has been is what will be, . . . and there is nothing new under the sun' (1: 9), and 'that which is, already has been' (3: 15). Furthermore, as J. Marsh points out, the O.T. Jews were more concerned with the *content* than the *chronology* of Time.[4] On this particular point we come close to African notions of Time in which the actual event is far more important than its chronology as such. A radical difference is, however, introduced by the Jewish eschatological hope which increasingly permeates the later writers of the Old Testament and of which we find not even the remotest idea or parallel in African background. Yet even this Jewish twofold dimension of History, with its 'This Age' and 'The Age to Come', is not strictly three-dimensional. It compresses Time into two constituents.

The Incarnation means, *inter alia*, that in Jesus there is an irreversible intrusion into and interruption of the Jewish expectations. The two Ages coincide in Him, and take on an entirely new perspec-

[1] Cf. Ellis' (note 1, p. 38 *supra*) discussion of Lk. 3: 16f.; 9: 27 and 23: 43, concluding that there is a juxtaposition of present and future Eschatology which is found in these and other Lucan passages, and is present in Markan and Q materials as well as in the Johannine tradition (pp. 40 f.). Cf. also an examination of Matthaean Time, by J. Kingsbury (note 1, p. 38 *supra*), which approaches the conclusion reached by Ellis concerning Luke.

[2] The examination of Time clauses in the Fourth Gospel by J. E. Bruns (note 1, p. 38 *supra*) is useful, but limited to the chronological and symbolic aspects of Time.

[3] See, for further discussion of personalized eschatology in the Fourth Gospel, C. F. D. Moule, 'The Individualism of the Fourth Gospel', in *Novum Testamentum*, Vol. V, Fasc. 2/3 (1962), pp. 171–90; and more fully, P. Ricca, *Die Eschatologie des vierten Evangeliums* (1966).

[4] J. Marsh, *The Fulness of Time* (1952), 21, 24 ff., *et passim*. This view is endorsed by J. Mánek (note 1, p. 38 *supra*).

tive. That new perspective cannot be explained away exclusively by a single or linear conception of Time, however much illumination we might derive from scholars like Cullmann, Moltmann and others.

The Eschatology of the New Testament derives its meaning and content from the Incarnation, of which the Cross is the heart. As such the Ministry of Jesus moves towards a climax on the Cross, and nothing can halt that event: '. . . so must the Son of Man be lifted up' (Jn. 3: 14 f.). In turn this gives birth and life to the eschatological community which moves in all directions—whether futuristic or past—from the Cross. When Jesus declares that 'I, when I am lifted up from the earth, will draw all men to myself' (Jn. 12: 32), this cannot be directed only to those who come historically into existence *after* the Cross. It is a cosmic declaration which sweeps in all directions of Time, like a giant radar installation. Upon the Cross all that needed to be fulfilled and revealed to usher in the New Age is realized, and Jesus rightly cries 'It is finished' (Jn. 19: 30). His Resurrection occurs both in Time and beyond Time, so that He becomes the first fruits (I Cor. 15: 20) of those who are destined to the Age of Fulfilment. New Testament Eschatology becomes a phenomenon of christological Fulfilment and Revelation—fulfilled promises of God and the revelation of the mysteries of what in Christ has all the Time been a reality, but of which 'it does not yet appear what we shall be' (I Jn. 3: 2).[1]

But for Jesus Himself, the Age to Come does not simply commence at His Death-Resurrection event. He brings it in His own person, as the Gospels bear witness (Mt. 11: 12–14, Lk. 16: 16, etc.).[2] He submits to Baptism with the spirit of 'it is fitting for us to fulfil all righteousness' (Mt. 3: 15). The same note is struck at Nazareth (Lk. 4: 21); and He begins His Galilean ministry in a similar key:

---

[1] J. Moltmann, in *Theologie der Hoffnung* (1965), is making an important distinction between Revelation (or unveiling, Enthüllung) and Fulfilment in connection with what Christ's future will bring. See pp. 125–209 for his fuller discussion of the matter.

[2] These verses, Mt. 11: 12–14 and Lk. 16: 16, are extremely difficult. Schweitzer was probably right when he wrote that 'this saying resists all exegesis' (*Mystery*, 111). It is almost certain that two epochs (in Luke's account, perhaps three in Matthew's) are pointed to: one lasting up to John, and the other starting from him onwards—so Dodd, *Parables*, 48; cf. Cullmann, *The Christology of the New Testament* (ET 1959), 44, on Mt. 11: 11. W. G. Kümmel sees a limit in ἕως ἄρτι when the Kingdom appears in the future, *Promise and Fulfilment* (ET 1957), 124. C. H. Kraeling sees three periods: of preparation, the present, and the future—in *John the Baptist* (1951), 156 f.

'. . . πεπλήρωται ὁ καιρὸς καὶ ἤγγικεν ἡ βασιλεία τοῦ Θεοῦ' (Mk. 1: 15). He is conscious that He is the Bringer of the Last Days, having come not to abolish the Law and the Prophets, but to fulfil them (cf. Mt. 5: 17, Lk. 24: 24–7).[1] So He proclaims the Gospel of fulfilment (Lk. 4: 16–21, Mk. 1: 14 f.), and His vocabulary of words like 'Kingdom', 'repentance', 'judgement', etc., is intensely eschatological. According to Bultmann, Mk. 1: 15 is the summary of Jesus' preaching. For Dodd, ἤγγικεν ἡ βασιλεία τοῦ Θεοῦ (Mk. 1: 15) is equatable with ἔφθασεν ἐφ' ὑμᾶς ἡ βασιλεία τοῦ Θεοῦ (Lk. 11: 20), and both imply the arrival of the Kingdom.[2] Kümmel, on the other hand, thinks that 'the Kingdom is expected as a future reality in Jesus' message.'[3] Both the present and future realities are essential characteristics of the Kingdom: it has come and it will come, and this is what constitutes its essentially eschatological and christological nature.

Repentance, to which both John the Baptist and Jesus call their hearers (Mt. 3: 2, 4: 17; Mk. 1: 15), is an eschatological phenomenon. It is announced over against the present (in Jesus) and coming judgement and salvation. As Wilder points out, the Kingdom is both Promise and Warning.[4] The time for the new heart, the New Covenant (Ezek. 11: 19–20; 34: 25; Jer. 31: 31–4, etc.) has arrived—it is fulfilled. The Passion of our Lord epitomizes the end of the old era, and the birth of the new. When he cries: 'I have a baptism to be baptized with; and how I am constrained until it is accomplished' (Lk. 12: 50), He refers 'to the release and victory that will mark the end of His present obedience, . . . involving Him now in constriction and ultimately in death', as Robinson remarks.[5] The new era presses hard upon the old, and the crisis that ensues has fateful demands.[6]

---

[1] It is wrong to argue that Jesus necessarily fashioned His life to conform to His awareness of Messiahship, or that He acted consciously to fulfil the details of O.T. or other references about the Messiah, the Servant of Yahweh, the Son of Man, etc. J. Marsh falls into this danger when he says that 'Jesus himself consciously acted, or consciously interpreted his actions, in fulfilment of Old Testament scripture' (*The Fulness of Time*, 83); and Schweitzer has similar tendencies.

[2] R. Bultmann, *Theology of the New Testament*, Vol. I (ET 1952), 5 (this work is cited here as *Theology* I, II). Dodd, *Parables*, 44. But see the objections to this interpretation, by J. Y. Campbell, note 3, p. 35 *supra*.

[3] Kümmel, op. cit., p. 43.   [4] Wilder, op. cit., Chap. IV.

[5] Robinson, *Coming*, 41.

[6] Wilder, op. cit., 179. Perhaps the idea of Jesus precipitating a crisis, as stressed by men like Bultmann, Dodd and Jeremias, has been over-taxed. Is it possible that our history of crises leads us to see crisis in the Gospels even when it is either absent or minimal?

John the Baptist is symbolically the dividing line between the Old and the New Aeon, so that 'before him, (are) the law and prophets; after him, the Kingdom of God. Any interim period is excluded', as Dodd argues in his *Parables*. Jesus points out the things which He is accomplishing as signs of the arrival of the Kingdom (Mt. 11: 4–5, Lk. 7: 22). But another dimension of the Kingdom is that it 'is not coming with signs to be observed' (Lk. 17: 20), nor can it be pin-pointed to either spatial (Lk. 17: 21) or temporal dimensions (Lk. 19: 11–27, Mt. 25: 14–30, Acts 1: 6 f.). But does not our treatment of Eschatology along linear concepts of Time all too often drive us aground on temporal sands?

Jesus brings the Kingdom of God into human history, and Dodd interprets the parables of our Lord in this light. But the realization of the Kingdom is not exhausted in the present: it retains more futurity than Dodd allows. This futurity is yet present in Jesus Christ; it is to be realized by the Church in terms of unveiling and fulfilment. According to Dodd Jesus does not look for a Parousia in the future. But Kümmel shows in *Promise and Fulfilment* (ET 1957), that even though the presence of Jesus is an eschatological one, 'the "little flock" receives the promise because it gathers as believers round Jesus and thereby enters into relation with the promised eschaton already in the present,' (p. 54); and the Parousia is pressing and may be at any moment (Mt. 24: 44b). Consequently, Kümmel takes to be referring to the future the parables of the Faithful and the Unfaithful Servants (Mt. 24: 45–51), the Thief in the Night (Mt. 24: 42–4), the Waiting Servants (Lk. 12: 39 f.), and the Ten Virgins (Mt. 24: 1–13). He also sees an interval between the Death-and-Resurrection of Jesus and a future Parousia.[1] But if there is a future to the Kingdom, it is a reality which cannot be divorced from its present effectiveness. This is where Dodd's contribution of 'Realized Eschatology' becomes so crucial, even if not sufficient.

In Jesus the Kingdom has come (Mt. 12: 28), but that is only the beginning which points towards the future consummation (cf. Mt. 24: 14)—also in Him. What in Judaism was yet to come has arrived in the Person and Work of Jesus Christ. He is the Messiah, the Son of Man, God's chosen in Whom He is well pleased (Mk. 1: 11 pars.). So on the Cross, the ultimate in significance is fulfilled, setting the Christian era in motion between two poles, viz., the End has come

---

[1] Kümmel, op. cit., 73 ff., cf. von Dobschütz, op. cit., 194 ff.

and paradoxically the End is yet to be. As a result of this, the Eucharist is celebrated as unveiling the whole eschatological drama from the
Cross to the consummation of the ages. As the Eucharist is Christocentric, so is also Eschatology.

The eschatological message of Jesus is first and foremost to 'this
generation', a wicked (Mt. 16: 4) and faithless generation (Mt. 17:17)
seeking for proofs (Mt. 12: 39). But a number of His hearers follow
Him, some of whom believe in Him and thereby enter into eternal
life (Jn. 3: 36; 5: 24, etc.)—a new non-temporal mode of existence. It
is in the Fourth Gospel that Eschatology is most intensely 'realized',
and the more so because it is intimately bound up with the Person of
Jesus Himself. The words *the Gospel* (τὸ εὐαγγέλιον) and *evangelize*
(εὐαγγελίζω) do not occur in this Gospel, but Jesus Himself is indeed
THE GOSPEL. It is He who personally confronts men and women—
Andrew, Peter, Nathanael, Nicodemus, the Samaritan woman, the
cripple by the pool of Beth-zatha, Mary, Martha, and others. In this
encounter, He brings both judgement and salvation (life), and the
result depends on men's response. They either pass from death into
life (Jn. 3: 15 ff., 36; 5: 24, etc.), or remain under judgement (3: 18 f.,
36, etc.). The Spirit is given to the eschatological community (14, 16),
and Jesus Himself comes after 'a little while' (16: 16) to be with His
followers. There is virtually no interval between the Resurrection and
Parousia of our Lord in the Fourth Gospel. He makes nonsense of
the Time rhythm as far as eschatological experiences are concerned.

In his *Apostolic Preaching*, Dodd argues out a strong case that it is
in Paul's epistles that full justice is done to 'Realized Eschatology'.
Paul's Eschatology in the Thessalonian epistles is largely futurist
and apocalyptic, being in main based on Jewish apocalyptic. In
later epistles (Romans, Colossians, etc.), it takes on a cosmic scope
embracing the entire creation in the purpose of God's redemption.
But we must emphasize that he does not dismiss the Parousia; and in
addition he uses other words like *reveal* (ἀποκαλύπτει), *revelation* or
disclosure (ἡ ἀποκάλυψις), the difficult τὸ πλήρωμα (*that which
fills, the fulness*), etc. We are the ones upon whom the end of the
ages (τὰ τέλη τῶν αἰώνων) has come (I. Cor. 10: 11), because the
last (ἔσχατος) Adam (I. Cor. 15: 45) has appeared in history, at the
fulness of time (Gal. 4: 4). Without dwelling on the work and teaching
of our Lord, Paul takes the Cross as his starting point in interpreting
and presenting the Gospel. For him the Age to Come has come with
the Lord's Resurrection, and the Kingdom of God has come in the

life of Jesus Christ.[1] Eschatological realities become meaningful only inasfar as they are christologically grounded, and as such they are both in and beyond Time.

Possibly as a result of circumstances,[2] Paul dwells at undue length on the futurist aspect of Eschatology in his epistles to the Thessalonians. But at this stage he is not a strongly 'realized' eschato-logist, and expects the Parousia in his lifetime and that imminently (I Thes. 1: 10; 2: 19; 3: 13; 4: 13–18; 5: 23; II Thes. 1: 7–10; 2: 1–4). While we may rightly agree with Dodd that the Parousia retires into the background in Paul's II Corinthians,[3] it is difficult to find such a precise time for the changeover as Dodd advocates. But the place of human institutions becomes increasingly important for the life of the eschatological community in the epistles to the Corinthians. By the time he writes to the Ephesians and Colossians, the community is here to stay and the Parousia must coincide with the reconciliation of all things in Jesus Christ (Col. 1: 20, cf. Eph. 1: 9-10). That ultimate goal is possible only through the Cross, by which we are delivered and transferred into His Kingdom (Col. 1: 13 f.) The unity of all things is achieved when Christ presents the Church, His own Body, complete before God (Col. 1: 22, cf. I Cor. 15: 24). This will be by bringing them into harmony with His will rather than by an act of suppression.[4] The process to that goal can only take place both in Time and beyond Time: it is both historical and metaphysical.

Since the Cross is for Paul the dividing line between the evil Age (Gal. 1: 4, Eph. 6: 12) and the Age to Come, it is with reference to the Cross that the new creation is brought into being (II Cor. 5: 17, Gal. 6: 15). Jesus Christ becomes the firstborn (Col. 1: 15), the nucleus of the new creation around 'whom the whole body, joined and knit together by every joint with which it is supplied, . . . makes bodily growth and upbuilds itself in love,' (Eph. 4: 16). But, simultaneously He is also the completion of that new creation, the Omega.

---

[1] Cf. C. H. Dodd, *The Apostolic Preaching and its Developments* (1936, cited here as *Apostolic Preaching*), 46 f. *et passim*.

[2] For further discussion, see C. F. D. Moule, 'The influence of circumstances on the use of eschatological terms', in *JTS*, Vol. 15, No. 1 (1964), pp. 1–15. One wonders whether Paul's notion of Time may also have changed as he deepened his experience in Christ and hence influenced his eschatological outlook.

[3] Dodd, *New Testament Studies*, 111.

[4] Dodd, op. cit., 124 f. Robinson comes to a similar conclusion, though via a different approach: 'the Parousia is clearly understood not as a separate catas-trophic occurrence, but as a continuous pervasion of the daily life of the disciple and the Church. The coming is an abiding presence . . .' (*Coming*, 176).

The Holy Spirit who is given as the eschatological guarantee ('Αρραβών) (II. Cor. 1: 22; 5: 5, Eph. 1: 13–14), forms the link between Jesus of Nazareth and His community the Church. It is the Spirit that really transforms the ultra-temporal perspectives of Eschatology into realities hoped for and experienced by the Church. This obviously rescues Eschatology from the limits of linear concepts of Time.[1]

So then, the Christian is crucified with Christ (Gal. 2: 20), raised with Him (Col. 2: 12, cf. Rom. 6: 3–11), glorified with Him (Rom. 8: 30), and is to come with Him (I Thes. 3: 13; 4: 17). The benefits of the Age to Come can be appropriated fully by the one who is in Christ, and apart from such relationship and experience the Gospel message is meaningless. Yet Paul's 'Christ-mysticism' does not replace his hope of glory, however real that may be. Dodd is rightly cautious that for Paul 'the foreground is more and more occupied by contemplation of all the riches of divine grace enjoyed here and now by those who are in Christ Jesus',[2] (Eph. 1:3; 3:16–19). The future is transposed into the present so that a life lived 'in Christ' is permeated and saturated with the power of the Age to Come, and lacks nothing except the final consummation. This is a consummation of God's promises and unveiling of mysteries hid in Christ. The eschatological Man (I Cor. 15: 45) mystically embraces the whole humanity and creation, bringing deliverance and life (cf. Rom. 8: 18–24). Yet we experience this only in hope and expectation. But what kind of hope and expectation, if one might dare to ask. Moltmann gives us an insight into what I believe to be the right answer. 'The Christian expectation is directed to no other than the Christ who has come, but it expects something new from Him, something that has not yet happened so far: it awaits the fulfilment of the promised righteousness of God in all things, the fulfilment of the resurrection of the dead that is promised in His resurrection, the fulfilment of the Lordship of the crucified one over all things that is promised in His exaltation.'[3]

The Church exists between two eschatological termini: the Cross and the Parousia. Between these points, it lives simultaneously as though it is travelling (in history) and has arrived (in the Parousia of Christ). This paradox defies a three-dimensional linear concept of

---

[1] Cf. article by W.H., 'Pneumatologie und Eschatologie', in *Kirchenblatt für die Reformierte Schweiz* (20 October, 1966), 324–6.
[2] Dodd, *Apostolic Preaching*, 149.
[3] J. Moltmann, *Theology of Hope* (ET 1967), 227.

Time. The Church is in the rhythm of realizing Christ's Lordship and reconciliation (Rom. 5: 10), of justification by faith (Rom. 5: 1) and transformation 'into His likeness from one degree of glory to another' (II Cor. 3: 18). These are real experiences, but they do not eclipse the Consummation from Paul's mind. The experience of these eschatological realities looks back to the Cross, derives its meaning and impact from Christ Himself and is mediated by the Spirit. But this same experience is in part and proleptic, whetting the appetite for the ultimate goal of glory to which all must lead in Christ (Col. 3: 4, Phil. 3: 20 f., I Cor. 15: 28, Eph. 1: 12 f.). What we now have is only the arrhabon of what is hidden in Christ and belongs to what will be fulfilled and revealed in Him at the Parousia (Gal. 4: 4, I Cor. 10: 11, etc.). Paul's eschatological experiences of the Christ are essentially the same eschatological realities as we find them in the Gospels, the main difference being that in Paul's epistles they are articulated in the context of their historical removal from the Jesus of Nazareth. Whereas in the Gospels they are concentrated in the Person of Jesus, in the post-Easter Church they are scattered about geographically and temporally, through the working of the Spirit.

The Eschatology of the Gospels is strewn not only in Pauline epistles but also throughout the New Testament. In the letter to the Hebrews, there is no doubt that the 'eschatological days' have come (1: 2) with the Incarnation, and the Parousia will simply consummate this process (9: 28). A new and better Covenant now replaces the old one (7: 22; 8: 6 f.; 10: 9 f.). It introduces a new and better hope (7: 19), so that man can draw near to God (7: 19; 10: 22). Jesus Christ has realized (8: 6–13) what Jeremiah had seen from a long temporal distance (Jer. 31: 31–4). The Cross, a once-for-all event, marks the end of the evil Age and the beginning of the Age to Come (9: 26; 10: 9).

In Hebrews, the power of the Age to Come (6: 4f.) is made available and can be appropriated through Faith and Baptism. It is enjoyed here and now. The experience is pictured as entering into the promised sabbath rest ($\sigma\alpha\beta\beta\alpha\tau\iota\sigma\mu\delta s$) (4: 9–10). 'The "Rest", precisely because it is God's, is both present and future; men enter it, and must strive to enter it. This is paradoxical, but it is a paradox which Hebrews shares with all primitive Christian eschatology'. So writes Barrett in his contribution to the *Dodd Festschrift* (1956).[1]

[1] C. K. Barrett, 'The Eschatology of the Epistle to the Hebrews', an essay in the *Dodd Festschrift* (1956), 365, 372.

But while the writer to the Hebrews is certain that these are the last days, the Parousia has not arrived. Between the Cross and the Consummation, Christians are still pilgrims walking by faith (6: 18–19; 10: 19, 22) as the (last) Day draws near (10: 25). Meanwhile, their experience is so intensely real that they 'have come to Mount Zion and to the city of the living God, the heavenly Jerusalem, and to innumerable angels in festal gathering, and to the assembly (Church) of the first-born who are enrolled in heaven, ... and to Jesus the mediator of a new covenant ...' (12: 22–4). In Christ the eschatological Covenant (8: 6–8) is both present and futuristic, revealed at the Cross but awaiting its full manifestation at the Parousia (9: 28). It is both a promise and a revelation. The Gospel in Hebrews is the realization of God's promises of the Old Testament, now fulfilling and replacing what was but a shadow of things to come (8: 5; 10: 1).

The author of I Peter is conscious that divine intervention in human history has occurred in Jesus Christ (1: 3 ff.). It is epitomized in the eschatological community which has been brought forth (2: 9–10). These are, therefore, the eschatological times (1: 20) into which the prophets had enquired (1: 10–12). Two eschatological activities are at work as a result of the Life, Death-and-Resurrection of Jesus Christ: Salvation (1: 5, 10, 18 f.) and Judgement (4: 5, 6, 17), and both have a universal application. Believers have only tasted (2: 3) their destiny (5: 10) through Baptism, for there is abundant grace yet to be received at the revelation (ἀποκάλυψις) of Jesus Christ (1: 13, the Chief Shepherd, 5: 4). Because He is already exalted (3: 22), the Holy Spirit is among them (4: 14; 1: 12). But that is not the end: for they are still 'aliens and exiles' (2: 11), living under the compulsion of great urgency because 'the end of all things is at hand,' (4: 7). The Last Day will both unveil what is radically new and consummate what is already being appropriated now.[1]

The writer of II Peter is positive that believers are granted to partake of divine nature (1: 4), though their (historical?) entry into the Kingdom is still future (1: 11). The Day of the Lord will be accompanied by a physical upheaval in which the universe will be incinerated (3: 10–12). But behind this destruction lie 'new heavens and a new earth' (3: 13), ready to replace the old. This is the promise for which believers must wait. The author introduces a chronological

---

[1] For further discussion on the Eschatology of I Peter, see E. G. Selwyn, essay on 'Eschatology in I Peter' in the *Dodd Festschrift*, 394–401. Cf. his commentary 1946).

element (3: 8) in trying to combat mockery concerning 'His Coming' (3: 3–9).[1] His reply amounts to the fact that God's patience is for the benefit of all to repent (3: 9). Nothing is said about the cosmic implication of the Gospel. On the whole, this book is atypical of N.T. Eschatology.

There is little Eschatology in the epistle of James, and what there is is futuristic. The 'last days' are still in the future (5: 3). The great event is not primarily what happened on the Cross but 'the coming of the Lord' (5: 7), which is, however, at hand (5: 8). Yet a new day dawned when God 'of His own will brought us forth by the word of truth that we should be a kind of first fruits of His creatures' (1: 18). Therefore, the new faith is 'the faith of our Lord Jesus Christ, the Lord of glory' (2: 1). Believers are to wait patiently for the final Consummation (5: 7 f.), but practise the true religion of love and obedience (1: 22, 27; 2: 8).

In I John, the Lord Jesus is central. The message is written in 'the last hour' (2: 18), when Jesus Christ as the Life is already made manifest (1: 2). The believer appropriates this eternal Life by abiding in Christ (2: 5, 6, 28, etc.).[2] The old order is passing away (2: 17). The believer is already the child of God (3: 1, 2), sharing in the salvation brought by the only Son of God (4: 9, 14), and the Spirit is resting upon him (4: 13). All that remains for the believer is that 'it does not yet appear what we shall be, but we know that when He appears we shall be like Him, for we shall see Him as He is,' (3: 2). This will also give him confidence 'for the day of judgement' (4: 17). The End only winds up what already is the experience of those who abide in Christ. Once more we see how intensely christological are these eschatological realities, and as such they fall within and beyond the confines of linear notions of Time.

The Eschatology of Revelation is almost exclusively futuristic, with difficult apocalyptic language and pictures. The accomplished work of Christ is allowed only a minor place, and the world is placed on the verge of God's immediate, sudden and almost merciless retribution. Yet, through the blood of Jesus, Christians are 'made . . . a kingdom, priests to His God and Father' (1: 6) and 'share . . .

---

[1] Cf. Cullmann who feels that 'the purpose is to assert, not the timelessness of God, but rather the endless character of the time of God . . .' (*Christ and Time* 69).

[2] Three key words in this epistle are significant: μένω used twenty-three times ζωή used thirteen times, ἡ ζωὴ αἰώνιος used six times.

in Jesus the tribulation and the kingdom and the patient endurance' (1: 9). The author uses ὁ ἔσχατος (1: 17) about Jesus, but in a sense different from that of Paul in I Cor. 15: 45. The promises to the Seven Churches are given on condition that they 'overcome', rather than because Jesus has overcome on the behalf of all. Their reward is for the future (2: 7, 11, 23, 27, etc.). The Jerusalem above is yet to come down (3: 12; 21: 2), and is unlike that in Hebrews. The reign of the ransomed community is not 'realized' but 'futuristic' (5: 9–10). Saints under the altar still cry 'how long?' (6: 10) as they wait for the eschaton to arrive. But the book has a cosmic scope for the Gospel. All nations accord praise to Jesus (6: 9; 7: 9 f.); all creatures recognize Him (5: 13); and the Gospel is proclaimed to all (14: 6). At the end all things are made new (21: 1, 3); and Jesus appears as a mighty Conqueror, not so much because He has already accomplished His victory on the Cross, but because He is yet to accomplish it. Thus the book of Revelation emphasizes a 'Futurist Eschatology' at the expense of 'Realized Eschatology'.

The Acts of the Apostles shows clearly the conviction of the early Church that the Age to Come not only has dawned in the life of Jesus Christ, but is hidden in Him. The age of fulfilment has come (2: 16; 3: 18, 24; 10: 36, 43; 13: 32 f.) through Jesus Christ (2: 14–39; 3: 13–26, etc.). The Holy Spirit is a sure sign of this realization (2: 33; 5: 32), so that He is both the eschatological promise (2: 16–21, Joel 2: 28–32) now fulfilled, and the mystery of God now unveiled in Christ. But the future consummation is an essential element of the Kerygma, because there is still the 'not yet' (3: 21; 10: 42), although some would deny this part of the Kerygma.[1]

Even from this short survey it is clear that fulfilment and consummation in Christ are the main polarities of New Testament Eschatology. They are the irreducible denominator without which Eschatology is meaningless. It is these that give the unique teleological content to Christian Eschatology. The very life of the Church is a clear witness to this fulfilment and expectation of the consummation. Time is an important factor in any consideration of Eschatology, but a linear understanding of Time is not necessarily the emphasis of the New Testament. On the surface the Synoptic Gospels are more inclined to portray Eschatology in the light of a linear concept of

---

[1] For further discussion see Dodd, *Apostolic Preaching;* H. J. Cadbury, 'Acts and Eschatology', contributed to the *Dodd Festschrift*, 300–21; and T. F. Glasson, *The Second Advent* (1945), 153 ff.

Time, but a closer look at the situation seems to allow for other possibilities as well. The Fourth Gospel is almost indifferent to linear notions of Time, bringing to the foreground eschatological realities which are, instead, supra-temporal.

This same pattern is discernible in the remaining portions of the New Testament. In his earlier epistles, Paul has a clear vein of a linear concept of Time in approaching Eschatology, but in his later writings this is not so important. He keeps, however, to the two polarities of the Cross and the Parousia, both of which are intensely christological. It is significant that he and other writers of the New Testament increasingly move away from temporal to non- or semi-temporal terms and images like the Parousia (Mt. 24: 3, 27; I Cor. 15: 23; I Thes. 2: 19; Jas. 5: 7), the Revelation (Rom. 8: 19; I Cor. 1: 7; II Thes. 1: 7; I Pet. 1: 7), Appearing (II Thes. 2: 8, I Tim. 6: 14), Consummation (Mt. 28: 20), ἡ ἀποκατάστασις (Acts 3: 21) and others. The Early Church did not adjust smoothly or immediately to an Eschatology dominated less and less by linear concepts of Time; and the book of Revelation is one clear example of that difficulty in the canonical writings. It is, nevertheless, significant that the New Testament does not employ the linear temporal term 'the Second Coming', this being first used by Justin Martyr in the second century.[1] It is impossible to estimate how much harm may have been injected into Christian thinking by this otherwise useful and innocent distinction.[2] Only when we stretch out the eschatological polarities of the 'already' and the 'not yet' on a linear concept of Time, do we find the New Testament tension unbearably acute. Similarly, only then can we 'read' impatience into the so-called 'delay of the Parousia', which this threefold linear concept of Time has exaggerated beyond all possible evidence in the New Testament.

We have looked at the Akamba conceptual background and at the New Testament Eschatology. It remains now to see how missionary teaching has been propounded, involving the bringing together of these two backgrounds, and what has resulted from that attempt.

[1] Justin Martyr, *Dialogue with Trypho*, XXXII, LI, CX, in which he distinguishes two advents of Christ—one with suffering and dishonour, and the other with glory.

[2] Cf. L. W. Barnard, 'Justin Martyr's Eschatology', in *Vigiliae Christianae*, Vol. 19, No. 2 (1965), pp. 86–98. One finds it hard to accept this writer's conclusions that Justin's two advents of Christ are biblical. He, however, rightly points out the influence of circumstances upon Justin's views—a factor found also in the New Testament.

(c) Africa Inland Mission (A.I.M.) teaching on Eschatology

It is unnecessary to dwell at length on the teaching of the Africa Inland Mission concerning New Testament Eschatology. A few examples will suffice to illustrate the teaching which would then speak adequately for itself. The type of Eschatology so presented is exclusively 'futurist', as stated in the 'Doctrinal Basis' of the Africa Inland Church. Accordingly, members are required or expected to believe in:

'The Personal, visible and premillennial return of the Lord Jesus Christ;
The literal resurrection of the body;
The eternal blessedness of the saved, and the eternal punishment of the lost.'[1]

The Kikamba *Catechism of Christian Teaching* (n.d.), elaborates the same teaching in the following manner:

Item 50: 'Will Jesus ever come again?
Yes, He will come again. He will first come to the sky to fetch His saints. I Thes. 4: 16 . . .
Afterwards He will come to the earth together with His saints. I Thes. 3: 13 . . .
51: 'What will take place when Christ comes to fetch His Church?
(1) Those who died in Christ will be raised first, I Thes. 4: 16 . . .
(2) The Christians who will be alive when He comes will be changed and raptured to go and meet Christ in the sky, I Thes. 4: 17 . . .
(3) All believers will at that time receive "clean"[2] (holy, glorious?) bodies, Phil. 3: 21.
52: 'What will happen when believers are snatched away to be with Christ?
They will appear before the judgement seat of Christ to receive payment (Kik, *ituvi*)[3] according to their works, I Cor. 3: 11–15.
54: 'What will happen here on earth when Christ has fetched His Church?
(1) The Great Tribulation will then take place, Mt. 24: 15, 21 . . .
(2) Afterwards Christ will return to reign upon the earth for a thousand years. Rev. 20: 1–6 . . .
(3) And then He will give back (or return) the Kingdom to His Father. 1 Cor. 15: 24–6. . . .'[4]

---

[1] *Constitution, Rules and Regulations* of the Africa Inland Church (1954), items 14–16 of the 'Doctrinal Basis', p. 5. The revised edition (1962) is the same here.

[2] The Kikamba adjective *-theu*, means 'clean', but in Christian circles it is used for 'holy'. In Akamba life a 'clean' body is praiseworthy, so it is natural that they would here think in terms of bodies clean from dirt, dust, etc.

[3] The Kikamba word *ituvi*, means 'payment', though the context here means 'reward', and hearers would be led to believe that they have to work for such payment'.

[4] The Kikamba version of the Catechism, n.d., pp. 20–4. A new and revised edition in Swahili and English came out recently (n.d., 1962?), but as this is not yet

That is the main body of A.I.M. teaching in Ukambani concerning Christian Eschatology. A few observations and comments deserve mentioning, before we come to the hymns that are used to supplement this teaching.

Items 50 and 54 (2) of the catechism teach in effect that the Messiah will come visibly to this earth *three* times (including the Incarnation, before and after 'the Great Tribulation'). On this linear scale of Time, it is taught that 'the Great Tribulation' will take place in the period between the Rapture of the Church and the Millennial reign of Christ. But while on earth the unbelievers are being tortured, the saints will be safely enjoying their Marriage Feast or Messianic Banquet in the sky. I find no biblical or metaphorical support for this form of exaggeration!

I Thes. 4: 17 is quoted in support of item 51 (2), but this verse says nothing about Christians 'being changed'. A better passage would have been I Cor. 15: 51 f. which gives hints about Christians being 'altered' at the Parousia. Similarly Phil. 3: 21 as support for item 51 (3) is irrelevant since it speaks only about changing the bodily form (singular) and not about receiving clean (or holy) bodies (plural), as taught in this doctrinal item. In support of item 52 the passage quoted is I Cor. 3:1 1–15, which makes no reference to 'the Judgement Seat' of Christ as such. An appropriate passage would be II Cor. 5: 10.

If we scrutinize further this teaching and the scriptural support advocated, we discover more discrepancies. Mt. 24: 15 which is quoted in support of item 54 (1), says nothing about a (the) 'Great Tribulation'. The verse is concerned with the events of the siege and fall of Jerusalem (A.D. 67–70) and not with the Parousia as such. The same applies to Mt. 24: 21, even if we allow the time of distress to be one of the eschatological signs. The passage from Rev. 20: 1–6 does not refer to a further (and third) 'return' of our Lord, as taught in item 54 (2).

The use of hymns is an effective medium of conveying Christian or missionary teaching. Akamba Christians are very fond of singing. They may sing up to a dozen hymns at one Church service; they sing as they work in the fields, they sing in buses, they sing along the roads and the footpaths, they sing in their kitchens, they sing everywhere and almost at all times. If they don't know the words, they

in use in Ukambani we have to stick to the Kikamba version for our reference here. The scriptural quotations are nearly all the same in the three versions.

hum the tunes, or whistle. All their hymns have been translated by missionaries, from American and English hymnals. There are 211 hymns in the Kikamba hymnal, and at least ninety of these mention something about 'eschatological' matters, along the interpretation of the Africa Inland Mission. A few illustrations will suffice here, given in a literal rather than poetical retranslation from Kikamba:

Hymn 20:   'Jesus Christ is coming again,
              To take us up above to our home;
              I will not be with those who are left here,
              I will be taken, when He fetches us here . . .

              What of you sinners, when He comes here,
              Will you be punished because of disobedience?
              You will be paid for evil,
              You will not be excused, when He comes here . . .'[1]

Hymn 61:   'When the trumpet of God is sounded, and the
                      time ends,
              When we will see the dawn of the coming day,
              When the saved ones gather on the other side of
                      death,
              When Jesus comes to fetch them, I will be there.

                When the trumpet is sounded we will hear it,
                When Jesus comes and we are met,
                When up above we will be gathered together,
                With Jesus, I will also be there.

              The elect dead ones will be raised that morning,
              And we who are alive here will have our bodies
                      changed,
              Being raptured (caught up) together with them,
                      being met by Jesus,
              When all are being counted, I will be there.

              Let us press on to do the work of Master Jesus,
              Showing His love and mercies;
              And when we finish our work and lives here on earth,
              When we are being paid above, I will be there.'[2]

---

[1] Translated from the hymn by W. O. Cushing, 'There'll be no dark valley when Jesus comes . . .'.

[2] Translated from the hymn by J. K. Black, 'When the trumpet of the Lord shall sound . . .'.

Hymn 94: 'Time is coming to an end, the kingdom is near;
          I believe in Jesus so that I may have life later.
          In the past I was in darkness, but now it is dawn:
          The great light is at God's home up above.'[1]

Hymn 168: 'He is coming, and He says it is very soon,
          We will see Jesus that day;
          If you are not generous and faithful
          What will you tell Him, when you see Jesus?...'

          'When we shed tears as we serve Him,
          The promised date for rejoicing in the heart is coming;
          When we meet Him we will be like Him.
          Then we will rejoice for ever and ever.'[2]

Hymn 180: 'It maybe in the morning, Jesus will return,
          Or at noon, or in the evening,
          Or in the darkness of midnight,
          We will see His bright light.
              Jesus, do come now
              And fetch Thine own:
              We will rejoice with joy
              Now, unknown;
              Yes, great joy . . .'[3]

Such then is the substance of Christian Eschatology as taught by the Africa Inland Mission and as received by Christians in Ukambani. It is contained in their Church Constitution as part of the Doctrinal Basis which each member is required to accept. Candidates for Baptism must learn it as part of their catechumen instruction. And all believers are constantly reminded of it in sermons and hymns. The subject plays a leading role in the life of the Church, and believers expect the Return of our Lord to be at any moment. They speak often about it and about the end of the world, Heaven and Hell. Both the missionaries and Akamba Christians find many 'signs'—and scriptural verses to support their findings—indicating that, according to this teaching, the 'End' is very near. We shall mention some of these 'signs'.

---

[1] Translated from the hymn by A. R. Cousin, 'The sands of time are sinking . . .'.

[2] Translated from the hymn by K. Shaw, 'Sowing in the morning, sowing seeds of kindness . . .'.

[3] Translated from the hymn by H. L. Turner, 'It may be at morn, when the day is awakening . . .'.

Famines (Mk. 13: 8 pars.) come very often and regularly in Ukam-bani, and are the historical signposts of oral tradition.

Earthquakes (Mk. 13: 8 pars.) are not unknown since the country lies close to volcanic regions of Mt. Kenya, Mt. Kilimanjaro, and the Great Rift Valley. The people also get news of earthquakes in other parts of the world, such as Japan, Greece, Agadir, Iran, etc.

Wars and rumours of wars (Mk. 13: 7 pars.) are a common 'sign', especially since the Second World War.

An increase of knowledge (Dan. 12: 4) is very evident as a result of formal education and the invasion of science and technology.

Many 'run to and fro' (Dan, 12: 4) on bicycles, in buses, planes, spacecraft, etc. These fast means of communication are particularly impressive in a country where walking from one area to another, has always been, and is still largely, the chief method of human movement.

Preaching the Gospel to all nations (Mk. 13: 10 par.) is taken as an already fulfilled prophecy, even if not everyone has accepted the Gospel.

The return of the Jews to Palestine, and their setting up of the State of Israel, are understood as fulfilling passages like Is. 43: 5–7, Jer. 23: 3; 29: 14; 31: 8–10, Ezek. 11: 14–17, etc.

There are many other favourite passages which are taught as evidence for more 'signs', such as II Tim. 3: 1–5, II Pet. 3: 3–4, I Jn. 2: 18, 22, 23; 4: 1–3, Jude 18 f. Some people even go as far as finding 'signs' in eclipses, colourful sunsets, burning meteorites ('falling stars'), unusual cloud formations and freaks of the weather, for which they obtain encouragement, if not strong support from apocalyptic and other sections of the Bible like Is. 13: 10, Ezek. 32: 7–8, Joel 2: 10–11, 30–1; 3: 15, Zeph. 1: 15, Mt. 24: 29, Mk. 13: 25, and Lk. 21: 25. The classical hunting grounds for 'signs' are Mt. 24, Mk. 13, Lk. 21, I & II Thes., II Tim. 3, and the book of Revelation. These passages, together with others like Jn. 14, I Cor. 15, II Pet. 3, are also used to stir up both encouragement in Christian living and strong expectations of a speedy 'End of the World'.

Because these so-called 'signs' seem so obvious and plentiful, some individual believers go as far as setting dates for the 'End'. This historical indulgence is something into which Christians have ceaselessly fallen all through the centuries, in spite of clear warnings in the Scriptures. It is chiefly the result of failing to understand Christian Eschatology, and of interpreting it exclusively on a linear concept of Time.

That this missionary teaching has had a tremendous impact upon Akamba Christians cannot be questioned. It is worth mentioning here that the same teaching is taken even more seriously by members of the relatively new sect, *The Friends of the Holy Spirit*, the majority of whom have broken off from the Africa Inland Mission/Church. An analysis of their hymns indicates that at least 94 per cent of them speak about eschatological ideas relating to Heaven (as the place where trouble and sorrows end, full of rest and riches), Hell and fire, imminent intervention of the Saviour, Pilgrimage and receiving rewards. These hymns have a deep sense of urgency, asking or expecting Jesus to return immediately in order to redeem the members from sorrow and oppression. The hymns are patterned after those of the Africa Inland Mission, but directed more to the needs of this minority group, which considers itself to constitute the Lord's pure and holy ones.[1]

(d) Conclusions and Observations

We have shown how, in their traditional thinking, Akamba and other African peoples, do not conceive of the end of the world. For them History moves 'backwards' from the intense moment of the 'now-period' towards the increasingly distant past (*Tene*). Time is chiefly a two-dimensional phenomenon, defined also chiefly by its events rather than its mathematical content. Linguistically there is only a very brief future, and even then it is an extension of the now-dimension (*Mituki*) of Time. Apart from the involvement of the *Mituki* in the future, there is no third dimension of Time in Akamba thinking. There are, however, phenomena that fall into the unchanging rhythm of nature, such as day and night, seasons, birth and death. These are more or less out of Time since they must occur: they do not point either to a teleology or end of the world. They are rhythmically constant; and as constant phenomena of History, there is nothing teleological about them or their occurrence.

We have seen that there are no myths of the future in traditional African societies. This is another indication that African concepts

---

[1] The only published source to date on *The Friends of the Holy Spirit* is D. N. Kimilu, 'The Separatist Churches', in *Dini Na Mila: Revealed Religion and Traditional Customs* (Kampala, December 1967), Vol. 2, No. 2/3, pp. 17–61. The article gives also an English translation of nearly all the hymns used by this sect in Ukambani.

of History are not oriented towards the future, but towards the past (to which innumerable myths refer).

We have also reviewed New Testament Eschatology, pointing out particularly the importance of its christological orientation. Eschatology can only be understood as a christological phenomenon, based on fulfilment in Christ. This fulfilment, which is partly revealed in the Incarnation, is also partly being experienced by the Church—itself an eschatological reality—and is yet to be unveiled as constituting the consummation of God's mysteries in Christ. A historical process can neither be ignored nor made the sole dependence of this otherwise supra-historical phenomenon. The New Testament incorporates but does not necessarily emphasize a threefold linear concept of Time in relation to its Eschatology. A metaphysical element is an essential constituent of New Testament Eschatology, and to miss this is obviously to sway far from the centre of Eschatology.

The teaching of the Africa Inland Mission in Ukambani has stressed almost exclusively a few aspects of the futurist element of Eschatology, thereby (a) coming into a serious conflict with the linguistic and conceptual understanding of the Akamba, and (b) stressing what amounts to a minor part of New Testament Eschatology. Lest I be accused of 'attacking missionaries', I let evidence speak for itself here, and it does not require much imagination to reach an unbiased assessment of the situation.

Resulting from the two points raised in the preceding paragraph is a false spirituality among Akamba Christians regarding the matter of Eschatology—and hence of the Gospel at large. Having set their expectations on an immediate realization of this futurist Eschatology, many are deeply disappointed and shaken when they begin to realize that early generations of Christians are passing away and the (immediate) end of the world does not come. Sorrows continue to bombard them, but Jesus does not return immediately to 'rapture' them from this world. Heaven which they now have discovered as a future place for them, does not snatch them away quickly and give them the riches, comfort and bliss they miss here on earth. They have discovered a new future, they hope to attain it immediately, but paradoxically it seems as far away as the physical heavens themselves. For many, to be a Christian is to get a passport into Heaven: but Heaven seems to retreat faster than their hopes and expectations can follow it.

To sacrifice New Testament Eschatology on a threefold linear concept of Time, is to crash land it on barren ground. The tragedy is much worse when this is based only on one of the three dimensions, and especially when the conceptual background of the peoples concerned allows only a very short future. Thus, to tell Akamba Christians that 'Jesus will come' has to be expressed in one of the following ways:

(1) *Yesu nukauka* = Jesus will come (using the Far or Remote Future tense); or

(2) *Yesu nukuka* = Jesus will come (using the Immediate or Near Future tense); or

(3) *Yesu akauka (akooka)* = Jesus will come (the Indefinite Future or Indefinite Near Future tense).

If the idea that 'Jesus will come' is expressed by means of tense 1, it would be understood to mean that the Lord is going to come after a few months. In any case, the event of His coming must take place within the period of not more than two years from now.

If method 2 is used to express the same idea, it is understood that the person announcing this news has in effect left the Lord only a short distance away, and that He will arrive within the next few hours. The tense here strikes a note of immediacy and certainty: the event must take place 'today' or 'tomorrow' morning.

When tense 3 is used, it means that there is a certainty about His coming, but the exact moment may or may not be fixed. It would happen any time from tomorrow onwards. The event of the coming must await the sequence of other events. In situations of this awaiting, the Akamba use a proverb that *Weteele ndakusaa*, i.e., 'he who is waiting does not die', the point being that the event awaited will certainly come before one's death. This shows also the temporal nearness of the event, even if it cannot be given a concrete date.

Sometimes it may be necessary to use (4), the Present (or Present Progressive) tense: *Yesu niwukite* (cf. Rev. 1: 7). This conveys the idea that He is just outside 'the house', right on the road coming, and can even be seen approaching the homestead where the speaker is situated.

This linguistic illustration indicates some of the difficulties encountered not only on the purely grammatical level of translating phrases, but more on the deeper level of Akamba conceptual understanding which must be fathomed by any serious communication of Christian teaching. In a threefold linear concept of Time, a futurist content of Eschatology must be conveyed in any one of the three or four ways outlined above. And this applies not only to a simple phrase like 'Jesus will come', but to the entire range of ideas that constitute the New Testament understanding of the Consummation. Where is one to draw the line? That is the crux of the matter.

It would be an immense task, even with the help of a computer, to go through the Kikamba Bible and hymnal analysing the frequencies of these four tenses in connection with Eschatology. A fairly random check in the Kikamba Bible seems to indicate that 3—the Indefinite or Indefinite Near Future—is most frequently used, followed by 2, then 1 and finally 4. Examples of the frequency may be cited as follows:

1: Lk. 21: 27, I Cor. 15: 26;
2: I Cor. 15: 23, 49, 51 (b), I Jn. 3: 2;
3: Jn. 14: 3, Acts 1: 11, I Cor. 15: 52 (b), II Cor. 5: 10, Rev. 22: 12, 20;
4: Rev. 1: 7.

A random check in the hymnbook gives more or less equal frequencies of tenses 3 and 4, while tenses 1 and 2 are hardly employed.

It is interesting to note that, in its hymns, the Friends of the Holy Ghost sect which uses the same Kikamba Bible as the members of the Africa Inland Mission/Church, makes an even greater use of tense 4, which heightens the expectation of the followers.

In both denominations, it is clear that urgency and immediacy are the key notes, and that Eschatology is nearly all in terms of the immediate coming again of Jesus. This belief and the expectation that goes with it, clearly influence, if not govern, which grammatical tense is employed to express the idea of an eschatological futurity.

There is little one can do with the grammatical hurdles of this problem. But on the conceptual level perhaps a solution is possible, and the New Testament itself is not, evidently, unaware of this immensely great problem. In the Early Church there were, no doubt, those whose future horizon had been aroused and exten-ded by the expectation of an immediate return of the Lord. These died before their hopes were realized, just as Akamba (or African) Christians see more and more of the early believers dying before the arrival of the Parousia. These experiences seem to produce a number of results. As in the days of the Early Church, there are people who hold that the whole teaching is false, otherwise the Lord would have by now returned. Others feel that He may have 'changed His mind' and will never come after all; and consequently, 'let us eat and drink, for tomorrow we die'. More serious, however, is the apparent intensification of the expectation, particularly in the light of the numerous 'signs' which are interpreted as pointing to the nearness of the Parousia.

It may not be possible to gauge precisely the depth of these attitudes towards the so-called 'delay of the Parousia'. But among Akamba Christians the intensification of the expectation is more evident than any disappointment over the delay. We have already mentioned the rather extreme evidence of this among members of the independent sect, The Friends of the Holy Spirit. Certainly it belongs to the ethos of the New Testament to hold the Parousia imminent. But it is a false spirituality to escape into the Christian world of the hereafter at the expense of being a Christian in the here and now. This false spirituality seems to have overtaken many Christians, not only in Ukambani, but also in other parts of Africa; they have discovered a future which, they expect, will suddenly bring them to a land of bliss, comfort and long life.

Grammatically the Kikamba and other African languages may still be static or slow in accommodating this future dimension of Time. But a future is nevertheless in front of the people. This future is partly in this world and partly in another. In this world it is directed towards acquiring formal education, mastering the physical environment and tapping the resources of nature on local and national levels. But the future in another world dominates Christians more than other people. Futurist Eschatology is chiefly reponsible for this type of future in another world. In its extreme manifestation it represents Christ as the Purveyor of individuals from this world to the (future) next. The Kikamba hymnal has many examples of this type of teaching.

This is not the place to give a lengthy discussion of how the discovery of a future in another world, and the disillusion which comes when this world is not immediately realized, seem, *inter alia*, to be responsible for the incredibly large number of break-away sects in Africa. There were six thousand of these reported in 1968.[1] Whatever

---

[1] According to D. B. Barrett, *Schism and Renewal in Africa* (1968). The author advanced different reasons for this proliferation. It is interesting to note that apart from a few sects from the Roman Catholic Church, the rest are all from the Anglican-Protestant complex of Churches which advocate the translation and free use of the Scriptures, and put more emphasis on futurist Eschatology than does the Roman Catholic Church.

else may be their immediate causes, acquiring the dignity of independence, whether around a central figure or 'doctrine', gives the followers at least a partial realization (or incarnation) of their future
and what they hope in that future—even if that may only be shallow
or even naïve when judged by outsiders, or in the light of the New
Testament. In their new sect they find here and now at least an
exchange for what otherwise they have hoped to reap when they get
to heaven. The concept of Time is very much at the root of this
proliferation of African Church sects.

The New Testament seems to offer clear hints of dealing with questions concerning both future and present dimensions of Eschatology,
without sacrificing the whole issue on the rocks of a mechanical
threefold linear concept of Time. It makes it absolutely clear that Time
is subject to Eschatology and not vice versa. Whenever Christians
have reversed this order of priorities, they have ended up with a false
Eschatology as useless as the face of a clock without hands. Time helps
us to understand the horizontal dimension of Eschatology; but
Eschatology has also the vertical dimension which is non-temporal
and which defies all attempts to 'horizontalize' it. In presenting this
dimension of Eschatology, the New Testament uses a materialistic
language, the liturgical life of the Church, and insights into what
might be termed the 'nearness of the spirit world'.

It is my conviction in this work that this New Testament approach
to the problem not only adequately handles the so-called 'delay'
of the Parousia, but has given Christianity an Eschatology incorporating but not dependent upon a linear concept of Time. It is an Eschatology firmly grounded on Christology and hence capable of being
conveyed and understood in other historical and cultural situations
such as the African background against which we are making this
study. The Christian Gospel is intensely eschatological, and if the
interpretation or presentation of Eschatology is distorted, so would
the Gospel itself also become distorted. We shall return to this
relationship between Eschatology and the Gospel in a later chapter.
We must now start examining how the New Testament employs
various methods to present the non-temporal dimension of Eschatology and how this shows itself against the African background
before us.

CHAPTER III

The Use of Materialistic Language in Eschatology

(a) The Problem

IT is neither by accident nor in desperation that the New Testament does in fact use a materialistic language as one of the devices for portraying eschatological truths. We have stated that Time is an integral part of Eschatology, and that it aids us in understanding (chiefly) the horizontal or historical dimension of New Testament Eschatology. We need, therefore, neither dismiss Time nor be unduly enslaved by it when we discuss Eschatology. But there are other aspects of Eschatology which do not lend themselves naturally to a temporal consideration or understanding. There is nothing embarrassing about this, and for that reason the New Testament generously employs materialistic images as a means of conveying aspects of eschatological truths which cannot otherwise be easily or as effectively expressed.

All too often it has been said that Hebrew thought forms are concrete while Greek ones are abstract. Admitting that this distinction is obviously an exaggeration, it is nevertheless hardly questionable that the materialistic imagery in New Testament Eschatology is derived chiefly from a Hebrew background. This imagery is, however, Christianized and where possible, christologized, thus acquiring its usefulness and uniqueness as far as New Testament Eschatology is concerned. The imagery must also be judged and understood as symbolic, speaking about realities beyond the symbolism. If the symbolism and the realities are merged we get into difficulties.

We have shown in the previous chapter that Akamba, and other African peoples, are discovering a conceptual future which, at least for the Christians, is both of this world and in another, heavenly, world. The basic notion of 'the next world' is found in all African societies, as far as one knows. It is the hereafter beyond physical death. This is pictured exclusively in materialistic terms which make that world more or less a carbon copy of the present. Furthermore, geographically it is not far from the physical world. We shall return to a fuller discussion of this subject in a later chapter. But for our immediate purpose here, it is necessary to mention that for the Akamba, and other African peoples, that world of the hereafter is in the Time dimension of *Tene* (the Past), rather than the otherwise extremely short 'future'. At death, as we pointed out in Chapter II (a), a person moves 'backwards' from the *Mituki* (contemporary) period into the *Tene* period. Thus, in temporal terms, African hereafter is not in the future but in the 'past'. As such it is conceived in concrete mythological terms, and it is no wonder that that world is more or less a carbon copy of the human physical world. Man does not depart from his physicalness even if he dies, but becomes a living-dead and finally a spirit.

But African contact with the Christian Message has produced an area of conceptual inversion. First, for African Christians the hereafter is switched from the *Tene* period (past) to the growing or newly discovered future. Secondly the world of the hereafter is switched from this earth to the sky or heaven 'above'. In Time and geography there is a conceptual inversion in African Christian outlook. But that new hereafter and new world remain fundamentally materialistic. This point is immensely relevant and important for our study: for here, perhaps more than elsewhere, we have some common ground between the New Testament use of materialistic language and African conceptual understanding of the hereafter. Furthermore, there are ample grounds indicating that early Hebrew and traditional African thought forms have many similarities. But similarities need not produce the same results, and it must be borne in mind that there is a deeper and more complex level than the similarities might indicate on the surface.

Akamba (or African) Christians consider their hereafter in basically materialistic terms. There are three main explanations for this. (a) As we have pointed out, in their traditional concepts, Africans consider the hereafter to be physical and materialistic, even if those who inhabit that world are in 'spirit' form. (b) Christian Eschatology employs materialistic symbols and imagery, *inter alia*, to portray the hereafter. But whereas the New Testament uses this language as a means of conveying realities beyond the symbolism, African Christians seem to stop at the symbolism and take that to be the reality. (c) Strong emphasis on an exclusively futurist Eschatology in the process of evangelizing Ukambani forces people to discover a conceptual future which eludes all language other than materialistic. For the Christians this is a glorious future, a utopia to which they may escape at death or at the Parousia. For the unbelievers it is to be a future of pain and sorrow—an equally materialistic, if negative, future.

We shall consider eight eschatological symbols and words, to see how their meaning is understood in the Bible and by Akamba (and other African) Christians. In carrying out this analysis we shall also be examining how far an African language can contain biblical concepts. In the countries of the old Christendom many of these words have lost their power and purpose through long historical usage. But where the Church is young, this vocabulary is still a vivid and powerful medium of communication,[1] one of the vehicles for conveying Christian Eschatology. Therefore it is not enough simply to translate the imagery in a literal sense from one language to another; the whole conceptual meaning has to be translated, if its eschatological depth is to be fathomed and appreciated.

(b) Gehenna

According to Akamba concepts of the hereafter, there are no separate places for the 'good' and the 'evil'. The same applies to other African societies, apart from a few vague notions of retribution being meted out to those who in life have waged anti-social activities against their fellow men. Thus, for example, the Lodagaa (of Ghana and Upper Volta) believe that at death the spirit of the departed must cross a river: and if a person led a good life, he crosses it easily, but if he led a wicked life, he is punished and his crossing is made difficult. On arrival in the next world, thieves, sorcerers, murderers and rich people are tormented more than everybody else, though this tormenting by older spirits seems to be meted out to everybody, like an initiation ordeal, regardless of former life; there are, however, no separate places for different categories of the departed.[2] Among the Yoruba (Nigeria) it is thought that at death each individual

---

[1] We are reminded of the significance and importance of this imagery by A. N. Wilder, 'Eschatological Imagery and Earthly Circumstances', in *NTS*, Vol. 5, No. 4 (July 1959), pp. 229–45. In recent years 'the Debate about God' has called in question many of the terms used in Christian images. It is one thing to question their effectiveness, but it is another thing to deny the purpose of their usage.

[2] J. R. Goody, *Death, Property and the Ancestors* (1962), 371 ff.

appears before God or His deputy, to give account of his earthly life: those who lead a good life continue to live happily, whereas those who are wicked enter into more wretchedness.[1] Hell or Gehenna and its associations with punishment or torment are, by and large, an entirely novel introduction into Akamba (or African) thinking.

The Kikamba Bible transcribes the Greek γέεννα into *Ngienani*[2] in the N.T.; but speaks of *the valley of Hinnom* for the Hebrew גֵּי הִנֹּם in the O.T. According to missionary and Church teaching in Ukambani, the hereafter is divided into two possibilities: either Heaven for a life of joy and ease, or Gehenna for a life of misery and torture. This is stated in the *Constitution, Rules and Regulations* of the Africa Inland Church, item 16, p. 5, as part of the cardinal belief in 'the eternal blessedness of the saved and the eternal punishment of the lost'. A number of Kikamba hymns situate the hereafter also in these two geographical locations. There is no evidence from other parts of Africa to indicate that Christian teaching on this issue is radically different. Naturally, this is a useful psychological device in evangelism, but we must not be content with Gehenna only at that level.

As Jeremias points out in the *TWzNT*, the N.T. background to Gehenna derives from the O.T. and apocalyptic literature, although the word γέεννα as such is unknown in the LXX.[3] According to Rabbinic teaching, Gehenna was created by God.[4] It is enormously large[5] with three gates and seven compartments, and is possibly situated underground.[6] Its fire is sixty times hotter than any earthly

---

[1] E. B. Idowu, *Olodumare: God in Yoruba Belief* (1962), 199 ff.

[2] Properly, the Kikamba should read: *Ngiena*, since the *-ni* is a prepositional suffix of locality meaning 'in, at, on'. But some of the substantives of Kikamba acquire this *-ni* where others would not normally have it.
Cf. Delitzsch's Heb. N.T. in which he renders γέεννα rightly as גֵּי הִנֹּם

[3] J. Jeremias, on γέεννα in the *TWzNT*, Vol. I (1933), 655 f. The sources he cites include Jer. 7: 32, I En. 90: 26 f.; 27: 1 ff.; IV Ezr. 7: 36, etc., with the conclusion that 'das ist die Stufe der Entwicklung, die das NT widerspiegelt.'

[4] Some thought that Gehenna was pre-existent: cf. Mt. 24: 41, Jeremias (*supra*), Sotah 22a (cited in the *J.E.*, Vol. 5 (1903), p. 582); and others that it was created on the second day: Pesahim 54a (cited in the *J.E.*, ibid.). See further in the *J.E.*, Vol. 5, pp. 582 ff., the article by L. Blau; Jeremias (*supra*); and R. A. Stewart, *Rabbinic Theology* (1961), 157 ff.

[5] According to Pesahim 94a (cited in the *J.E.*, Vol. 5, p. 582), the earth is 1/21,600th part of Gehenna.

[6] Stewart, op. cit., 157 ff., but as he points out, there are other opinions. Some think that it is above the firmament, others that it is behind dark mountains (Ta'anit 32b), according to the *J.E.*, ibid. In I En. 28:1, it lies farthest to the West just as Paradise lies to the East).

fire (Berakot 57b),[1] and there is a great darkness.[2] It is the lot of kings (I En. 38: 1–6), sinners, heretics, and others like them.[3]

Thus, what in Jos. 15: 8, Neh. 11: 30b, etc., is the valley of the son of Hinnom, has by N.T. times acquired apocalyptic imagery and dramatic descriptions. Jesus may have accepted current notions about Gehenna without necessarily endorsing them all. In the Synoptics Gehenna is undoubtedly a state (or place) of terrible punishment (Mt. 10: 28; 23: 33, Mk. 9: 43b, 47), and should be avoided at all costs (Mt. 5: 29, 30; 18: 9, Mk. 9: 43, 45, 47). God can punish offenders by casting them there (Lk. 12: 5, cf. Mt. 25: 41). It is perhaps the most terrifying and serious symbol of punishment in our Lord's teaching.

Gehenna need not be confused with Hades in the N.T. Hades is the LXX (ἄδης) rendering for שְׁאוֹל. In the O.T. it is a dark (Job 10: 21 f.), eternal (Job 7: 9 f.) abode of the dead (Ps. 89: 48, LXX, 88: 48, Is. 14: 9), but, as Jeremias brings out, in the N.T. Hades is a clean, intermediate, and temporary abode of the dead before the final resurrection (Mk. 5: 39 pars., Mt. 11: 23 par., 12: 40, Act. 2: 26 f., 31, cf. Rev. 20: 2 f., 7).[4]

The N.T. lays great emphasis on punishment in Gehenna, symbolizing it by the element of fire (Mt. 5: 22; 18: 9 par., Jas. 3: 6). At the same time it is clear that that final punishment is a continuation of present judgement (Jn. 3: 18, 36; Rom. 5: 18; 6: 23; Mt. 3: 12 par., 13: 30). The punishment in darkness (Mt. 25: 30), is for the wicked (Mt. 18: 34) who will wail and gnash their teeth there (Lk. 13: 28). A still gloomy picture is drawn in II Peter 2: 4, Jude 6, 7[5] and Revelation. In Revelation Gehenna is a fiery place (19: 20; 20: 10, 14, 15; 21: 8), with darkening smoke (9: 2) and deadly locusts (9: 3–5).

To be apart from or without Christ (χωρὶς Χριστοῦ), is to be alienated from God, and a very serious condition for such a soul

---

[1] Fire is frequently mentioned as being associated with Gehenna: sulphurous I En. 67: 6; fiery abyss, I En. 90: 26; everlasting fire, I En. 90: 24, cf. Rev. 20: 2 lake of torment and oven of Gehenna, II Esd. 7: 36, cf. Bar 59: 10; 85: 13, Siby Or. 1: 103, Mk. 9: 43, 45, etc.

[2] J.E., Vol. 5, p. 583, citing Yebamot 109b; cf. I En. 10: 4; 82: 2, Mt. 25: 30 22: 13, Job 10: 21 f.

[3] J.E., ibid., citing Berakot 8b, I En. 10: 6, Jdt. 16: 17; cf. Ecclus. 7: 17, Mk 9: 48, Jas. 3: 6.

[4] J. Jeremias, on ᾄδης in the TWzNT, Vol. I, especially 148 ff., and on γέεννα 655 f. The Kik. Bible has Seoli for שְׁאוֹל in the O.T., but vala maveva ma akw mekalaa ('where the spirits of the dead abide') for ὁ ᾄδης in the N.T.

[5] II Peter and Jude draw, at this point, a picture parallel to that of I En. 10 4–6, 12 f.; and the 'sinning' is probably from I En. 6.

The life that Jesus Christ brings to the sinner both now and hereafter is the heart of N.T. salvation. To reject Him is to remain in a state so terrible that the symbol of Gehenna and its associations is the most effective manner of warning that the Bible can use. Dwelling upon the geography of Gehenna leads not only to unbiblical fantasies, but draws away attention from the person of Jesus Christ. Like all other eschatological truths, Gehenna as a state is partly 'realized' now and is the only ultimate destiny of those who remain χωρὶς Χριστοῦ beyond the Last Judgement. Thus, Gehenna is a christological symbol, the negation of incorporation into Christ. It is dependent and conditionally 'everlasting' as long as anyone is apart from Christ. However vividly the rabbinic literature might paint Gehenna, in the Christian context it is a symbolic imagery and has no independent reality. The state of being χωρὶς Χριστοῦ is real and not symbolic, but Gehenna serves to convey the seriousness of that reality.

(c) Fire

In Akamba thought there is only physical fire for the purposes of cooking, heating, burning wood and grass in clearing new fields, smelting, etc. The spirits also use fire for similar purposes, but their fire is said to burn without consuming grass or wood as we know them in this life. Kanig, describing one of the dwelling places of Akamba spirits, wrote in 1902 'There they live. There one also sees from afar their fire and hears their conversation . . . But when one gets near, their traces disappear and one sees neither coal nor ashes.'[1] Fire has neither moral nor religious associations, now or hereafter, but it is a very useful element to both the living and the departed.

There is comparatively little information available about the religious associations of fire in other African societies. There are, obviously, myths and stories of how man invented or first acquired fire. Some societies like the Zulu (S. Africa) trace it to God as His gift to men; others like the Bavenda (S. Africa) connect it with God, and when it is produced in lightning they take it to be a sign of His intentions to communicate with their chief. There are many societies among whom a 'holy fire' is kept. For example, in Baganda (Uganda) temples a fire always burned day and night and was cared for by vestal virgins. The Herero (S.W. Africa) have a sacred fire constantly

---

[1] G. Kanig, *Dornige Pfade eines jungen Missionars in Ukamba* (1902), 17 (my own translation).

burning at their altars in each village. This fire is the symbol of national life and prosperity, and acts as an intermediary object in making prayers or contacting the unseen world. Part of the Gikuyu (Kenya) ceremony for purifying crops before harvest, includes the lighting of the holy fire which officiating elders carry to all the district. People look upon it as a 'purifying flame', and eagerly wait to take portions of it to their homesteads where already old fires have been extinguished. The new fire is not allowed to die until the next season.

In all these cases fire is treated or regarded as a useful tool both physically and religiously. In no way is it elevated to a metaphysical level, or used as a means of punishing offenders in the next life. Only in one instance, that of the Lodagaa (Ghana–Upper Volta), is the heat of the sun employed in the next world to torment every new arrival, the period of torture varying from three months for everybody to three years for witches and rich men. As a relic of Christian teaching in the sixteenth and seventeenth centuries, some of the Bacongo (Angola) believe that at death wicked people go to the sun where they are burnt, but without being consumed.

We have given something of the African background concerning fire, and must now return to the biblical uses of fire. In addition to its physical value, fire has other purposes in the Bible, as briefly listed in BDB *Lexicon* under אֵשׁ and further discussed in the *TWzNT*.[1] But our concern here is chiefly with its association with God's judgement, for which there are innumerable references in the Bible and other Jewish literature, e.g. Gen. 19: 24, Joel 2: 3, Ecclus. 45: 19, IV Mac. 12: 12, Tes. Zeb. 10: 3, Mt. 18: 8, Rev. 19: 20, etc. Such fire is heavenly in origin and nature. In Kittel's *TWzNT*, Lang traces the background and function of fire as a symbol of eschatological judgement, and reaches the conclusion that 'the term "everlasting fire" for the punishment in Hell is not used in the Old Testament'. But in the N.T., fire as a symbol of the wrath of God is a familiar figure, due to the O.T. influence (Pss. 79: 5; 89: 46, Jer. 4: 4; 5: 14; Ezek. 21: 32; 38: 19, Zeph. 1: 18, Nah. 1: 6, etc.). Lang points out also that it was associated with judgement by members of the Qumran sect.[2]

---

[1] BDB, p. 77, give six meanings of אֵשׁ and combinations which include supernatural fire, altar-fire, and God's anger; a similar but fuller treatment is given by F. Lang in the *TWzNT*, Vol. VI, pp. 927–48, on πῦρ.

[2] Lang, op. cit., 936, 938; his references from the Qumran writings include I QS 2: 15, I QH 6: 18 f.; 17: 13, I Qp Hab. 10: 5, 13, etc.

Fire and judgement are closely related as an eschatological concept in John's preaching (Mt. 3: 11 f. pars.);[1] and in Jesus' teaching (Mt. 5: 22; 13: 40–2, 49–50; 18: 8 f.; 25: 41, Mk. 9: 43, 45, 47 ff., Jn. 15: 6). It is very frequently used as a symbol of judgement in Revelation (8: 5, 7 f.; 9: 17 f.; 11: 5; 14: 10; 16: 8 f.; 20: 9 f., etc.). Paul makes reference to it (I Cor. 3: 13), as does also Jude (7, cf. 23 with I Cor. 3: 15). In II Peter fire will dissolve the elements (3: 7, 10–12) before the new heavens and earth appear.

While fire is thus clearly connected with the last Judgement, it is essential to relate it to the present as well as the future. Since eschatological judgement is both present and future, this fire is already lit and cast upon the earth by the presence of Jesus Christ in the world (Lk. 12: 49). To be detached from Him (cf. Eph. 2: 12)[2] is in effect to be immediately 'thrown into the fire and burned' (Jn. 15: 6), since judgement is at work already (Jn. 3: 18 f., 36). He baptizes with the Holy Spirit and with fire (Mt. 3: 11, Lk. 3: 16, cf. Act 2: 1–4). Indeed 'God is a consuming fire' (Heb. 12: 29, cf. Deut. 4: 24, Ex. 3: 2, Jud. 6: 21). He who reveals the Father must necessarily cause men to enter into the fire of judgement (Mt. 13: 40, 43; 18: 8 f., etc.). At the Parousia, this eschatological fire will be fully revealed (II Thes. 1: 7 f., cf. Is. 66: 15 f., Heb. 10: 27). When related to New Testament Eschatology fire is a christological symbol: it saves or it destroys according to one's relationship with Christ. What matters most, therefore, is the reality which the fire symbolizes. It is noteworthy that the destructive symbol of fire is intimately linked with Gehenna.

Akamba Christians believe strongly in a literal and future fire by means of which unbelievers will be tormented after the final Judgement.[3] But as V. Taylor cautions us, Jesus is 'not to be credited with

---

[1] Mk. 1: 8 (Cf. Jn. 1: 33) omits 'fire' and the instrumental (?), ἐν—though the latter omission may not be significant since his grammar is not always 'upright'. If 'fire' is for cleansing rather than judgement, it echoes Is. 6: 6 f., Zech, 13: 9 and Mal. 3: 2 f. (the last reference applies to John and not to Jesus). For the Baptizer, salvation and judgement run concurrently.

Note, T. F. Glasson's short statement that the threefold reference to water, wind and fire might be traceable to an Orphic tradition, in *NTS*, Vol. 3, No. 1 (Nov. 1956), pp. 69–71, article entitled: 'Water, Wind and Fire . . .'.

[2] The phrase, χωρὶς Χριστοῦ is the approximate opposite of ἐν Χριστῷ. It is a hapax legomenon, but two other phrases are paralled to it: χωρὶς Θεοῦ in minor MSS of Heb. 2: 9, and χωρὶς ἐμοῦ in Jn. 15: 5.

[3] Cf. Augustine, *De Civitate Dei*, XXI. 2, 9, 10—where he holds strongly to a view of material fire. He says: 'that hell, which also is called a lake of fire and brimstone, will be material fire, and will torment the bodies of the damned, whether men or devils. . . . One fire shall be the lot of both . . . '(XXI. 10, ET by

later ideas of eternal punishment which are alien to His teaching concerning God and man, but, on the other hand, His words must not be explained away as a picturesque metaphor. By contrast with the phrase "to enter into life" the words "go into Gehenna" indicate spiritual ruin and perhaps destruction.'[1]

As with Gehenna we have to look beyond the material symbol of fire to the message intended and thereby conveyed. Ultimately it matters little whether this eschatological symbol is interpreted literally or figuratively. The seriousness of remaining apart from Christ is vividly and universally dramatized by the symbol of fire, whether that fire is to burn now, or in the next world. It has to be remembered also that fire is used in the Bible as a symbol of purification and refining, even if that is an intensely hot process. Hell fire alone will not convert people or turn the world upside down. If people are threatened with being cast into a lake of fire in the next life, the effectiveness of the symbol is largely lost and the Christian Gospel is reduced to negative threats which have no lasting impact upon those who receive or reject the Gospel. The eschatological use of fire must not be sacrificed on this threefold linear concept of Time. The symbol must be timeless if it is to be effective and to make sense in Christian evangelism and living.

(d) Treasure

Jesus made several allusions to 'treasure(s) in heaven' (Mt. 6: 20; 19: 21, Lk. 12: 33) The phrase, ἐν τοῖς οὐρανοῖς must mean: of the quality of eternal nature; originating in and from God. To encounter the risen Lord is to come into contact with Him 'in whom are hid all the treasures of wisdom and knowledge' (Col. 2: 3). He urged men to seek first the Kingdom of God (Mt. 6: 33) of which He was the Bringer. Likewise Paul directed his readers to the heavenly things where Christ is (Col. 3: 1 f.). This is the 'treasure hidden in a field' and the 'one pearl of great value' (Mt. 13: 44, 45), for which all other types of treasure must be sacrificed. On the side of God, it was through the Cross that 'the riches of His glory' (Rom. 9: 23) were made open and available to both Jews and Gentiles. This meant a complete self-emptying act on the part of Jesus (Phil. 2: 6–8), to the

M. Dods, 1871, Vol. ii, pp. 435 f.). Many other Christians have held similar convictions, as a result of, or independent of, Augustine's influence.

[1] V. Taylor, *The Gospel According to St. Mark* (1959), 411. (This work is cited here as *Mark*.)

effect that 'though He was rich, for our (CK) sake He became poor, so that by His poverty we might become rich' (II Cor. 8: 9). This is God's treasure *par excellence*, distributed to all who are in Christ. The same heavenly treasure is described sacramentally in the Fourth Gospel, that Jesus gives 'living water . . . welling up to eternal life' (Jn. 4: 10, 14), He Himself being 'the Bread of Life' so that 'he who eats my flesh and drinks my blood has eternal life' (6: 54).

So now, in the eschatological dispensation of the Spirit, the treasure 'in the heavens' has been revealed and made available to those who are in Christ Jesus (cf. I Cor. 2: 9). Saints became partakers of His riches in glory here and now, but only in anticipation so that 'in the coming ages He might show the immeasurable riches of His grace in kindness towards us in Christ Jesus' (Eph. 2: 7). The present experience is only the paradoxical foretaste of our full inheritance (cf. Eph. 1: 13 f., II Pet. 1: 4). And yet our inheritance must include much more than the insights we catch through this foretaste.

The term 'treasure in heaven' seems to be both misrepresented and misunderstood in Ukambani. People think of it in the form of material goods to be possessed by believers after this life. This is partly because of linguistic limitations and conceptual barriers, and partly because of theological (mis)interpretation.

Both treasure or storehouse ($\theta\eta\sigma\alpha\nu\rho\acute{o}s$), and wealth or abundance ($\pi\lambda o\tilde{v}\tau os$), are translated *uthwii* in the Kik. Bible.[1] While the two words are related, it is unfortunate that they should both be rendered by the same Kikamba word which means 'riches, wealth, possessions.'[2] Traditionally *uthwii* is reckoned in terms of cattle, farm produce, land, and household members. But it is not simply an individual possession: it is primarily a corporate possession, since the individual is only a corporate member of wider circles of the community (household, 'gate', clan, etc.). Members of the wider circles may take and use, by force if necessary, practically any goods belonging to the individual. The living-dead and the spirits have a share in the goods of this life, and can (and do) return to claim them from ordinary people (especially those of their former household). But a person

---

[1] Exceptions are: Mt. 2: 11 where $\theta\eta\sigma\alpha\nu\rho\acute{o}s$ is rendered *miio ya vata* ('precious goods'); Mt. 12: 35; 13: 52, and Lk. 6: 45 where the same word is rendered *kyumbanisyoni* ('the gathering-place' or 'store-house').

[2] Another Kikamba word for wealth is *mali*. But it can be used collectively for any number of possessions, and conveys the basic meaning of 'ownership'. *Uthwii* on the other hand, specifically means much *mali*.

cannot invest his goods now in order to draw interest in the hereafter; the rich here will be rich there, and the poor here will be poor there. Human beings, however, have no claim on the goods in the next world. And while there are no 'customs restrictions' at the border, goods from one world cannot be transported into the other.[1]

Information about other African societies seems to show that even where the dead are buried with some of their possessions, the goods of this life are not transferable into the next. Without any clear explanation, however, many societies believe that if a person is rich in his human life he will continue to be rich in the next life, just as the poor, or thief, or kind-hearted person, etc., continues to be as he was here. Thus economic and social statuses are inheritable in the next world; and a person (the living-dead or spirit) can improve or fail to improve his lot in the hereafter, the same way that he might in this life. The majority, if not all, of African peoples do not expect any rewards or treasures or other forms of elevation, on the basis of individual merits or otherwise, when a person dies. Only on the grounds of what a person is or has in this life does he become the same in the next: and this is not a reward to be hoped for, it is simply in the 'nature of things', according to African notions of the hereafter. It is a 'physicalization' of the spirit world which, as we have pointed out before, is generally a carbon copy of the human world.

Christian teaching in Ukambani has generally emphasized that believers will find *uthwii* in Heaven, the amount of which will be in proportion to individual labour, faithfulness and generous giving in this life. It is thought of purely in terms of houses, furniture, clothes, etc. Traditional concepts about material goods in the land of the living-dead, which is in the *Tene* period (past), are readily transposed to the life of Christians in the hereafter, and in the future. It is also understood that whereas in traditional life a person could not invest goods now for the spirit world, a Christian may invest both goods and labour in order to reap the profits in Heaven. So his present life here becomes a full scale 'insurance' business, if he enters into it fully.

---

[1] It is not customary among the Akamba to bury people with their possessions. Occasionally, however, an old man may be buried together with his snuff box (cf. J. Hofmann, *Geburt, Heirat und Tod bei den Wakamba* (1901), 23). In a good number of cases in the past, the dead, especially children, were not buried. The Akamba do not pay any attention to the graves. But some African societies bury articles (and formerly, human beings) with the corpses, and many turn the grave into a shrine for family rituals and libation.

A number of the Kikamba hymns instil this hope in the hearts of
the believers, e.g. hymn 168 (which is sung during the taking of
collection) says

> If we begrudge the living Jesus,
> We shall reap as (what) we have sown.
> He loves a generous giver,
> And He hears him when he prays.[1]

chorus 21 says

> When this life is over, when this life is over,
> We shall find furnished houses at Jesus' home,
> Which will be ours wherein to live (always).

Further teaching on the heavenly 'riches' (treasures) includes the
following items, according to Kik. hymns:

A very big house, comfortable (useful) home—hymn numbers 17, 20, 42,
57, 74, 81, 137, 144, 185, 199, 202, chor. 21;
riches in Heaven—23, 85, 86, 101, 129, 181;
we will be paid—61, 168 (go to Heaven as a result of serving Him), 195;
trouble, pain, etc. will end there—57, 86, 98, 127, 144, 161, 166, 199.

Similarly, as expressed in their hymns, members of The Friends
of the Holy Spirit, look forward to material rewards as soon as the
Lord has come for them. At the same time they reject or despise
the things of this world. Thus, they sing for example in hymn 39 (on
Kimilu's list)[2]

> The day of the Lord is near
> Those who rejoice in the worldly matters
> Will weep bitterly
>
> We who are on earth together with those in heaven
> Let us wait for the day of the Lord
> For that is the day of receiving our rewards.

In hymn 42, they sing:

> I know well when on earth
> My house is in heaven
> Our troubles and earthly joys shall end
>
> My home is in heaven
> A nice (fertile) country where I shall enter
> There are no troubles but joy.

[1] From the hymn by K. Shaw, 'Sowing in the morning, sowing seeds of kindness . . .'.
[2] See Chapter II, p. 56 note 1.

The same themes of house, comfort, joy, end of sorrows, and treasure in Heaven, occur frequently in these hymns.

From these examples and many others that we could not possibly quote here, it is clear that Akamba Christians believe that 'treasure in heaven' will be in terms of concrete material goods. One suspects that the same attitude is found among other African Christians, though as yet no studies of the problem have been made in other parts of Africa. It is relatively easy to transfer one's wishes for material benefits from the immediate environment of deprivation and want to a dreamland which in this case is identified with heaven. But since such heaven is highly mythological, nobody could prove to the believers its non-existence or otherwise. Jesus is nevertheless looked upon as the intermediate Agent who conveys the believing group from the earth, a place of material want and pain, to Heaven, regarded as the opposite, full of rewards and riches. Therefore the hope of gaining these heavenly rewards and treasure, and the fear of losing them, become the dominant motive in Christian life and service.[1] Thus, the whole concept of heavenly treasure or riches is entirely divorced from Christ except insofar as He conveys people from the world of material deprivation to that of rewards and riches. What seems to be happening, therefore, is that the extension of the future is not possible in terms of Time *per se*, but only in a materialistic projection of people's experiences and wishes in this life. Even God is oriented towards the production or creation of that type of future— an intensely anthropocentric and physicalized future.

New Testament emphasis is clearly on Jesus Christ being the One in whom, through whom and by whom 'heavenly treasure' is to be understood and inherited both in this life and the next. In His Incarnation (Jn. 1: 14, I Jn. 1: 2), He was made materially or physically available in the richest possible reality. As such He cannot and does not take mankind to any other form of heavenly treasure or reward: for in Himself all the riches of God converge and are available. To put Him in the position of an intermediate Agent amounts to a blatant rejection of Himself and a corruption of His Gospel. As the final and ultimate expression of God, He can only lead men to God and not to anything created: and beyond God there is no room for anything or anyone else. As symbols of fellowship with God, both

---

[1] So also in the Early Church, see C. N. Moody, *The Mind of the Early Converts* (n.d., prefaced 1920), 16.

'reward' and 'treasure' are vividly powerful. But they are symbols and not the reality itself.

If that reality is stretched on a linear and threefold dimension of Time, it is dangerously exposed to a misunderstanding and a reversal which make the symbol eclipse the reality.

(e) City

Both Judaism[1] and Christianity share the hope of an eschatological city (Jerusalem). Jesus' life and ministry ended in the earthly Jerusalem, but the same city was also the starting point for the Church, His Body (Acts 1: 4 f., 8; 2: 1–4). The heavenly Jerusalem is the destiny of the Church (Heb. 14: 14, cf. 12: 22, Phil. 3: 20 f.). The two cities are symbolically linked (cf. Gal. 4: 25 f.).

Yet, through spiritual experience, a person who is in Christ is already a member of the heavenly state or commonwealth (πολίτευμα) which previously was reserved for Israel but is now through the Incarnation declared open to all (Eph. 2: 12 f.) This is an eschatological experience for the present, as well as for the future since the final realization of our πολίτευμα belongs to the metaphysical order of things (Phil. 3: 20).

Speaking about the eschatological city, the author of Hebrews maintains a Platonic dialectic: the city is both present and future, earthly and heavenly. In its Time dimension it is linked with the old covenant since Abraham looked forward to it (11: 10), and the O.T. saints died before arriving there (11: 16).[2] But the eschatological days have come (1: 2), and freed it from its temporal bondage. Therefore, through faith and baptism the saints now 'stand before Mount Zion and the city of the living God, heavenly Jerusalem' (12: 22 NEB). They have realized their eschatological home in part, and they are still pilgrims (13: 13 f., I Pet. 1: 1; 2: 11). The experience, however, is so real that believers 'are no longer strangers and sojourners, but you are fellow citizens with the saints and members of the household of God' (Eph. 2: 19, cf. I Pet. 2: 9 f.). This status has dimensions both in Time and beyond. It is truly eschatological.

[1] E.g., Ezek. 40 ff., Hag. 2: 6–9, Zech. 2, I En. 90: 29, IV Ezra 7: 26; 8: 52; 13: 36, II Bar. 4: 3–6; 32: 2, etc. (though these last two books may be post A.D. 70).

[2] Cf. II Bar. 4 where it is shown to Adam, Abraham and Moses, and in chap. 51 the righteous enter it after judgement; the city is built by God, according to I En. 90: 29. See also, U. Simon, *Heaven in the Christian Tradition* (1958), 223.

Two eschatological Jerusalems are described at length in Revelation. As Charles distinguishes them, one is 'heavenly' (21: 9 to 22: 2), and the other is 'new' (3: 12; 21: 2–4; 22: 3–5).[1] But while the general description of these cities may be paralleled from Jewish apocalyptic a Christian differentia is introduced. The New (καινός) Jerusalem[2] belongs to the rejuvenated order of existence (21: 1, 5a, cf. Is. 65: 17), realized by God through his Son. It is not simply the Messianic capital of Jewish apocalyptic: it is the symbol of perfect fellowship between God and His people (22: 3–5). And this experience is a reality so intense that it has dimensions for the present (cf. Heb. 4: 16) and the hereafter. The Way to that 'city' is none other than Jesus Christ (cf. Jn. 14: 1–7; 10: 7, 9).

Past generations in Ukambani had no cities. Akamba ideas of cities and city life are derived from towns in Kenya that have come into existence since the end of the nineteenth century.[3] The city is an ambivalent place. On the one hand, it contains all the modern problems and experiences of 'rapid social change', represented by shortage of housing, slums, unemployment, impersonal relationships, loneliness of the individual, crime, sexual immorality and the like. On the other hand, for the younger generation living in the countryside, the city is their symbol of hope, civilization, prosperity, easy life and social freedom; and whether or not young people realize this expectation the city is nevertheless an immensely attractive myth.

The Kikamba word for town or city is *musyi* which, in its traditional context, denotes 'home, homestead, family'. The physical *musyi* may be moved from one spot to another, or individuals may change their homes (e.g. when a girl gets married). But on the conceptual level, *musyi* is both the place and symbol of familyhood, family ties, unity, communion, integration, security, resting, and the endlessness of human life. The *musyi* is where all the generations

---

[1] R. H. Charles in his two-volume commentary on Revelation (1920). Note the very materialistic description of the Heavenly Jerusalem, and the negative description of the New Jerusalem.

[2] Cf. I En. 90: 29 where Jerusalem is the 'new house greater and loftier than that first . . . all its pillars were new, and its ornaments were new', but it is doubtful whether the author(s) meant two distinct Jerusalems as in Revelation.

[3] Mombasa and other coastal cities date from ancient times. Even though Akamba traders frequented them and especially Mombasa, urban life as such remained unknown in Ukambani. Machakos (1892) and Kitui (1893) are the two main towns of Ukambani, but there are many smaller towns, railway stations, and trading centres all over the country.

converge, and it is also where the procreation of mankind takes place, and is preserved and respected. *Musyi* is the symbol of the beginning and the end for the individual, it is the place of birth and death, the symbol of old age and renewal.

That is the traditional image and experience of *musyi* for Akamba and many other African peoples. Through contact with Christianity and technological society, the word has acquired a much wider application, being used to refer not only to 'home' but also the 'city'. For the majority of people, *musyi* means two places (and two sets of ideas): a home in the countryside, which has its traditional associations and historical depth; the other is the town itself whether one has a home there or not. Many who live in towns still think of 'home' as being a place in the country, where they have a piece of land, keep livestock or own a house. They are thus living in a *musyi* (town) but far or away from *musyi* (home). Similarly, individuals who live entirely or chiefly in the country, regard their home as *musyi* and look to the town as a *musyi* (town), but not as their *musyi* (home). In this case, the city (town) is a stranger who comes to them through relatives living and working there, through the goods that come from there, or governmental orders that are legislated there.

When Akamba (or African) Christians come across the notion of heavenly city (*musyi*), their concept of it is strongly coloured by both traditional and modern ideas of *musyi*. Through the emphasis on an exclusively futurist Eschatology and a prolongation of the future dimension of Time, many Christians have come to believe in a physical and colossal city hanging up somewhere in the distant heavens, waiting for them to go there just as Nairobi and Mombasa wait for young people to go there when they finish their schooling. This physical city promises and provides all the good material things that people cannot acquire in this life; and these are to be earned through faith, generous giving in Church collections, and witnessing for Christ in this life. Many of the Kikamba hymns, as used by followers of both the Africa Inland Mission/Church and the Friends of the Holy Spirit, not only portray this picture but urge and encourage believers to hold this expectation.[1] Jesus is brought into the picture as the Agent of conveying believers from this earth to the city in Heaven; and the Christian Faith is the only

---

[1] For example in the Kikamba hymnal, numbers: 17, 20, 42, 57, 74, 76, 78, 86, 144, 185, 202, etc.

passport to that city of prosperity. But how much this heavenly *musyi* is a *home* and not simply a *city* for them personally, is hard to gauge.

(f) Country

An eschatological country is spoken of in Hebrews. O.T. saints sought it (11: 14, 16), and by faith 'greeted it from afar' (11: 13). But what was promised in the O.T. is, in a temporal context, now realized and fulfilled in Jesus Christ, the leader or pioneer (ἀρχηγός) and perfector (τελειωτής) of faith (12: 2). Consequently, the pilgrims have arrived at their fatherland (12: 18 f., 22 ff.), and the writer can plead with those who, through faith, participate in Jesus, to 'be grateful for receiving a Kingdom which cannot be shaken' (12: 28). But, because this is an eschatological experience, it is only a foretaste in expectation: Christians can go 'to Him outside the camp' (13: 13), but they are still pilgrims (13: 14 cf. 12: 1 f., I Pet. 2: 11). Jesus Himself, having initiated the eschatological era (9: 26), will 'appear a second time' to unveil and bring salvation to a consummation (9: 28).

Paul does not speak specifically of a heavenly country. But he draws attention to 'things that are above' (Col. 3: 2 f.), and to the eschatological Man from 'heaven' (I Cor. 15: 45, 47 f.). The new humanity bears the image (εἰκών) of the heavenly Man as a necessary prerequisite to inheriting the Kingdom of God (I Cor. 15: 48 ff.).

In II Pet. 3: 12 ff., the saints are awaiting 'new heavens and a new earth', which will replace the old. Likewise in Rev. 21: 1 ff., the new creation replaces the old, and the New Jerusalem becomes the 'fatherland' for the saints. In I John, the believer is so firmly settled in the fatherland through abiding in God, that it is the world which must pass away (cf. 2: 17). Those who abide in Him have reached their permanent home which cannot be eroded by Time: and the passing away of the world only removes that which, in contrast and by virtue of being in Time, is transient and temporary.

The Gospels make no explicit reference to the heavenly 'homeland', but it is clear that a reality is pictured as the 'heavenly land' where God's will is done (Mt. 6: 10), and from whence 'the Son of Man' descended (Jn. 3: 13, cf. 31). There are 'heavenly things' (Jn. 3: 12) which are apparently hard for us to believe, but they are precisely the order of eternal existence brought into historical realization in the Incarnation (Jn. 1: 14, cf. I Jn. 1: 1 f.). And, as Dodd comments, 'beyond the vision of God we cannot aspire.' So in Jesus Christ, we come to our fatherland both now and at the Parousia.

The Kikamba word for country is *nthi*. It also means: floor, ground, land, continent, earth, world. At death, the living-dead go to the country of the departed. But this is almost an exact replica of the land from which they come—with fields, rivers, mountains, etc. An early missionary, Hofmann, rightly recorded the attitude of the Akamba to the land of the departed: 'they are of the opinion that it must be beautiful, because nobody returns from there'.[1] Nevertheless, it is not a goal to which the living look forward, nor is life there on a higher or better level of existence even though the departed receive a new 'spirit-' power.[2]

The item of an eschatological 'fatherland' has been readily and enthusiastically received in Ukambani, as it links with traditional beliefs. Christians look forward to it with great joy. But instead of having it on this earth, it is in 'Heaven'; and it is infinitely better than the traditional land of the departed—for there is no sickness, hunger, etc. It is exclusively pictured in materialistic terms: fertility, water, singing, etc. Missionary teaching has greatly encouraged this picture, mainly through the hymns, e.g. number 199:

> There is a very fertile land (country), far far away,
> Where God's people will go:
> Joyful songs will there be sung
> Jesus is (will be) praised always.
>
> Let us all to that fertile land go,
> Let us face there without doubting:
> We shall never see pain and sorrow,
> Because we shall dwell in Jesus' home (country) . . .[3]

Similar examples can be quoted from the hymns of the Friends of the Holy Spirit. Members of this sect consider themselves to be pilgrims travelling through a barren land, which is full of troubles, sorrows, opposition and hardship. But they look forward to the end of their journey and arrival in the fertile land, with plenty of water, comfortable homes, and secure from sorrows and troubles.

---

[1] J. Hofmann, *Geburt, Heirat und Tod bei den Wakamba* (1901), 24. (My own translation.)

[2] So also Hofmann, ibid. More will be said on this subject in Chapter V.

[3] The Kikamba version of: 'There is a happy land . . .', by A. Young. Other examples are found in hymns 17, 42, 57, 61, 96, 98, 101, 127, 129, 166, etc.

Meanwhile, they urge and expect God to sustain them and come quickly for them.

To Akamba people, what constitutes 'good land' (or country) is its fertility. If a country is not fertile, and hence agriculturally profitable, it is for them useless and 'bad'. Fertility of the land means productivity in terms of crops, livestock and human beings. Only when a land or country is productively fertile do the people consider it to be 'good', 'beautiful', 'valuable' and 'desirable'. In Kikamba 'beautiful' and 'good' are expressed by the same word -*seo* (adjectival stem); but land is first and foremost 'fertile' if it is to be considered valuable and to be appreciated. Therefore, when in English one sings or speaks of a 'beautiful country', the Akamba automatically think or speak of a 'fertile country'.

Most of the fertile land in Ukambani is occupied and utilized intensely. People are, therefore, short of fertile land, and wherever it is available they do their best to acquire a piece of it. Since their traditional concept of the land of the departed (or the hereafter) is basically the same as that of this present land, there is no contrast, in terms of fertility, between this and the next 'country'. When Christians speak about an eschatological country which is 'fertile', in the 'future' and 'heavenly', this makes a strong contrast with the traditional ideas about the land of the departed. It conjures up every possible myth about the 'goodness' of that land, and the way it will meet all the happy expectations that go with the idea of a 'fertile' land. Christians escape, at least in their hopes and minds, from this earth (which in Akamba experiences and history is often afflicted with famines due to lack of sufficient harvest when there is not enough rain or when locusts devastate the crops), to a mythological country which is much more fertile and hence more productive and attractive.

These notions and hopes about a purely materialistic country clearly create a false spirituality. They encourage an attitude of indifference to the world in which Christians are called to live; they encourage them to escape from physical reality to a largely fictitious reality; and their Faith is embarrassingly immature. Certainly a heavenly country is a vivid and appropriate metaphor to use in describing eschatological realities, especially in a land and at a time when Palestine depended so much on what the country could produce. But, as we have pointed out before, this is only a metaphorical way of expressing a reality, and the metaphor cannot replace the reality behind it. An abiding relationship with and fellowship in Christ, made historically possible through the Incarnation, are realities which can only be expressed metaphorically by the use of these materialistic terms. There can be no heavenly country apart from Jesus Christ. Incorporation into Him, and fellowship in Him, amount to both the eschatological country itself and arrival there. He is both the end of the journey and the road on which that journey is made. Therefore that land or country is both temporal and beyond Time, both historical and metaphysical, both present and yet to be. This metaphor points to the reality, expresses something of the reality, and stands for a reality already unveiled, historicized and yet still veiled and beyond history. Therefore the metaphor is not the reality itself, and to hope for the metaphor alone is to miss the reality. The New Testament does not leave believers in Christ on the level of the metaphor: it leads them right into the reality itself, into both pilgrimage and arrival in Christ. Again we must see this eschatological country as a christological phenomenon. In the next chapter we shall argue that it is chiefly in the two Sacraments of Baptism and the Eucharist that the Christian participates in this eschatological homeland, paradoxically both in Time and beyond Time.

(g) Eating and Drinking

According to Akamba beliefs, the inhabitants of the next world work in the fields, herd cattle, prepare meals, eat and drink, feast and dance . . . just as people do in this life. They are generally pictured as eating more, working harder, etc., than we do at present. They are also particularly fond of merry-making, and when 'seen' by human beings they are usually dancing.

Information about other African societies indicates the same range of beliefs, namely that life in the next world is much like the present. It is only natural, therefore, that eating and drinking should form part of the life of the living-dead and the spirits, since their world is thought to be like ours. There is nothing, however, special about eating and drinking in the hereafter, since these are regular, normal and necessary activities.

The New Testament speaks also about eating and drinking at the Messianic Banquet (Lk. 22: 29 f., Mt. 8: 11 f. par., Rev. 19: 9, cf. Mt. 22: 1–14, Lk. 14: 15–24). This was a familiar notion in Jewish

Eschatology.[1] But the N.T. does not indulge in sensuous and materialistic hopes of the type found in some Rabbinic teaching. This Messianic meal is a metaphorical vocabulary describing spiritual fellowship between God and the redeemed community: 'He who comes to
me shall not hunger, and he who believes in me shall never thirst'
(Jn. 6: 35, cf. Rev. 7: 16, Is. 49: 10). While the N.T. allows room for
a future Banquet, it is explicit in declaring that already in Jesus Christ
the time for the Banquet has arrived and men must come to Him
to eat the Bread and drink the Water of life (Jn. 4: 14; 6: 27, 33–5,
48–58; 7: 37, Rev. 21: 6; 22: 17, cf. I Cor. 10: 4). The Holy Eucharist
is nothing less than an appropriation of this Messianic Banquet,
the sacramental means of spiritual sustenance.

We have seen that according to the teaching of the Africa Inland
Mission in Ukambani, there will be a 'personal, visible and premillennial return of the Lord Jesus Christ' (*Constitution* of the A.I.C.,
item 14, p. 5). At this point He will 'catch away His Church' to the air,
during which time there will be on earth the so-called 'Great Tribulation'. Christians will, however, receive their rewards before the
Judgement seat of Christ, in the air, before He once more returns to
reign on the earth for a thousand years (*Catechism*, Chapter 17, pp.
39 f.). This is the time when, it is believed, the Christians will enjoy
the Messianic Banquet in the air, whose food and drink will be of
material substance but more tasty than anything known on earth.
Several Kikamba hymns (e.g. numbers 144, 166, 190 and 199) instil
this belief, and one has heard preachers in Ukambani elaborating on
the same belief. The symbol of the Messianic Banquet has now become
'materialized' and 'futurized'.

Here again we see how far a materialistic symbol has lost its
effectiveness when the reality is fused with the symbolism. Eating and
drinking as eschatological symbols are most meaningful only in their
sacramental and christological context. But once they are viewed
simply as a future hope they become empty theologically and spiritually. It is here that we must anticipate our discussion of the Eschatology of the Sacraments in the next chapter. The fellowship, communion, union and tranquillity with which eating and drinking are

[1] Cf. the Qumran: 'The Manual of Discipline for the Future Congregation of
Israel' (col. ii), T. H. Gaster, *The Scriptures of the Dead Sea Sect* (ET 1957),
285 ff.; known also as 'The Messianic Rule' (G. Vermes, *The Dead Sea Scrolls in
English* (1962), 118 ff.); 'The Rule of the "New Covenant" ' (A. Dupont-Sommer,
The Dead Sea Scrolls (ET 1952), 45 ff.); cf. J. M. Allegro, *The Dead Sea Scrolls*
(1956), 115 ff., 146 f.

associated, begin already to be the experience of Christians as they participate in the Sacrament of the Eucharist. This supersedes both the dimensions and limits of Time.

(h) Tears and Pain

In the New Jerusalem, God is to put an end to tears and pain (Rev. 21: 4, cf. Is. 25: 8; 35: 10). But this process is already at work in Jesus Christ (Mt. 11: 28 f., Jn. 6: 35). He experienced sorrow, agony and death on our behalf (Mk. 10: 45, II Cor. 5: 21, Heb. 2: 9, I Pet. 2: 24, etc.).[1] To be 'in Christ' is to have access to 'the Father of mercies and God of all comfort' (II Cor. 1: 3b f., Heb. 4: 16; 10: 19–25). But this comfort may involve, paradoxically, a participation in the sufferings of Christ during the interim period (I Cor. 1: 5 f., cf. Col. 1: 24), when the Christian is subject to Time. Nevertheless, the entire powers of the age to come are thrust 'back' (or 'down') so that we can appropriate them here and now as we anticipate the End (Heb. 6: 4 f.; 10: 25). This experience means wiping away tears and removing pain which otherwise are the nature of life without Christ. In the End those who are in Christ must inherit the comfort whose full range is part of God's mysteries, but is yet to be unveiled.

Life in Ukambani is full of tears and pain from a variety of causes —sickness, bereavement, accident, famine, etc. These are often, if not always, attributed to magic, witchcraft, curse and (to a much less extent) the living-dead and spirits. Suffering is mostly of a physical nature, and traditionally the Akamba have no concern over 'spiritual' agony. Death brings physical suffering to an end, but the next world has its quota of pain and joy, experienced as much as these are experienced by human beings. So there is no final escape or comfort from 'tears and pain', and this is the accepted lot of mankind in both worlds. Since God is not the cause of suffering, then it is not His business to remove it—so the logic goes. The same experiences and beliefs are reported in other African societies.

---

[1] This is not the place to engage in a discussion on the question of the Suffering Servant, about which there is superfluous literature. Note the attention drawn by Moule to the fact that both Jesus and 'the New Testament writers themselves make startlingly little use of the Servant Songs' (*The Birth of the New Testament* (1962), 81 ff.). See also the discussion by W. Zimmerli and J. Jeremias on 'παῖς Θεοῦ' in the *TWzNT*, Vol. V (1954), 653–713 (ET: *The Servant of God*, 1957); and T. W. Manson, *The Teaching of Jesus* (1931), and *The Servant-Messiah* (1952).

In the type of teaching followed in Ukambani, Christians are encouraged to escape, howbeit psychologically, from this world of suffering to Heaven which now they visualize as a place where tears and pain are to be blotted out. A good number of hymns used by both the Africa Inland Church and Friends of the Holy Spirit, paint this type of picture and expectation. For example, in the Kikamba hymnal number 57:

> We will dwell with Him for ever and ever
> Singing hymns in heaven, and forgetting pain;
> They (the hymns) are of resurrection nature, resurrection;
> I speak saying, 'Let us abide with Jesus'.

Hymn number 86 has a deep longing to get to that heavenly abode:

> Up above there is a beautiful (good) home (city),
> Which cannot be destroyed:
> The owner is Jesus, our Redeemer.
> The faithful are cared for there.
> When shall I see that home (city)—
> The home (city) of our Saviour?

Parallel examples can be quoted from the hymns of the Friends of the Holy Spirit. Thus No. 15 admonishes that:

> Great joy will be found in heaven
> Those who have overcome in the earthly battle . . .
> They will never remember the earthly troubles
> When they see the beloved Jesus our King
> Coming in His glory and the might of His Father . . .

In hymn 34, the singers urgently wish to escape from here:

> My Lord the earth is like a wilderness
> With much trouble and hunger
> I am waiting for you in great thirst . . .
> Your servants are ever tired . . .
>
> I beseech Thee Father, remember me
> Lest I give up my journey . . .
> Help me to be victorious in your work.
> When the Lord's day comes,
> I will receive a crown
> Together with the saints.

In their traditional beliefs Akamba and other African peoples do not know of ways in which one may escape from pain and sorrows either in this or the next world. So now the Christian Message, as they hear, understand and receive it, promises them precisely that solution. Consequently that expectation is in a concrete, material and literal sense; and it is hoped that it would take place in a world detached from the present but placed in the skies above and for all practical purposes conceivable only in terms of the future dimension of Time. As far as this world, life and the present dimension of Time are concerned, the Christian Message is irrelevant except in supplying a psychological escape from the sorrows and pain of daily experience. This expectation, furthermore, makes Heaven *per se*, self-contained in the sense that, for Christians, simply by getting there, all the good things automatically become available and all the bad things automatically disappear. Then, Jesus Christ might as well retire from the scene at that point! And that is precisely what comes out of this false spirituality, however genuine and sincere its feelings might be.

(i) Heaven

Heaven(s) is a vast subject in the Bible and Jewish–Christian thought, as brought out in writings like U. Simon's *Heaven in the Christian Tradition* (1958); and the article in the *TWzNT* (V, pp. 496–543) on οὐρανός (etc.) by H. Traub and G. von Rad. It means: (i) the physical universe besides and beyond the earth, and (ii) the symbolic dwelling 'place' of God, His angelic hosts and the redeemed. Our chief concern here is with Heaven as it relates to the redeemed community.

In the New Testament, Heaven is symbolically regarded as a 'place'. Thus: a great reward is in Heaven (Mt. 5: 12), Christ's followers are to lay up treasures in Heaven (Mt. 6: 20, cf. Lk. 12: 33), children have their angels in Heaven (Mt. 18: 10), Jesus 'ascended' into Heaven (Lk. 24: 51 (A B W O, Text. Rec.), Acts 1: 11, 'The Apostles' Creed'), and will 'descend' (I Thes. 4: 16) in the clouds of Heaven (Mt. 24: 30). In Revelation there are innumerable references to Heaven in locational terms.

But while the majority of the allusions to Heaven in the N.T. give a spatial picture of it, emphasis is laid upon fellowship centred around God. So Jesus taught us to pray: 'Our Father in heaven ...' (Mt. 6: 9 *NEB*). It is this 'theocentric' life that Jesus Christ came to manifest and impart to the world (Jn. 1: 14; 6: 33; 10: 10 *NEB*, I Cor. 15: 45b, etc.). The 'life eternal' is absolutely and intensely

7

the normal life of Heaven, but in Christ it can now be appropriated in all its fullness (Rom. 10: 6–9, I Cor. 15: 47 ff.,[1] etc.). The experience is so real that Paul can write that 'your life is hid *with Christ in God*', and again that Christ is our life (Col. 3: 3 f.).

This is man's destiny, and the eschatological imperative is: 'Put on the Lord Jesus Christ' (Rom. 13: 14), the Man from Heaven (I Cor. 15: 47, Jn. 6: 38). But because this is an eschatological experience, it makes sense mainly or only in the dimensions of present appropriation and future consummation. The goal is pictured as: being with the Lord always (I Thes. 4: 17b, Jn. 14: 3, cf. Phil. 1: 23b), receiving our inheritance (Eph. 1: 14, cf. I Pet. 1: 4), putting on immortality (I Cor. 15: 53 f.), dwelling in the New Jerusalem (Rev. 22: 3-5), living in the house of the Lord (Ps. 23: 6, Jan. 14: 2 f.), etc. In temporal terms this goal will, however, be realized in comparatively 'new Heaven(s) and a new earth' (Rev. 21: 1, II Pet. 3: 13, Is. 65: 17; 66: 22). But in spite of this temporalization the supreme accent is upon theocentric worship and fellowship (Is. 66: 23, Rev. 4). This is the true Heaven-ly existence which defies description in terms of Space and Time, as it is the very essence of and participation in the Beatific Vision.

The Kikamba word for heaven(s) is *itu* (pl. *matu*). Conceptually and linguistically it simply means the vast mantle of space 'overhanging' the earth. Although the Akamba do not know precisely where God dwells, they associate Him with the Heavens, saying that He dwells beyond the clouds (*mathweo*, and *matu*). When a person dies, he (now as a living-dead) goes to the land of the departed which is on this world and next to that of human beings but invisible to men. There is no expectation or belief that the living-dead or spirits dwell with God: they are creatures and belong to their places of abode wherever these may be; but God as Creator exists or dwells on an entirely different plane and mode of existence.[2] People neither desire,

---

[1] Theologically, both φορέσωμεν (p⁴⁶, א A D G etc.) and φορέσομεν (B I Tex. Rec.) are possible in I Cor. 15: 49—one is for the present realization, and the other is for the future; but textually the latter reading is to be preferred.

[2] Hofmann, op. cit. 24, reports the Akamba (1901) as saying, concerning the departed: ' "The dead are now come to God". Later on the dead come to their place, and from time to time they assemble once more before God.' I have not come across this saying or belief, and it is possible that Hofmann confused the Kikamba he heard (God is *Mulungu* in Kikamba; but occasionally the plural *milungu* is used to refer to important family and clan members who have departed this life).

nor hope, nor intend nor expect to live with God or share in His type of existence, when they depart from this life.

Information from other African peoples supports, and is on the whole much like, these Akamba ideas. It is accepted by African peoples that God dwells in or is associated with the sky, clouds, or heavens, even if, according to many, He may have other modes of being especially in His immanent aspect. With only a few exceptions, African peoples do not consider the departed as living in the sky: somewhere on or in the earth is their dwelling place. They are associated with earthly objects and phenomena (like mountains, waterfalls, bushes, and human experiences), just as, in contrast, God is associated with heavenly objects and phenomena (like the sky, sun, stars, rain, etc.). In a number of African languages, the name for God (or for one of His attributes) means 'sky, heavens, above, up, sun, or of clouds'.[1] From available traditional concepts, Heaven is not the final dwelling place for the departed.

Christian teaching in Ukambani as channelled through the Africa Inland Mission and Church has emphasized the geographical, locational and physical interpretation of Heaven. That God dwells there is not a new element as far as Akamba (and other African) Christians are concerned, since this was already known in traditional beliefs. The new element, however, is that Heaven is the geographical home for the Christians, just as Gehenna is thought to be the unfortunate home for non-believers. The dwelling place of the departed is now switched from the traditional place on or in this earth, to two other areas removed and different from this earth. These are reachable either on one's death, or at the end of the world. The traditional dwelling place for the departed is now to be deserted and evacuated. It is also to be no longer in the *Tene* (past) dimension of Time, but in the new and ever lengthening future dimension. As people orient their thinking from the *Tene* period to the future, they also remove the land of the departed from this earth to Heaven (or Gehenna for the unfortunates). This is another area of both temporal and psychological inversion in the thinking of Akamba and other African peoples who have been exposed to this type of Christianization.

It is chiefly in the hymns that the picture of Heaven is painted in the most elaborate and sensuous terms. This applies to the hymns

---

[1] I have collected considerable information concerning God in relation to heavenly objects and phenomena, in my book, *Concepts of God in Africa* (1970), chapter 12.

used both by the Africa Inland Mission/Church and the Friends of
the Holy Spirit. Some of the main ideas about Heaven include:
houses built there for Christians, a comfortable mansion, a furnished
home, a place without sorrow or anguish, full of riches and the place
where Christians receive only rewards. It is not necessary to quote
many of the hymns to substantiate these facts, and a few verses will
here suffice. In the Kikamba hymnal chorus 21 reads:

> When this life is over, (twice)
> We shall see ready made houses at Jesus' home,
> And they will be ours wherein to dwell . . .

Hymn 202:

> A comfortable (good) dwelling place He has made,
> Which is in the big city (home) of God;
> And it will be dwelt by the clean in heart,
> Who are ever willing to be cleansed by the Holy Spirit.

Hymn 144 strikes the same note:

> We are going to our home in Heaven,
> We are going to Jesus' home;
> Sorrows will end there,
> We are going to Jesus' home.
>
> We are going to our home in Heaven . . .
> There is a fully furnished home . . .
> Jesus will come to fetch us here,
> Jesus will come soon (the tense also means 'tomorrow').
> We will be rejoicing and praising Him,
> And we will never suffer again.
>
> We will never hunger or feel greedy
> When we arrive at that clean (holy) home (city);
> And nothing will spoil (damage) the heart,
> Or cause us to stumble.

Hymns used by the Friends of the Holy Spirit contain the same ideas
and expectations about Heaven.

The New Testament and Christian hope do indeed make room for
and encourage believers to view the Heaven-ly life in contrast with the
present. But, as we have pointed out, Heaven for its own sake is
not heavenly, and has no independent reality as such. New Testament
emphasis is on Jesus as the One through whom and in whom life is
Heaven-ly. This is the nature, quality and scope of the life He has
mediated to our physical existence. It defies both history and geo-

graphy, even if it is and may be mediated within the temporal and spatial confines of our nature. To localize it, even if in Heaven, and to 'temporalize' it (by confining it to a future dimension of Time), is to restrict it within limited dimensions. And such Heaven has neither attraction nor meaning, except perhaps to societies that might feel oppressed and deprived, and hence the need to escape psychologically to such a myth. The New Testament is explicit that Jesus never promised us a heavenly utopia, but only His own self and His own companionship both in Time and beyond, both in space and beyond (cf. Jn. 14: 3, Mt. 28: 20b; 18: 20). Indeed He emphatically demolished the notion that men could see or know God (the Father), apart from seeing, knowing and encountering God in Jesus Himself (Jn. 14: 6–11). Just as in Jesus God has become as near and visible as possible, so also in Him Heaven becomes as tangible and available as possible, within and beyond Time. In Him, therefore, Christian Eschatology becomes practical Eschatology. The Church participates in it and the Church anticipates it. Therefore, also, the Church cannot afford to let Eschatology slip into the future or any single dimension of Time or Space. The Church is part of that eschatological phenomenon of the New Testament, and these two cannot be viewed separately. It is another method of the New Testament, to communicate its eschatological message through the liturgical life of the Church, experienced best and most intensely of all in the Sacraments of Baptism and Eucharist.

Before proceeding to the Eschatology of the Sacraments we might briefly recapitulate our findings in this chapter. From the examples we have cited, it is evident that the New Testament employs a materialistic language as one of the means of communicating or depicting its eschatological message. This language is, however, employed symbolically and christologically. The language is not the reality but only a vehicle of communicating what otherwise is beyond the dimension of human understanding. As far as Ukambani is concerned, this method of using a materialistic language to convey eschatological truths, has for all practical purposes failed to relay the realities behind the symbolism. Instead, the symbolism has been interpreted on its literal level so that it is confused with the realities it represents. Consequently there is, among the Christians in Ukambani, a false spirituality resulting from this false separation of Eschatology from Christology.

Many of the biblical concepts we have examined are alien to Akamba ideas, as far as their theological content is concerned. The same seems true about these ideas in other African societies. In attempting to reach some understanding of the ideas in this materialistic language, Akamba people have created a similarly materialistic future located away from the earth: in Heaven (for Christians) or in Gehenna (for non-believers). The same world is also imagined to be a contrast, for better or worse, to this earth. People have little or no notion of how to relate this life to the life in that other world, except insofar as they can psychologically escape to that dreamland. This whole conceptual area is new to Akamba and other African peoples, in that traditionally they never thought of or expected a future world situated somewhere in the heavens. Both in terms of Time and geography, African peoples are undergoing a radical change in their conception as far as their understanding of the hereafter is concerned. On the individual and psychological level, this new world has facilitated the discovery and experience of the *ego*, of the 'who I am' (now and in the future), as distinct from the corporate 'we' (of the *mituki* and *tene* periods). This new world is the world of the 'I' as an individual, for it is a world dependent much on the individual decision, conception, Faith (or lack of it), work, and projection of the ego. This development will almost undoubtedly get rid of the mythical world but retain the individualism it is cultivating, once the proper psychological balance is attained.

On the theological level, this discovery of a new world seems to have eclipsed the place and person of Jesus Christ in the eschatological drama. It is here that the Sacraments of Baptism and the Eucharist become crucial in conveying the eschatological message via not only material language but also material elements. They are the nexus between the material or physical realities and the eschatological realities which the materialistic language attempts to convey on the conceptual level.

CHAPTER IV

The Eschatology of the Sacraments

THE New Testament employs a materialistic language on the conceptual level as one method of conveying its Eschatology. But, as we have seen, this use of a materialistic language poses difficulties in the communication of the Gospel truth, even though behind the materialistic symbols and images lie important eschatological and christological realities which must be discerned. The second method of the New Testament is to put Eschatology in the liturgical context in which the central act of worship is at the same time a means of communicating the realities of Eschatology.

It is at the Sacraments of Baptism and the Eucharist that Christian worship is most intense and real. At these Sacraments both the physical and spiritual worlds converge, as do also the dimensions of Time. The materialistic language of Eschatology meets here with the non-material realities which it endeavours to convey symbolically. Thus, the Sacraments are the most effective media of demonstrating, via material objects, those eschatological and christological realities which are conveyed only in part on the conceptual level. We are to examine here how far these two Sacraments contain and convey eschatological realities, and how the use of this method of the New Testament fits into an African background.

(a) Sacrifice and Worship among the Akamba

In the strict Christian sense, worship is almost unknown in traditional Akamba life. There are, however, many acts which are in the nature of worship, and we shall take some examples of them. On the individual level, offerings and libation are made by elderly men at meal times and during drinking parties. This is not done at every meal; and the recipient of the food and drink is normally one or more of the living-dead and some of the important pillars of the family or clan. Only in rare and difficult occasions would these ordinary offerings be addressed to God. Words are uttered, not in form of prayer but to the effect that ' May you (living-dead) receive this beer or piece of meat!'. Another formula is: 'We give you, the community of our grandfathers, this little amount of beer so that you may drink it with us!'. The Kikamba word for this part of the ceremony is *kwathiisya* which means 'to direct an idea or event by means of one's words or wishes'. It is different from praying which is *kuvoya*.

Another act in the context of worship on a personal level is the giving of blessings. This is always done by a senior person, by virtue of age or social status, to a junior person. It is generally done when one is departing from another, and the person giving the blessing spits lightly on the recipient, invoking words like: 'May you go a cool (peaceful) journey!', or 'May God go with you!', or 'May you live to see your children's children!'.

On a national level, there are traditional acts of worship particularly in times of dire need, such as epidemics, drought, locust invasion or war; and in times of prosperity, such as planting and harvest time, and during the *rites de passage*. Formerly there were many shrines all over Ukambani, but these are increasingly disappearing or being abandoned. The shrines are found under sacred trees, especially the wild fig tree and the sycamore, at sacred groves, and around sacred rocks. During a public act of sacrifice, people in a given area are informed of the date for the occasion, and a one-coloured sheep, goat or cow is chosen for the purpose. A single colour (which could be any) symbolizes purity and holiness, as well as the unanimous agreement or intention of the people making the sacrifice.

The ceremony of making a sacrifice is conducted by the oldest male member of the group. He slaughters the animal, pours down its blood as libation, and members of the group share in eating all the meat there and then. The oldest man, acting as the priest for the occasion, presents the sacrifice at the foot of the sacred tree (or wherever the shrine might be), while other men and women watch from a short distance. Afterwards he joins them, and reports that 'I have just been with the "Man", and he said that he was very pleased and would like you to come on another occasion. The "Man" told me to share this food with you.' The word 'man' (*mundu*) simply stands for 'the other party', without specifying whether that is the living-dead, spirits or God. It is the recipient, acting or pictured anthropomorphically. When the smoke from the roasting of the sacrificial meat goes up vertically, this is taken as indicating that the sacrifice has been accepted. The rest of the food and drink (milk and beer) is shared among all those who are present, and everyone goes home afterwards. If this is on a large national scale, the women stage a dance known as *kilumi* to mark the occasion.

The making of offerings and sacrifices is widespread in African societies, and I have not come across one where it is entirely unknown. There are some societies which do this regularly and at given formal occasions, but many do it only when there is a special need or to mark a special occasion. I would wish, for this study, to distinguish sacrifices as those acts which involve the shedding of blood or killing of an animal; and offerings as those acts in which blood is not involved, and in which food, drink and other items are merely 'offered'. Animals for sacrifices as used in African societies include: cattle, sheep, goats, chickens, dogs, wild animals, and human beings (formerly, though there are still a few areas, such as in Nigeria, where this has not stopped altogether). Items for offerings include foodstuffs, beverages, domestic articles, money, plant parts, ornaments and clothing. Places of worship include temples, shrines, altars, homesteads, groves, rocks, caves, waterfalls, hills and mountains. Times of worship include occasions of individual and national needs, festivals, ceremonies, before or during or after an undertaking, and whenever the individual or community feels like making sacrifices or offerings. As a rule, prayers and invocations accompany the making of sacrifices and offerings. There is, in short, no place and occasion when African peoples may not perform acts of worship or of reaching into the spiritual realm, through offerings, sacrifices, prayers or invocations. One may also generalize that the recipients of these acts are: God, divinities, spirits or the living-dead. Where the object is other than God, that recipient is often regarded as an intermediary through whom man establishes a link with God or with the spiritual realm. These are, however, generalizations for which there are always exceptions, but I make them here from a study of acts of worship among more than two hundred African societies. It is not in the scope of this work to go into details here, but these paragraphs are presented simply to form a wider background to our discussion of sacrifices and worship among the Akamba.

And so we return to the Akamba and consider more of their religious ceremonies. Water does not play a significant role in their religious life. Instead, they use a semi-magical and medicinal concoction known as *ng'ondu*, for nearly all their domestic and local ceremonies. *Ng'ondu* is made from a mixture of barks and roots of various plants[1] plus the contents of a goat's stomach. All purification rites require the use of *ng'ondu* administered by either the oldest member of a given community, or the medicine-man. These rites are performed after births, funerals, epidemics, serious illness or following a serious breach of custom. *Ng'ondu* is also used for formal blessings on a family or community level, e.g. at the arrival home of a child and its mother when the child is born away from its parents' home, after circumcision rites, when an epidemic is over, etc.

We should here mention two other occasions which are given religious significance, and which are relevant for our discussion later. Shortly after the birth of a child, the family makes a feast to mark the name-giving ceremony, and to have the household cleansed from the religious impurities of birth. The ceremony of name-giving is known in Kikamba as *kuimithya*, which means 'humanization'. It is through this ceremony that the child is formally accepted and acknowledged to be a full human being and thereby a full member of the human society. Prior to that occasion, the child is simply an IT, a thing; but the ceremony incorporates the child into the community of human beings—it 'humanizes' him, transforming a *thing* into a *person*.

When the child is between the ages of about five and fifteen, the circumcision rites take place, these being in two parts for everybody. The purpose of circumcision (or clitoridectomy for girls) is threefold: (i) it is an indelible physical and social mark of separation from the cradle, from babyhood; (ii) it provides an opportunity for the candidate to be secluded from society for a period of up to ten days (this might be compared with the idea of death—death from one status, that of childhood); (iii) after the period of seclusion the candidates are re-integrated into society, they are born anew, they are given new responsibilities in society. This is like the symbol of rebirth, which is effected when they return to their families as new and mature men and women.

What, we may now ask, is the religious meaning of these ceremonies and rites in Akamba life? Several observations can be made. First, it is significant that God is rarely brought into the picture, except

---

[1] The plants include (in Kikamba names): 'mulinditi, muvu, waithu, ikwasyi ya kiongoa, mui wa mutuva, ithinza, mutheke, ikwasi ya kiindiu, mukenya, mutaa wa kuminzangisya' (according to D. N. Kimilu, *Mukamba Wa Wo* (1962), 93).

on major occasions when people solicit His intervention and assistance. And even on such occasions, it would be incorrect to assert that the people experience a spiritual fellowship with God, which could approximate the Christian sense of worship. God is 'utilized' rather than 'worshipped', and, with perhaps a few exceptions, the same distinction might be made about African societies. Even the prayers made at these occasions, and at other times, are requests to God to give or do something of a material nature.

Secondly, when sacrifices and offerings are made, at which the food is eaten by the participants, a sense of sharing between human beings and either God or other spiritual beings, is created. Unlike some African societies, the Akamba do not put much emphasis on God's participation in such sharing, since they do not consider Him to have anthropomorphic desires. It is an occasion for people to make their requests known to God, and that is the main purpose for the sacrifice. This is, however, different with regard to the relation between the living and the departed. Both formal and informal offerings of food and drink are made to the living-dead, as signs of fellowship, hospitality from their human families, and as symbols of remembrance. It is at these occasions that the living formally *remember* the departed, and in act as well as in mind, recall them in the *Mituki* (Now) period, and thus proclaim their personal immortality. Here we see how significant the concept of Time is, with regard to the idea of the survival of the departed. The living must retain the departed within the *Mituki* period, thus contemporarizing them, and because the departed are contemporarized, people feel that they have to extend their hospitality to them just as they would if they were still alive in human form. The physical act is a human response to the non-physical presence of the departed. Via the material elements of food and drink, human beings keep in contact with the spirit world in its contemporaneity. I do not consider these acts to have sacramental meaning either among the Akamba or other African societies, but this might be a matter of opinion.[1]

Thirdly, the rituals and ceremonies of cleansing, at which the *ng'-ondu* is used, are aimed primarily at ceremonial and taboo impurities, and do not, as far as I can gather, have implications of cleansing from

---

[1] Cf. R. R. Marett, *Sacraments of Simple Folk* (Cambridge, 1933), who would find sacraments where perhaps a Christian theologian might not. It is noteworthy, however, that anthropologists do not speak of sacrifices as sacraments when describing African religious life.

sin or spiritual stain. Ritual harmony is restored once the cleansing ceremony is satisfactorily carried out.

Fourthly, we have already pointed out the significance of the naming and the initiation ceremonies, which mark the incorporation of the child (as an IT) into the human society, and the eventual incorporation into the full responsibilities of society when the circumcision (and clitoridectomy) ceremonies are performed.

These, then, constitute the main area of Akamba religious activities. They do not contain sacramental ideas or intentions. We may, therefore, conclude that in their traditional life, Akamba people have no sacramental concepts or practices. As far as God is concerned, their acts of worship are few and always utilitarian in character. They have, however, innumerable occasions when they perform religious rites and ceremonies which have parallels with Christian ceremonies, even if their meaning may not be equated. We turn now to the New Testament for an examination of the Christian view of the Sacraments and worship.

(b) The Eschatology of Baptism

In its origin, Christian Baptism has obvious similarities with John's baptism, but it derives its fullest essence and meaning from the Death–Resurrection event of Jesus Christ. Johannine baptism itself has points of similarity with, and departure from, Jewish proselyte baptism and the Essene and Qumran lustrations. Although there is no unanimity of opinion on this issue,[1] it seems almost conclusive that Jewish proselyte lustrations are inevitably the social-religious background, if not predecessor, to both the Qumran and Johannine practices.

The Jews (and probably the Gentiles?), are required to undergo John's baptism 'unto repentance' (Mt. 3: 11, cf. pars.), which is pregnant with the eschatological urgency of the appearing of God's Kingdom in the New Age. It anticipates the imminent Messianic

---

[1] J. Jeremias in *Infant Baptism in the First Four Centuries* (ET 1960), thinks that the connection between proselyte baptism and Christian Baptism is as strong as 'parent and child' (pp. 24–37). Others who favour a pre-Christian date of proselyte baptism include W. F. Flemington in *The New Testament Doctrine of Baptism* (1948), 15 ff.; T. F. Torrance (cautiously) in 'Proselyte Baptism', *NTS*, Vol. 1, No. 2 (Nov. 1954), pp. 150–4; and G. R. Beasley-Murray in *Baptism in the New Testament* (1962), 11–31. A contrary view is expressed by, among others, T. M. Taylor, 'The Beginnings of Jewish Proselyte Baptism', *NTS*, Vol. II, No. 3 (Feb. 1956), pp. 193–8.

Baptism with the Holy Spirit (Mt. 3: 11 pars., cf. Acts 1: 5; 2: 1–4, 14–21, Joel 2: 28 f.). As Lampe rightly points out, the eschatological hopes and ideas of the Old Covenant converge upon John's symbolic rite of baptism.[1]

Without hesitation, Jesus consents to undergo the baptismal rite in the hands of John. From the point of view of His life and ministry, this rite foreshadows His Passion. It is a necessary and essential part of His Mission. Therefore He regards it as 'a baptism to be baptized with' (Lk. 12: 50, Mk. 10: 38 f.). From His followers' point of view, however, it is the means of entry into the Kingdom (Jn. 3: 5, Eph. 5: 26 f., Tit. 3: 5 ff., Heb. 10: 22, cf. Ezek. 36: 25 ff.). Consequently, the moment Jesus undergoes this rite, He destroys the Johannine baptism, not by annulling its effectiveness and necessity, but by superseding and fulfilling it. He signals Christian Baptism to transform Johannine baptism and take over from it. From that moment on, only Christian Baptism counts, whether or not it is given oral dominical support. Already the whole life of Jesus, between His baptism in the hands of John and His Resurrection, is a baptismal act by means of which men must be incorporated into Him. This is the theological ground on which Christian Baptism stands, despite the arguments that may be put forward in support of or against any dominical authority in Mt. 28: 19 and elsewhere. Any dominical authority for this Sacrament rests on the whole theological momentum which culminates in the Resurrection of Jesus. By itself Mt. 28: 19, is the result of the sacramental transformation already enacted in the life and ministry of Jesus. We can view the Eucharist in the same way, as we shall see later. Mt. 28: 19 contains an authentic dominical instruction implementing, however, the act of Christian Baptism already authorized and enacted in the life of Jesus. This oral dominical authority does not institute Baptism as though the latter came as a postscript before the Lord's visible departure. Rather, Mt. 28: 19 gives Christian Baptism its well deserved imprimatur. Therefore, Christian Baptism does not stand or fall on the ground of Mt. 28: 19 as such. Its theological and christological meaning must be sought nowhere except in the Jesus of Nazareth.[2]

---

[1] G. W. H. Lampe, *The Seal of the Spirit* (1951), 32 (cited here as *The Seal*).

[2] I am aware that there are arguments contrary to some of the views I express here, but in spite of the genuine difficulties raised over Mt. 28: 19, Baptism as a dominical sacrament instituted by the Lord and observed from the earliest days of the Church is accepted by a great number of scholars, including Flemington, op. cit., 115–29; D. M. Baillie, *The Theology of the Sacraments* (1957), 73, 75 ff.;

In content and intention, Christian Baptism is intensively eschato-logical. In his essay, The 'Judgement Theme in the Sacraments', Moule clearly brings out the content of divine judgement in the two Sacraments. Speaking about Baptism, he says that the candidate in effect pleads guilty, accepts God's verdict on sin, and the death sentence is executed. But he is not annihilated. Rather, he is raised alive, since 'Baptism, in short . . . is an epitome of the indicative of the Christian Gospel which states "Ye are dead, and your life is hid with Christ in God" (Col. iii.3).'[1] From this anthropological starting point implications on a cosmic scale are evident, namely, that on the Cross of Jesus the whole universe was baptized.[2] Christian Baptism is the means of mediating the implications of Christ's Death and Resurrection, both on individual human and cosmic levels. One of these implications is the execution of eschatological judgement which tolls the death knell to the law, to sin, and to the old man.

Another eschatological implication is that through Baptism the Christian is resurrected to a new life (Jn. 5: 24), a new heart (Rom. 2: 29, II Cor. 4: 6, Heb. 10: 22, cf. Ezek. 36: 27), resulting in a totally new man (II Cor. 5: 17, Eph. 2: 15; 4: 24). Forsyth aptly summarizes the outcome, that Baptism 'does not simply wash away; it floods with new life . . .'.[3] Temporal limitations are neutralized, so that the soul arrives at its spiritual 'Promised Land', and is enabled to derive sustenance from the powers of the Age to Come (Heb. 6: 4 f.). But this experience is only an eschatological signal of the trans-formation (cf. II Cor. 3: 18) which points to the Parousia (cf. I Jn. 3: 2). It is a Sacrament of birth (Jn. 3: 3 ff., cf. I Pet. 1: 3, 23, Barn. 6: 11, 16: 8), by which the regenerated individual (Tit. 3: 5) is incorpor-

C. F. D. Moule, *Worship in the New Testament* (1961, cited here as *Worship*), 47 f.; G. R. Beasley-Murray, *Baptism in the New Testament* (1963), 77 ff.; T. F. Torrance, *Conflict and Agreement in the Church* (1960), Vol. II, pp. 115 f. On the other hand, R. Bultmann, *Theology of the New Testament*, Vol. I (ET 1952), 140 f., 311, considers Christian interpretation of Baptism as participation in Christ's death and resurrection, to have been influenced by Hellenistic mystery religions. J. Wheeler Robinson regards it as 'prophetic symbolism', in 'Hebrew Sacrifice and Prophetic Symbolism', *JTS*, Vol. XLIII (1942), pp. 129–39.

[1] C. F. D. Moule, 'The Judgement Theme in the Sacraments', essay in the *Dodd Festschrift*, pp. 464–81. (The essay is cited here as 'Judgement Theme').

[2] So also O. Cullmann, *Baptism in the New Testament* (ET 1950), 23 ff.; J. A. T. Robinson, *Twelve New Testament Studies* (1962), 158–75; and briefly A. Richard-son, *An Introduction to the Theology of the New Testament* (1958), 341.

[3] P. T. Forsyth, *The Church and the Sacraments* (1917), 180. He adds concerning Baptism, that 'it regards the whole soul in its whole destiny—in its past, present and future'.

ated into the eschatological community. This initiatory nature makes Baptism, in the words of Forsyth, 'the Sacrament of destination'.[1] It neutralizes temporal dimensions but does not erase them. Therefore Baptism thrusts the Christian into the eschatological tension of the 'already' and the 'not yet'. As one raised with Christ (Col. 2: 12, cf. Rom. 6: 3 f.), he is sealed with the Holy Spirit, and bears anew (cf. Gen. 1: 26 f.; 2: 7) the 'Imago Dei' (cf. I Cor. 15: 49). The whole process occurs in terms of being *in Christ*, which itself is an eschatological phenomenon[2] that sets in motion a series of dynamic spiritual activities, the marks of a new life. They include the forgiveness and cleansing of sin (Acts. 22: 16, I Cor. 6: 11, Heb. 10: 22, II Pet. 1: 9, cf. Justin, Apol. 61: 10), sanctification (Jn. 17: 17, I Cor. 1: 2, Eph. 5: 26, etc.), regeneration (Tit. 3: 5), enlightenment (Jn. 1: 9, Eph. 1: 18, Heb. 10: 32) and the bestowal of the Holy Spirit (Acts. 2: 38, I Cor. 12: 13, Eph. 1: 13 f., cf. Jn. 3: 5).

Through Baptism, the individual is made an integral member of the eschatological community which bears the Messianic character. By being given what Lampe calls the 'badge of divine ownership',[3] he is assured of salvation both now and on the day of Judgement, and meanwhile the Name of God (or Christ) protects him against evil powers. As a full heir of God's Kingdom (Rom. 8: 17, I Pet. 3: 7), he is entitled to all the rights and the benefits thereof (Col. 1: 12 f.). He is adopted as a son (Gal. 4: 5 f., Eph. 1: 5, cf. Jn. 20: 17), whereby he may claim the use of the christological prayer: 'Abba! Father!'[4] (Rom. 8: 15, Gal. 4: 6), and can join the family prayer: 'Our Father . . .' (Mt. 6: 9 ff.). This is the full range of his experience while waiting for, and growing towards the full manifestation of his corporate adoption, υἱοθεσία (Rom. 8: 23).

---

[1] Forsyth, op. cit., 193.

[2] Bultmann, op. cit., pp. 311 f., argues rightly that the formula 'in Christ' has not only an ecclesiological meaning, but at the same time an eschatological one as well. See also L. S. Thornton, *The Common Life in the Body of Christ* (1941/2) saying that 'to be "in" the risen Christ is the whole of Christianity', pp. 253 ff.

[3] Lampe, op. cit., 14 ff.; and likewise Bultmann, op. cit., 137.

[4] The word *Abba* has been a subject of discussion, with emphasis being drawn particularly to the intimacy and reverence contained in its usage. See, especially, C. F. D. Moule, *Worship*, 76 ff.; *The Phenomenon of the New Testament* (1967), 47 ff.; J. Jeremias 'The Lord's Prayer in Modern Research', *Ex T*, Vol. LXXI, No. 5 (Feb. 1960), pp. 141 ff.; and most fully, Abba: *Studien zur neutestamentlichen Theologie und Zeitgeschichte* (1966), appearing in English as *The Prayers of Jesus* (1967).

Baptism is the sacramental mark of identification in the New Covenant, just as circumcision was the physical mark in the Old Covenant. Paul speaks of it as a 'circumcision made without hands' (Col. 2: 11 f., cf. I Pet. 3: 21), of the heart (Rom. 2: 29), marking off the eschatological Israel of God (Gal. 6: 16, cf. Phil. 3: 3) and without reference to physical birth (Gal. 3: 27 ff., Rom. 10: 12). Therefore it is unnecessary for Gentiles to be physically circumcised, (Acts. 15: 5–11, 28 f., I Cor. 7: 19, Gal. 5: 6; 6: 15). The Christian is now entitled to the heavenly commonwealth (Phil. 3: 20, cf. Eph. 2: 12), living as he does in the eighth Day, between Baptism and the Parousia (Barn. 15: 9), for upon him the end of the ages has come (I Cor. 10: 11). Sunday, the Lord's Day, stands as the antitype of the Age to Come,[1] paradoxically the eighth day of the dying Age and the first day of the coming Age. Therefore, through Baptism the eschatological Israel enters the promised Rest, σαββατισμός[2] (cf. Heb. 4: 9 f.). The community proleptically arrives at Mt. Zion and the heavenly Jerusalem (Heb. 12: 22 ff.), and must live according to a new set of morals inscribed upon the heart (Rom. 3: 21–6; 10: 9 f., Jer. 31: 33 f., cf. Heb. 8: 7–13).

The bestowal of the Holy Spirit is an integral part of Christian Baptism (cf. Mt. 3: 11), and begins historically at Pentecost (Acts, 1: 5; 2: 1–4, 14–21, 37–9).[3] He provides the environment for Christian communion with God, and mediates participation in Christ (Jn. 14: 18, 23, etc.). As the Guarantee, 'Αρραβών, donated to the eschatological Body (II Cor. 1: 21 f., Eph. 1: 13 f.), He makes eternal life 'realized' in our present existence. He makes it possible for believers to become His or God's temple (I Cor. 3: 16 f.; 6: 19). Through Him the essence and character of the heavenly life permeate into the present life and experience of those in Christ. It is He who floods and saturates the believer's life with 'the powers of the Age to Come', separating him from the Old Aeon and incorporating him into the New. At the same time He precipitates judgement (Jn. 16: 8,

[1] See further discussion, Barrett, op. cit., pp. 370 f.
[2] The eschatological significance of Sunday as a day of rejoicing and rest (not physically), is shown by the fact that around the end of the first century it had already become 'the eighth day' in Christian circles (cf. G. Dix, *The Shape of the Liturgy* (1943), 336). This was long before Constantine's edict of 321 made it an official day of rest.
[3] In the early Church, the Holy Spirit generally came upon the believers at or after Baptism (cf. Acts 19: 1–7), though not always subsequent to the rite (e.g. 10: 44 ff.).

11), since He is associated with judgement (κρίσις) and conviction (ἔλεγχος), as Moule tells us.[1]

At the believer's Baptism, the Baptism of Jesus is re-enacted through the Spirit, recalling and implementing the act of Salvation. Christian Baptism becomes then, the applied kerygma of the Gospel. The Holy Spirit makes the rite both a Christocentric and an eschatological Sacrament, different from the baptismal rites of the Mystery Religions,[2] and from any other ritual lustrations. The faith of the candidate is grounded in Jesus Christ, in whom the believer finds the source of spiritual vitality. Therefore, Baptism rightly deserves to be called a 'sacrament of inaugurated eschatology',[3] a rite which 'means birth' as the Eucharist means 'nourishment and growth'.[4]

The two Sacraments are thus intimately related, both theologically and christologically, and one pre-supposes the other.[5] He who is born anew through Baptism, must grow by nourishing his life through the Eucharist. So Baptism points to the Eucharist, the foretaste of the Messianic Banquet.

(c) The Eschatology of the Eucharist

The Eucharist was instituted in an eschatological setting. At the Last Supper, the Lord introduced a new meaning into what a number of scholars consider to have been a Passover Meal.[6] Although the Eucharist, a 'paschal festival' of the New Covenant (I Cor. 5: 7 f.),

[1] Moule, Judgement Theme, 474 f.

[2] Whereas Bultmann sees many similarities with the Mysteries, he recognizes the difference as a result of relating Baptism to the Death and Resurrection of Jesus Christ, op. cit., 140 ff.

[3] N. Clark, *Theology of the Sacraments* (1956), 61; cf. J. A. T. Robinson in *Coming* (1957), 118–39.

[4] Moule, op. cit., 476.

[5] It is not laid out in the N.T. explicitly that participants in the Eucharist must be baptized first; but the tempo of sacramental theology would make it necessary, and the practice came into the Church at an early date, see: Did. 7: 1, 4; 9: 5; Just. Apol. 66: 1; cf. E. Schweizer, *Church Order in the New Testament* (ET 1961), 142.

[6] See, for example, J. Jeremias, *The Eucharistic Words of Jesus* (ET 1955, cited here as *Eucharistic Words*), 1–60; and more briefly, A. J. B. Higgins, *The Lord's Supper in the New Testament* (1952), 9–23, and repeated in 'The Origins of the Eucharist' (*NTS*, Vol. I, No. 3 (Feb. 1955), pp. 200–9). Both men consider the Last Supper to have been a Passover Meal, but they also deal with the contrary views. For a comparison with the Qumran Communal Meal, see the essay by K. G. Kuhn in *The Scrolls and the New Testament*, ed. K. Stendahl (British edition 1958), 65–93.

became the experience of Christians only after the Crucifixion and Resurrection, it was already anticipated and re-enacted in the life and ministry of Jesus. It is rightly marked by a dual polarity: the Cross and the Parousia, when put within the framework of Time.

The presence of the Lord at the Eucharist makes it the means and moment of the most intimate communion between Him and His eschatological community. His presence neutralizes temporal limitations, making the Sacrament a remembrance (ἀνάμνησις) to be repeated constantly, without losing either its effectiveness or its freshness. Meeting the Lord at His Messianic Banquet is cause for the deepest possible joy, as the Apostolic Church experienced (Acts 2: 46). At the Eucharist the Church experiences the Lord in all His contemporaneity and futurity. Participation in the Eucharist is a rich experience of the 'Eschatology of bliss' (die Heilseschatologie), so completely different from O.T. ways of worship. Any disappointment over the delay of the Parousia is neutralized by the Eucharist; for in the experience of the Eucharist the Church penetrates proleptically (cf. I Cor. 11: 26), into the very hour of the Parousia. Not surprisingly then, we find little if any evidence to show that the Early Church was shaken or disappointed by the delay of the Parousia. At the Eucharist the Church is too preoccupied in the Parousia to have any room for disappointment. At the Eucharist, the Church comes to the Lord who stands before the Father,[1] representing mankind in Christ. So the eschatological community sends up in unison the eucharistic 'Marana tha' cry (I Cor. 16: 22, cf. Did. 10: 6)[2] which is simultaneously the sigh of fulfilment and expectation.

The Lord is present to judge and to save. That is the dual function of His presence as it is paradoxically experienced by the participants of the holy mysteries. On the one hand the sinner is barred from taking the holy things for the holy ones[3]; but on the other hand, precisely because he is a sinner, he is sick, and needs what Ignatius of Antioch called the medicine of immortality and the antidote (remedy) against death (Eph. 20). Therefore, warns Paul, 'let a man examine himself, and so eat of the bread and drink of the cup' (I Cor.

[1] Dix, op. cit., 262 ff.; O. C. Quick, The Christian Sacraments (1927), 198; Robinson, op. cit., 185; and Doctrine in the Church of England (1938), 160 ff.

[2] See C. F. D. Moule, 'A Reconsideration of the Context of Maranatha', NTS, Vol. VI, No. 4 (July 1960), pp. 307–10, and Worship, 70 f., where, among other things, he questions whether it is eucharistic or not. Cf. Clark, op. cit., 69 f.

[3] Greek Orthodox, The Divine Liturgy, 29, perhaps echoing Did. 10: 6.

11: 28, cf. 10: 16 f.); for in this Sacrament are the very realities of ultimate being. We are reminded by Moule that I Cor. 11: 27–34 is set in judicial language; but it is 'remedial' and 'redemptive' judgement, rescuing the participants from the final condemnation.[1] It is at the Eucharist that the Church most intimately stands absolutely naked before the Father, in rehearsal for, and as prelude to, the final day of Judgement. Here the Church enters and anticipates the End drama simultaneously in and beyond Time.

But blessings abound at the Messianic Banquet, the Meal distributed as the true and life-giving Manna from heaven (Jn. 6: 32, 35, etc., cf. the desert manna, 6: 31, 49, Ex. 16: 4 f., 13 ff.). The participants anticipate their final reclining with the Patriarchs (Mt. 8: 11 par.). As Jeremias calls it, the Eucharist 'is the marriage feast where fasting is abolished.'[2] Every guest sits at the place of honour (cf. Mk. 10: 37–40), appropriating the heavenly benefits. Jeremias rightly comments that 'this is Christ's last and greatest gift,' observing that at the Last Supper the words and actions of Jesus aim at assuring 'the disciples of their possession of salvation.'[3] This is the assurance which is repeatedly brought to memory at every Eucharist (I Cor. 11: 24 f., cf. Lk. 22: 19 (the latter part is omitted by D, etc.)) and experienced in real fellowship with the exalted Lord. It is the blessing of infinite value which must neither be abused nor rejected. Since through Baptism the participants have come to Mount Zion (Heb. 12: 22 ff.) the eucharistic Bread and Wine are truly the food and drink of the Promised Land, the means of assimilating the bodily reality of Christ's 'flesh and blood' (I Cor. 10: 16 f.; 11: 23–6). Thus, ignoring the polarities of Time, the Eucharist thrusts 'back' the supra-temporal realities of God's Kingdom, into our historical realm of the present so that we who are in Christ can appropriate and enjoy them now.

The Bread and Wine are the manna and water anticipated in the wilderness (Ex. 16 f.) but realized in Christian life and, if Schoeps' contention is valid, merged together (I Cor. 10: 3 f.).[4] These eschatological metaphors of fellowship are full of meaning, in spite of their frequent use in other literature.[5] At the Last Supper the disciples are rightly assured that 'it is to your advantage that I go

[1] Moule, 'Judgement Theme', 470 ff.

[2] Jeremias, *Eucharistic Words*, 137.

[3] Jeremias, op. cit., 159, 174.

[4] H. J. Schoeps, *Paul: the Theology of the Apostle in the Light of Jewish Religious History* (ET 1961), 115 f.

[5] Jeremias, op. cit., pp. 153–7.

away' (Jn. 16: 7, cf. 14: 18), for in this sacramental fellowship the Lord means to be closer to His Church than would have been the case otherwise (cf. Jn. 14: 23). Here then the whole Gospel is visibly and mystically epitomized (I Cor. 11: 24 f., Lk. 22: 19, cf. Jn. 14: 26; 16: 13 f.). The Eucharist is a one act drama portraying comprehensively all the events, both historical and supra-historical, from the Incarnation to the Glorification of Christ. Only in this perspective can eternal realities of existence and being emanate from His life-giving 'flesh' and 'blood' (Jn. 6: 53–8, cf. I Cor. 15: 45).[1] Therefore, to eat and drink the Eucharist elements is to participate in the very total body, $\sigma\tilde{\omega}\mu\alpha$ of the Lord (I Cor. 11: 24 ff., cf. 27; 10: 16 f., Mk. 14: 22 ff. pars.).

At the Eucharist, Time is recalled in its three dimensions of past, present and future. Time is simultaneously eclipsed and intensified. And in that context the World to Come is momentarily pre-viewed within the framework of its two termini of the Resurrection and the Parousia. The early Church rightly began to observe Sunday rather than the Sabbath as the Lord's Day (Rev. 1: 10) since it 'marked the periodical manifestation in time of the reality of eternal redemption in Christ.'[2] It was the day when the Eucharist was regularly celebrated and, as Moule cautiously observes, it was 'sufficiently reminiscent of "the Day of the Lord" in the Old Testament sense to sound the overtones of judgement.'[3] The victory and vindication of Christ are thus brought to memory (cf. Col. 2: 13 ff.) on this the 'eighth day' (Barn. 15: 9), 'until He Comes'. It is here and now on this eschatological day, that the Age to Come most intimately overlaps This Age. But the overlapping, being transacted in Time, points to the consummation when This Age completely disappears and gives way to the Age to Come in all its full splendour and intensity.

So, at the Eucharist the participants eat of 'the tree of life' (Rev. 2: 7; 22: 2, 14, 19, Gen. 2: 9, cf. 3: 22, 24, I En. 25: 4 f.), the food off

---

[1] Cf. E. Stauffer, *New Testament Theology* (ET 1955), 164, saying that 'in the Eucharist meal there takes place a sacramental reincarnation and indwelling of the Logos', and that the 'body' is 'His flesh in a strict ontic sense.' This is clearly an overstatement, for which there is no justification in the N.T. Cf. Schoeps, op. cit., 118, that the eucharistic elements 'become a means of extending the incarnation of Christ'; and more mildly, Baillie, op. cit., 64 ff. Dodd in *Parables*, sees the Eucharist 'in its origin and in its governing ideas . . . as a sacrament of realized eschatology,' p. 203.

[2] Dix, op. cit., 336.

[3] Moule, op. cit., 475 f.

'an altar from which those who serve the tent have no right to eat' (Heb. 13: 10). Here they drink 'the water of life' (Rev. 22: 17, Jn. 4: 14; 6: 35; 7: 38, cf. Is. 55: 1). But with all its sacramental richness, this experience remains one of an imperfect (ἀτελής) fellowship, imperfect not ethically but eschatologically, because it is staged in Time. Yet the eternal order is brought into the temporal, though only sacramentally; the invisible world is made visible though simply through 'a mirror dimly' (I Cor. 13: 12). So the celebrating community recalls the 'it is finished' (τετέλεσται) of the Cross (Jn. 19: 30) announcing its salvation. But it repeats the eucharistic prayer, μαράνα θά (I Cor. 16: 22, Did. 10: 6, cf. Rev. 22: 20).[1] This is the eucharistic paradox, in which the participants attain what is promised and yet cannot rest so long as the desperate wail of ἕως πότε continues from under the altar (Rev. 6: 10). At this point the Eucharist must remain truly a 'mystery', a rite that is best celebrated only by faith mixed with joy, fear and trembling.

As at Baptism, the Triune God is present in the midst of His people at the Eucharist. The Church, immersed *in Christ* stands before the Father, partaking of the Body and Blood of the Son and appropriating the benefits of eternal life through the mediation of the Holy Spirit. It is the sacramental moment when the 'Ecclesia militans' becomes absolutely one with the 'Ecclesia triumphans' (cf. Heb. 12: 22–4). So the eucharistic action is staged in the heavenly realities, in the presence of God, the Church and 'the whole company of Heaven.' But it belongs to the eschatological nature of the Eucharist that what is mediated in and through it is both a fulfilment and a promise. It is a fulfilment of what faith in Christ can see and appropriate. But it is a promise of the much more which in the limits of temporal dimensions cannot be conceived even by the most saintly participant.

(d) The Sacraments as the Epitome of the Gospel

We have seen that the two Sacraments of Baptism and the Eucharist are intimately linked together, both christologically and eschatologic-ally. Just as the Baptism of Jesus was ultimately fulfilled and univer-salized on the Cross (cf. Lk. 12: 50), so also Christian Baptism finds

---

[1] Is it not possible for the Church to pray, at the Eucharist, 'Marana tha' (O, our Lord, come!) and 'Maran atha' (Our Lord has come), at the same time? See discussion in Moule's *Worship*, 70 f., 75, and K. G. Kuhn in the *TWzNT*, Vol. IV (1942), 471–5.

its fulfilment and completion at the Eucharist. The early Church rightly administered the Eucharist immediately after Baptism so that 'it was daybreak before this solemn ceremony came to an end'[1] on Easter Sunday.

The Sacraments are Christocentric in their institution and practice. They epitomize the whole Gospel, from the Incarnation to the Parousia. In the Johannine view, they proclaim what has already happened historically and eschatologically, and anticipate what will happen at the End. The same can be said about Pauline theology of the Sacraments. They are by their very nature, the essence and centre of Christian life and worship.

From the very early days of the Church, it became clear that the Church was in its strongest form at the hour of sacramental worship. This was the point which cemented together the faithful with one another and with their Lord (cf. Did. 9:4). It is at this point throughout the centuries that the Church recalls what in Christ it ought to be, and anticipates what in Him it will unquestionably become. At this point also, the Church commemorates the two christological dimensions of its origin and its destiny. Therefore, the worshipping Church must and does triumph, for it is here, more than at any other point of its existence, that the gates of Hades simply cannot prevail against the Church. This triumph of the Church is not by waiting until those gates of Hades come to wage an attack. Rather the Church at worship equips itself to invade and overthrow even the gates of hell (or Hades). This was the Gospel preached and experienced by the Church in the early centuries of its life,[2] and there is no doubt that the Church is still at its strongest when gathered for sacramental worship. The same Lord is mediated through the Sacraments, as effectively and sufficiently as He was in the Apostolic days.

Kümmel reminds us that, as a link between the two aeons, the Sacraments proclaim that the old has passed away and the new has dawned[3] (cf. II Cor. 5: 17). The Baptism of Jesus, begun in the Jordan and accomplished on the Cross, marks the sacramental realization of the Kingdom of God. Christian Sacraments then become the channels of grace, the milk and honey of 'the Eschatology of bliss', cele-

---

[1] L. Duchesne, *Christian Worship—its Origin and Evolution* (ET 1919), p. 315; so also Dix, op. cit., p. 338.

[2] For a fuller discussion of the 'Church at worship' in the early days, see C. F. D. Moule, *The Birth of the New Testament* (1962), Chapter II.

[3] Kümmel, op. cit., 119 ff.

brated with gladness on the eighth day (Barn. 15: 9). Therefore, through them the faithful lives in the Day of Judgement, experiences the Reign of God, participates in the Messianic Banquet, shares in Christ's exaltation, and enjoys communion with God and the whole 'festal gathering'. This is a complete act of transformation, both in temporal and spatial dimensions.

The use of material elements of water, bread and wine, in the Sacraments, foreshadows the ultimate 'sacramentalization' of the entire cosmos. The Bible is explicit that man in his totality is both matter and spirit. Man's redemption in his material component must also involve the whole of material creation of which he is part. Therefore, man's Salvation is a miniature and rehearsal of cosmic redemption (Rom. 8: 18–23, Col. 1: 20); and will be completed only in relation to the whole cosmos. Since these material elements are changed sacramentally to become an essential component of Salvation, is it possible that the entire creation is thereby earmarked to the same destiny?[1] In epitomizing and proclaiming the whole Gospel, the Sacraments 'pre-event' the ultimate manifestation of the 'new heavens and a new earth' (II Pet. 3: 13, Rev. 21: 1). These are 'renewed' through sacramentalization. This process is to be accomplished through the same Word of God as when He made the first creation (Gen. 1, Jn. 1: 3), and established the New Covenant (I Cor. 11: 25, cf. pars. in the Synoptics) in the economy of 'new things' (Rev. 21: 5, II Cor. 5: 17 ff., cf. Is. 66: 22). But what are these 'new heavens and new earth', except the elements that through Baptism and the Eucharist have been transformed, christologized and eschatologized?

The Sacraments, therefore, make the Church, the Body in which they are observed, a truly eschatological field in which the guarantee (ἀρραβών) of the ultimate is realized even in the temporal dimension of now. The Fourth Gospel in particular, shows how members of this eschatological community, born of water and the Spirit, experience and sustain their eternal life through the sacramental Bread and Wine.

So the redeemed community leads a sacramental life from beginning to end. This eschatological community lives paradoxically in its two

---

[1] The problem of cosmic redemption has not been given the attention it deserves, at least in western theology, though it is celebrated in the liturgical life of the Orthodox Churches. For a solitary discussion of the matter, see A. D. Galloway *The Cosmic Christ* (1951).

termini, and yet as if it had neither. For that belongs precisely to the nature of eternal life. The Holy Spirit mediates that life at Baptism by stamping the believer as Christ's property, and at the Eucharist by nourishing him with heavenly benefits. The Sacraments are intensely Christocentric and, therefore, provide the opportunity for the most intimate form of worship. To participate in them is to dwell in the very heart of Christian worship and to speak the most explicit language of fellowship capable of being learnt and spoken by all those who are called to be in Christ.

The Sacraments not only contain the entire substance of Christian Eschatology, but also epitomize the whole Gospel. So now, the sacramental use of material elements which can be touched, tasted, etc., makes them the media *par excellence* of proclaiming the Christian Message, and the means of keeping the lives of the faithful wholly Christocentric.

(e) The Meaning and Place of the Sacraments in Ukambani

In the practice followed by the Africa Inland Mission, when a person indicates his intentions to become a Christian, by professing the Faith, he enrols in a catechumen course. This is to prepare him for 'adult' Baptism, and subsequently the Eucharist. In the Kikamba catechism there are sixty main items of instruction, of which six deal with the Sacraments.

Concerning Baptism, the instruction is as follows:

(Item 55) Q: 'What is Christian Baptism?'
    A: 'Christian Baptism is an ordinance whereby, when a believer confesses in truth his faith in Christ, he is immersed in water in the name of the Father and of the Son and of the Holy Spirit. Mt. 28: 19 . . .'

 (56) Q: 'What does Baptism signify?'
    A: 'It is a testimony of the believer before people, that, because of the renewal of the Holy Spirit, he counts himself to have died and been buried with Christ, and raised with Him. Col. 2: 12 . . .'

Concerning the Eucharist, it is as follows:

 (57) Q: 'What is the Lord's Table?'
    A: 'The Lord's Table is a service for believers by which they remember the death of Christ until His coming. I Cor. 11: 23–26 . . .'

(58) Q: 'What are the elements at the Lord's Table?'
     A: '(1) Bread, a symbol of His body which was given. Mt.
        26: 26 . . .'
        '(2) The juice of grapes, a symbol of His blood which was
        shed.[1] Mt. 26: 27 . . .'
(59) Q: 'When was the Lord's Table instituted and by Whom?'
     A: 'It was instituted by the Lord Jesus Himself, the night in
        which He was betrayed. I Cor. 11: 23–26 . . .'
(60) Q: 'What should those who partake of the Lord's Table be in
        their character?'
     A: 'They should (always) be in fellowship with the Lord and
        with other Christians. I Jn. 1: 7 . . .'

Each individual is required to undergo at least two years' instruction,[2] but in practice the period is much longer. A person acknowledges verbally and publicly that he wants to become a Christian, and then he is enrolled as an 'adherent' in the local church. Immediately he begins to attend catechumen instructions, and the course may last for two to ten years before he is baptized.

Another requirement is that 'all candidates for baptism should be able to read, except those whose age, infirmity, or circumstances render literacy difficult.'[3] There is no 'Infant Baptism', and 'no man being a polygamist shall be baptized,' and 'a woman who, having had Christian instruction wilfully becomes a polygamous wife may not be baptized.'[4] Similarly, any 'adherent' who 'is guilty of theft, immorality, witchcraft, idolatry, drunkenness, the use of tobacco or other narcotics, participation in sacrifices, dances, circumcision, or other pagan ceremonies, . . . shall be suspended from the Catechumenate . . . until such time as there is evidence of genuine repentance, and . . . the period of instruction prior to baptism shall be lengthened.'[5] Many adherents are strictly disciplined according to these regulations, but not a few break them and get away undetected. Soon after Baptism, many find it burdensome to observe this 'tradition of the elders', and lapse into real or apparent 'heathendom'. This official list of regulations puts greater emphasis on why a person may not be baptized than on why he needs to be baptized and what that Baptism means. We have seen that Akamba religious

---

[1] The Kik. verb is in the active but used intransitively: *yetikie* ('which spilled').
[2] A.I.C. Constitution (1954), 19.
[3] Ibid.
[4] Op. cit., 27, 29.
[5] Op. cit., 29.

life lacks both sacramental ideas and practices. This factor has combined with that of improper missionary teaching, to create false ideas and misunderstandings about the Sacraments in Ukambani, as we shall see.

Akamba Christians look upon Baptism as the more important of the two Sacraments. This great significance derives not so much from the theological-spiritual value of the Sacrament, as from the cultural-social meaning attached to it. It is the most impressive rite of the new religion-and-culture.[1] From the very start of a full-scale evangelization, it was administered until recently (in the fifties) exclusively by missionaries. Thus in the eyes of the people, it was the main cultural contact with the apostles of a technological civilization.

At Baptism the 'adherents' acquire new names which become indelible marks that they have been in contact with the culture and religion from 'overseas'. Many of such names come from the Bible, but others are western names like Rosemary, Pius, etc.[2] From that date on, they want to be called 'Peter James', or 'Isabelle Livingstone'. Many parents, whether Christian or not, give their children these 'foreign' names at birth. The practice is reported in other parts of Africa.

The Akamba are very fond of getting and giving new names, and a person may have up to ten such names by the time he is old. In most cases these names have a meaning. E.g. Mwanzia (male) or Syonzia (female) is given to a child born when the mother is on the way or on a journey; Wambua or Syombua is given to a child born during the rains. If, as the child grows, it develops certain characteristics, a new name is given to indicate this change, e.g. Kakwasi (Small Potato) if the child is fond of potatoes; or Musembi (Runner)

---

[1] The first Baptism service by the A.I.M. in Ukambani was in 1905, when three men were baptized. It was reported to have been 'an impressive sight as Brother Hurlburt led these men into the water and baptized them. The banks were crowded with men, women and children . . .' (*Hearing and Doing*, Vol. X, No. 5 (Oct. 1905), p. 7; quoted also in Chapter I above). The services are still impressive.

[2] I know one family that gave their newly born son the name of 'Hitler', at the beginning of World War II, since Adolf Hitler's name was so publicized. When he grew up he stopped using it. This borrowing of names from another culture or religion is not a new thing. J. Jeremias points out that Jewish proselytes took the names 'of the patriarchs and matriarchs' upon conversion to Judaism, even before the introduction of proselyte baptism (*Infant Baptism in the First Four Centuries* (ET 1960), pp. 34 ff.). For a further discussion on the cultural significance of Baptism as seen by Africans, see F. B. Welbourn, *East African Rebels* (1961, *passim*), and cf. B. G. M. Sundkler, *Bantu Prophets in South Africa* (1949, *passim*).

if he is a good runner. When young people reach the age of attending dances, they give one another names which may reflect their personalities. But since those who go to dances are not considered Christian, they have no opportunity at Baptism to acquire new names by means of which they may indicate their contact with the new culture. So, the 'dance-names' (as they are called), are taken from objects and ideas associated with western culture, e.g. Kalamu (Pen or Pencil), Kalani (Clerk), Silingi (Shilling), Veneti (Bayonet), etc. When girls are about to get married, they give one another nicknames, which they retain in their circles as housewives. The names reflect outstanding features of individual personalities, e.g. Kakuvi (Short one), Ndanu (Cheerful one), Ngelemende (Sweets, because of her pleasant personality), etc. When a girl gets married, she must avoid using 'baby' names belonging to members of her new family circle, and has to refer to them by other names. She also acquires the title of *Ng'a*— ('Daughter of —'). The men also get new titles upon being married, and at beer parties. Older people give names to younger ones as a sign of respect and courtesy. Poets and singers give names to people featured in their poetry or songs. People in positions of leadership, whether indigenous or from overseas, are given names that befit their outstanding characteristics.

Thus, the giving and use of names have an important role in Akamba life. The same applies in many other African societies. Baptism has come to mean practically no more than simply a western rite of a 'naming' ceremony. The Christian 'adherent' works for this new name which ultimately identifies him with the process of the assimilation to western culture. He may not have many material symbols of identification such as a bicycle, a glass-windowed house, speaking English, etc., but he is enabled to take the white man's name or/and a biblical name. It is the certificate of marriage between the two cultures. He may be denied full acquisition of the new culture by circumstances of race, education, or economic standards, especially in the colonial days, but the names cannot be denied him. Baptism is the dividing and joining line between one culture and another. A baptismal name becomes a social badge, and the owner feels that he is no longer culturally 'heathen', uncivilized, uneducated, in darkness. He becomes aware of himself as a new person culturally, involved in the process of getting 'civilized' and 'educated', and living in the light. He becomes truly a 'reader', and adopts whatever of western culture is accessible and palatable to him.

At Baptism, most Christians have the only opportunity when they can acquire new names:[1] hence their longing desire to get baptismal names overshadows all the other aspects of this Sacrament. They feel that the 'old' or 'baby' names are washed away by the water in which they are immersed, which is usually running water in a stream. It also washes away the myth of *maundu ma TENE* ('the things of the Past', i.e. things associated with tribal culture and thought to be unacceptable as Christian and 'civilized').

At a Baptism service, the congregation and candidates are repeatedly told that 'Baptism does not take a person to Heaven, but only faith in Jesus Christ takes a person there.' Additional admonition may follow to the effect that Baptism 'takes you as far as the Lord's Table.' Two hymns are usually sung at baptismal services. One is number 92, 'There is a Fountain filled with Blood', by W. Cowper, of which part of the Kikamba version runs like this:

> There is now a river of blood, of Jesus the Son
>   of God.
> And when people are washed there, they are cleansed
>   from sin,
> They are cleansed from all sins, they are cleansed
>   from sin,
> When evil (bad) people are washed there, they are
>   cleansed entirely . . .

The other hymn, number 84, is 'O Happy Day, that fixed my choice', by P. Doddridge. Part of the Kikamba version reads:

> There was a happy day, When I took Jesus,
> The Saviour and my God; Let all people hear now . . .
>
> Yes, lead me my God, I will joyfully follow Thee,
> All the days that I shall be alive I shall praise
>   Thee my Redeemer.

Baptism is seen by many, therefore, to be the climax of a long period of preparation, the reward of passing the baptismal examination, and the end of a tedious parrot-like memorization of scripture verses. But it raises the social status of the 'adherent', as he now enters the circle of the initiates. The sacramental value of Baptism is alto-

---

[1] The Baptism service is about the only occasion when 'adult' Christians can publicly adopt new names which are recognized by everyone. The fact also that this is done ritually and in a 'European' fashion makes the occasion socially and culturally very significant, both for the candidates and the spectators.

gether unknown, partly because of lack of sacramental ideas in traditional life, and partly because of insufficient teaching on its sacramental value and meaning.

The Eucharist is likewise misunderstood and often associated with magical ideas. To the Akamba it appears like a social occasion when participants share little amounts of bread and drink. At every celebration the minister reads I Cor. 11: 23–34. The middle portion of this passage (especially verses 27–32) conveys what to the Akamba sounds like threats of magic and curse, to both of which the people are extremely sensitive. Perhaps unconsciously they transpose associations of magic and witchcraft with food and drink on to the elements at the Eucharist.[1] So the service becomes an occasion of fear and dread (cf. verses 29–34). Furthermore, the Eucharist has nothing physically striking[2] or outstanding either socially or culturally, nor does it bestow anything comparable to the name-badge of the rite of Baptism.

Since there are only a few ordained ministers, many churches do not celebrate the Eucharist regularly, and sometimes only three or four times a year. This factor tends to make the Eucharist appear like an unimportant service in Christian life. And even where it is held regularly every month, only a small proportion of the congregation participates. Church regulations similar to those governing the conduct of 'adherents', are applied with severity, and 'offenders' are disciplined by the authorities (or their own conscience), and forbidden to participate in the Eucharist.[3] In many cases these semi-excom-

---

[1] Cf. R. Bultmann, who feels that these verses (I Cor. 11: 27–32, and 15: 29) are not altogether free of magical associations (*Theology*, I, pp. 311 f.). See also, C. N. Moody, *The Mind of the Early Converts* (prefaced 1920), 16f. Cf. the (Roman) Catholic sacramental principle that a Sacrament confers grace *ex opere operato* on those who receive it rightly (e.g. in B. Leeming, *Principles of Sacramental Theology* (1956), 27 ff. *et passim*).

[2] The A.I.M. forbids the use of 'wine', and at the Eucharist bread and another fruit juice are used. In the catechism booklet, the term 'ngoyoo ya nzavivu' (the juice of grapes) is used in talking about the Eucharist Wine, thus avoiding the right Kikamba word, 'mbinyu', which is, however, used in the Bible. This misuse of language for doctrinal purposes is rather questionable. Sometimes (one is told), people add red ink to a fruit juice to make it look like blood before it is used at the Eucharist services.

[3] A.I.C. Constitution, 27, 29. No statistics are kept concerning those who do or do not participate in the Eucharist. But the situation gives the impression that it is comparable to that of the Church in Buganda. There, according to J.V. Taylor, the rule of exclusion from the Holy Communion in the Common Prayer Book, of the 'open and notorious evil liver', is applied to '87 per cent of married men in the church, and about 80 per cent of married women . . .' (in *The Growth*

munications are caused or suspected to be caused by the sin of sexual immorality, and some of those who attend the service do so lest their friends, neighbours and fellow Christians think that they have fallen into that sin.

Missionary teaching on the Eucharist creates the feeling that it is more dangerous to participate in the service than to refrain. The service is an occasion filled with warnings on the dangers of 'unworthy' participation. These warnings become a great deterrent to a people with such a sensitive magic-and-curse mentality.

Only one hymn is relevant to the Eucharist service, and it is sung at nearly every celebration. This is: 'Come, for the Feast is spread', by P. P. Bliss (number 203). The Kikamba version says nothing about the sacramental meaning of the Eucharist, other than inviting participants to come to 'the true food for the heart' and bring their needs to Jesus.

It is interesting to compare the sacramental ideas of the Friends of the Holy Spirit sect. The members have no formal catechumen instructions prior to Baptism, and 'converts are baptized at any time. They may even be baptized within a few hours after conversion . . . Proselytes have to be re-baptized. This re-baptism is known as the second Baptism of the Holy Spirit', referring to John the Baptist's words that he baptized with water while Jesus would baptize with the Holy Spirit. If the candidate has already taken a biblical or western name (at a previous Baptism), he abandons it and sticks to his Kikamba name. Those who come straight from traditional religion are baptized once, by immersion, and do not take on a foreign name at this (or other) occasion. At the discretion of the male member performing the ceremony, infants may be baptized if he feels so led by the Holy Spirit.

The Friends of the Holy Spirit combine the Eucharist with an agape meal, in the Kitui area, whereas in Machakos the Eucharist is not celebrated at all. In Kitui, the members meet at night in somebody's house to eat a meal together. This consists of meat, vegetables, fat, spices and a type of flat, thin bread (*kyavati*), with milk, tea and coffee. When the eating of food is over, one *kyavati* is consecrated by the senior elder in the group, and then shared among all the members present. 'Then brown coffee with sugar is prepared and

---

of the Church in Buganda (1958), 244). Since the A.I.M. tradition is more strict than that of the C.M.S., the numerical comparison in Ukambani is likely to be greater than in Buganda, and at least not less.

consecrated . . . to be shared by all members using only one cup. The reason for partaking the Holy Communion at night is to prevent the participation of non-members. To the Friends of the Holy Spirit the Lord's Supper is sacred and whereas true believers partaking it bring upon themselves spiritual blessings, the sinful members and unbelievers partaking it bring upon themselves condemnation. . . . All members of the congregation, baptized and unbaptized are allowed to partake the Supper.' Members contribute the food and drinks for the occasion.[1]

It is readily noticeable that some of the practices followed by the Africa Inland Mission/Church are rejected by the Friends of the Holy Spirit in the observance of both Sacraments. The rejection of biblical and foreign names is obviously a symbolic rejection of foreign control in Church life, since this sect has broken off from a foreign Missionary body. The foreign names, as we saw earlier on, are used as badges of identification with missionary culture; but now, a sect which has rejected foreign control must equally use the same effective badges to register its outward dissociation. Readiness to baptize converts and infants is prompted, perhaps, not by theological motives as such, but by the desire to increase the number of converts as rapidly as possible. It can also be an indication that people have become tired of the lengthy catechumen instructions in the Africa Inland Mission/Church, which hold up full Church membership for two to ten years after conversion. In their Baptism of infants, members of this sect show their concern for and better understanding of Christian community and the Body of Christ. They are unconsciously acting in an extremely theological manner.

Again, while the Friends of the Holy Spirit may not realize its theological or even historical importance, celebrating the Eucharist in the context of an agape meal not only recaptures the practice of the Early Church but greatly demonstrates and strengthens the meaning of the Eucharist as a Communion. Is this something that is lacking in the practice used by the A.I.M. and A.I.C.? We saw how warnings of condemnation and curse pervade the service of the Eucharist in the A.I.M. churches, and while this has its right place it can and may destroy the whole purpose of the Sacrament. Certainly a sense of fellowship is hard to cultivate under such circumstances. The Friends of the Holy Spirit are clearly groping for something of

---

[1] D. N. Kimilu, 'The Separatist Churches', in *Dini na Mila: Revealed Religion and Traditional Custom*, Vol. 2, Nos. 2–3 (December, 1967), pp. 51–3.

supreme importance in Christian life, even though they may neither realize its theological significance, nor reap its full benefits for lack of better understanding.

While it is not the intention of this work to deal with practical issues of evangelization, this question of Christian Sacraments in an African background, does call for a further discussion of the encounter between the New Testament theology of the Sacraments and the situation in Ukambani as we have outlined it above. Can the Sacraments of Baptism and Eucharist be presented meaningfully and intelligibly to a people whose religious background lacks sacramental concepts? This is the question with whose answer we have to conclude this chapter. It belongs to the fundamental issue with which we are concerned here, namely to discuss the methods which the New Testament uses to convey its eschatological message. A materialistic language is one method, and the liturgical practice is another which we are attempting in this chapter.

(f) The Practice of Christian Sacraments in an African Background

We have seen that Akamba traditional background is lacking in sacramental concepts and practices, and that the situation is probably the same in other African societies. We have seen also that according to the New Testament the Sacraments of Baptism and the Eucharist are intensely eschatological and christological, and that they epitomize and contain the whole Gospel. Christian teaching and practice in Ukambani within the context of the Africa Inland Mission/ Church and the Friends of the Holy Spirit, fall short of the New Testament theology of the Sacraments. The Church in Ukambani is obviously deprived of the most vital part of Christian life. We need to examine how the Sacraments could be effectively related to the traditional background and assimilated in Christian life.

During the instruction period prior to Baptism (or to Confirmation where this might apply), the Church in Ukambani has a magnificent opportunity to expound the whole Gospel radiating from the theme of the Sacraments. They could form the basis and skeleton of the entire curriculum. After all, catechism and confirmation classes lead finally to the Sacraments, and if this is the ultimate goal it is obviously of ultimate importance to keep the Sacraments constantly in the foreground. The Early Church came to its eschatological self-realization most of all in the observance of the two Sacraments. The same principle must apply equally today as it did two thousand years ago. In this perspective only would the Sacraments become the essential means of initiation into the Body of Christ and the growth of both the Christian individual and community, instead of Baptism being regarded as a badge of acculturation and the Eucharist as a semi-magical rite for the few holy ones. Studies of the independent Church movements in Africa generally point out the place given to Baptism and the comparative absence of, or little attention given to, the Eucharist. One wonders how far such Church groups exist theologically, when they pay attention to their sacramental birth but neglect sacramental growth.

It is well known that the question of Infant Baptism and its introduction in the Early Church has never been resolved, and continues to form the subject of theological debate. But in the Church situation in Ukambani, it would seem recommendable to practise Infant Baptism both for its theological desirability and as a point of contact for expounding and demonstrating the meaning of Christian Baptism. This need not exclude 'adult Baptism' for those who become converted at a later age. The apparent silence on Infant Baptism in the New Testament is not tantamount to a prohibition of the practice; and the whole tenor of the Scriptures clearly supports and sanctions the administration of this rite on the children of Christian families.

Infant Baptism in Ukambani would lend itself readily to the traditionally rooted ideas and practices of giving names to children and humanizing the new-born babies. As we saw, the rite of humanizing children is a formal ceremony of incorporating them into the community of human beings. Only when this rite is performed does a baby become truly a human being, a person and not just a thing or an IT. This traditional practice and the concepts that go with it, can be transposed to convey the central meaning of Christian Baptism as a Sacrament of birth and incorporation into the Body of Christ. In the New Testament context, Baptism makes the 'no people' (both Jew and Gentile) in the sight of God, into the true 'my people' of God: it is the act of humanizing those who otherwise are apart from Christ (χωρὶς Χριστοῦ), and hence dead and non-existent. From the moment of Baptism onwards, they become truly human, for they are reborn and incorporated into the only true Man.

At such a rite of Infant Baptism the child would (or should) be given a name, as a Christian, not simply for its physical life but more important for its spiritual recognition and existence. A new personality is stamped upon the child, the personality of Christ in whom and for whom the child is born anew. It is at this hour that the meaning of the Gospel can be driven home most forcefully, both through the theological content of Baptism and the drama of the occasion. People are very susceptible to mental, emotional and religious impressions at moments of crisis such as those connected with birth, marriage and death. Birth is, however, a moment of great joy, and why not seize upon it and demonstrate the theological significance of Baptism? In an earlier chapter we pointed out that Akamba people put great value on family and kinship ties. Infant Baptism presents an occasion to convey the transposition of traditional sense of kinship to the christological kinship created through Baptism. It is this community of kinsmen which then must be nourished and sustained through the Eucharist.

In an earlier subsection of this chapter we drew attention to Akamba use of names and their meanings. Here then is another area of fruitful contact between Christian teaching and Akamba traditional life. Christianity brings with it a whole range of rich vocabulary, both in personal names and religious concepts. It would be fitting to analyse the meaning of biblical names and concepts, so that when Akamba Christians use these names either for their children or at adult Baptism, they know something of the conceptual content of the names. More important, however, are the biblical concepts that are introduced in the process of evangelization, and these could be related to the Sacraments so that believers may realize and appreciate more fully the meaning of their conversion. After all, real conversion must involve the total man, including his thinking process and vocabulary.

One extremely effective method of disseminating Christian teaching is the use of music, hymns and songs, all of which play a vital role in any society. Traditional musical instruments and tunes are forbidden in Christian circles in Ukambani, as far as the congregations of the Africa Inland Mission are concerned. At Church services some congregations use harmoniums or accordions if there is a missionary to play them, since Akamba Christians are not taught how to play them; but the majority of congregations have no musical instruments and sing without any. All the hymns used by the A.I.M. and A.I.C. are translations from American and European hymns, chosen particularly to cover the doctrines of sin, salvation and going to

Heaven (or Hell). The music and words differ considerably from traditional Akamba music, especially in the area of musical notes, pitch, rhythm and intonation of words, and lack that vital spirit of spontaneous expression of emotions which is so common in African societies. Lyrics, songs, hymns, musical recitals and poetical pieces for use in the Church in Ukambani, could be drawn from the local background, loaded with Christian teaching and set to Akamba tunes, and mode of expression. The use of drums, flutes, whistles and other musical instruments would not only enliven the services but make Christian commitment relevant to every part of life. Only the vibrations of the drum can sufficiently arouse the entire musical and religious expression of a Mukamba (or any African for that matter): the piano and the harmonium are too gentle for that. The drum is probably the most powerful weapon of communication in traditional African societies. It creates solemnity, it stirs up exuberant joy, it aids the singers in learning their parts, and above all it epitomizes and creates the dynamic rhythm which is such an integral part of African life. The drum and other musical instruments are ready-made tools for use in Christian worship and their effect would be invaluable. For example, at Baptism they can be played to dramatize the meaning of dying and rising with Christ—with all the solemnity of death and the outburst of joy at the symbolic resurrection to new life. The same effect can be wrought at the Eucharist, to drive home the presence of the Lord, the fellowship around the Lord's Table, the vitality received from Eucharistic nourishment and the thanksgiving which accompanies this Sacrament. Even a small measure of clapping and dancing at these services may not be out of place, when employed with moderation. In a society which still has a large proportion of illiterate members, the power of music and hymns in the communication of the Christian message, cannot be underestimated. Its great potentialities must be harnessed, not only in the actual process of evangelization but also in Christian worship.[1]

[1] The subject of African music in the Church is increasingly gaining attention. See, among others, H. Weman, *African Music and the Church in Africa* (1960); S. Mbunga, 'African Church Music', in *AFER*, Vol. X, No. 4 (October 1968), pp. 372 ff.; L. Marfurt, *Musik in Afrika* (1957); J. Kyagambiddwa, *Ten African religious Hymns* (1963), *Ugandan Martyrs African Oratorio* (1964); P. Jans, 'Essai de Musique Religeuse pour Indigenes dans le Vicariat Apostolique Coquilhatville' in *Aequatoria*, No. 1 (1956); A. M. Jones, *Hymns for the African* (1931); A. Sandilands, 'Making Hymns in Africa', in *Books for Africa*, Vol. 25, No. 1

In the previous chapter we indicated the difficulties of using a materialistic language to convey eschatological realities. Broadly speaking, the Akamba think more in concrete than abstract forms. They have to handle, hear, taste, see and, if possible, smell the objects of their thought. They conceive God more readily as the Creator and generous Giver of children, rain, and good things, than as the metaphysical God of love, mercy, grace, etc. It is precisely here that through the Sacraments the New Testament provides us with an open channel of communication from the material to the spiritual. The elements (water, bread and wine) are perceptible through all the human senses. But by using them sacramentally the participants are hoisted from the realm of 'physicalness' to the realm of 'spiritualness', from the visible to the invisible, from the earthly to the eternal. This is the area of understanding which must replace much of the fear, dread, and 'magic-mentality' which, in Akamba minds, tends to shroud the Sacraments, especially the Eucharist. Furthermore, as we saw above, the Sacraments contain the whole Gospel, and when it is thus proclaimed in this concrete manner, its Message would penetrate the whole man through the total senses of his perception.

In addition to the tangible elements of the Sacraments, there is the spoken word. The Akamba recognize the power of the spoken word, and about this we shall speak briefly. Words have a tangible content, so that when invoked especially on solemn occasions and in rituals, or by 'specialists' like the medicine-men and magic-workers, they have what can only be described as physical force or power. This is the psychology which pervades much of Akamba (and other African) thinking. They know that when a senior person invokes a curse upon a junior person, that curse will undoubtedly come true if it is justly invoked. They believe that when a witch uses somebody else's hair, tools, food or other property, and makes a magical incantation against him, that person will meet with misfortune—unless he uses more powerful incantations to counteract those of the witch. For good purposes the medicine-man uses the power of the spoken

---

(1955); J. H. Nketia, 'The Contribution of African Culture to Christian Worship', in the *International Review of Missions*, Vol. XLVIII (1958), pp. 265–78; and the publications and newsletters of the Africa Music Society. For the power of hymns and music in evangelization and Church life, see: J. E. Rattenbury, *The Evangelical Doctrines of Charles Wesley's Hymns* (1941); and F. Hildebrandt, *From Luther to Wesley* (1951).

word in treating his patients, and when he gives them 'medicines' for treatment, protection or good fortune. The Akamba word for this action is *kwathiisya* which literally means 'to pilot or direct, by word, some action or word for a particular purpose'. This purpose can be either good or malicious. People fear it when others 'direct' (*athiisya*) wicked intentions towards them. For example, in a heated quarrel the parent might tell his disobedient teenage son '*woothi kutulika kuu utavikite kula uuthi!*' ('let it be that you break your leg before you reach where you are going!'). This is one such act of *kwathiisya*, and the *word* (as a substance in this case) has great effect: the son will almost certainly stop going where he intends to go, and will get reconciled with the parent. If he goes, he takes the great risk of breaking his leg, according to the word of his father. Akamba people are extremely susceptible to this type of power from the spoken word, for when a *directive* word is uttered under these solemn, ritual, medical or magical circumstances, it has to be realized in concrete forms.

With that psychological background we return to the administration of the Eucharist. This psychology poses both dangers and opportunities for the celebration of the Eucharist among Akamba Christians. The people are not incapable of realizing that the prayer of Consecration—the ritual word—and the physical actions that accompany the administration of either Sacrament, turn material elements of water, bread and wine, into something else, into sacramental vehicles of grace. But, at the same time, the words of the Institution which are read from I Cor. 11: 23–34, hover so much on the verge of 'curse' for the unworthy participant, that it requires little mental effort to tip the hearers over into the realm of magic and curse. In the sight of Akamba people, the division between sacramental grace and the effects of magic or curse, is extremely thin, however great the theological difference might be. No effort should be spared, therefore, to teach the people this fundamental difference. In both cases the spoken word is functioning and indispensable. But whereas in the case of curse or magic it is man's word which is believed to produce the desired effects, in the case of the Sacraments, it is the sacramental grace of God being mediated through, but subsequent to, man's word of consecration. In the one case, man manipulates through word; in the other, God acts in spite of but through man's humble prayer and action. We need to realize, however, that the quasi-magical understanding of the Sacraments cannot be eliminated easily, and that even wider Christendom has never freed itself entirely from that approach to the Sacraments.[1]

The Akamba rite of circumcision is an important point of contact in understanding and teaching about the Sacraments, particularly since Christian Baptism is in some respects linked with the meaning of circumcision in the Old Covenant (cf. Rom. 2: 25–9; 4: 11 f., Phil. 3: 3, Col. 2: 11 f., Gen. 17: 9–14).[2] The rite of circumcision (and clitoridectomy) incorporates the initiate into the community of adults, and entitles him (or her) to participate in all the activities of the nation. It is the highlight of one's life, qualifying a person to become a *complete* Mukamba. The skin is cut in a once-for-all act, obliterating the mark of *childhood* and leaving a scar which is the symbol of *adulthood* and *completeness*. We can draw parallels from Christian Baptism, with its purposes of incorporation, initiation, new birth, new Covenant, obliterating the old man and substituting the new, being a once-for-all act, etc. (cf. Col. 2: 11–13). Baptism entitles the candidate to full participation in the life of the Body of Christ. For those baptized as infants, their Confirmation period could be a substitute for the second phase in Akamba circumcision. It would not be out of place to take even adult baptisands on a 'retreat' (like the second phase of circumcision) and give them further instruction on Christian living. As circumcision is a rite of access to full identification with the Akamba as a people and an acceptance of responsibilities and national solidarity, so also Baptism is a rite of *access* (cf. Heb. 10: 19–22) to full identification with Christ (cf. ἐν Χριστῷ) and a participation in the benefits and responsibilities of His Kingdom.

But Baptism links the believer with God, which is a concept entirely foreign to Akamba thought. While in Akamba society everyone is related to other human beings in this world and to the living-dead in the other, it is never thought that this web of kinship could possibly be extended to the Creator. But the Sacraments make it possible,

---

[1] S. Angus, *The Mystery-Religions and Christianity* (1925), 252 ff. points out that in the Roman world, pagans brought magical and quasi-magical conceptions 'which have infected Christian theology and worship', and that 'magic laid hold also of Jewish and Christian formulae and holy names'. Cf. F. B. Welbourn, *East African Rebels* (1961), 150, where he refers to 'baptism by post' for people living too far away to be reached by other means; and reports from Independent Churches in Africa, of individuals who get baptized as many as ten times.

[2] See the discussion by O. Cullmann of Baptism and Circumcision in *Baptism in the New Testament* (ET 1950), 56–69.

and therefore bring into Akamba ontology a Christian differentia of stupendous implications. Baptism opens the door into the world of the I–THOU relationship between God and Man, bridged in the intense dialogue of communion. As we have argued, this dialogue is at its height in the Eucharist. It is the Eucharist which makes it possible for the eschatological community to realize fully and intimately its own self-awareness and the Lord Jesus in the midst of His people. It is this Christocentric emphasis which in the New Testament became a vehicle of eschatological realities. The same should be explained to the Akamba and implemented dramatically through the music, singing, words, and the whole physical environment of the eucharistic service. Jesus Christ as the Host to whom the faithful are related makes the Eucharist a true Messianic meal which draws them together (instead of repelling them), and through which they obtain spiritual sustenance and blessing rather than a curse. Therefore, every possible appeal through the senses should be made to excite their emotion, capture their imagination, direct their attention and focus their concentration upon Him at the Eucharist.

This reverses the traditional Akamba way of thinking in which the spiritual is merged into the physical, whereas the Sacraments point the physical in the direction of the spiritual. It is one of the methods of the New Testament, and this is a necessary reversal if Christian worship is to mean something much deeper and more intimate than the simple traditional rituals of sacrificing. Therefore, after the Cross of Jesus, all other sacrifices have become redundant and irrelevant. The believer with this understanding would approach the Eucharist as one who is now directly responsible to God and must conduct himself in a manner worthy of this new relationship. His concept of Salvation will be elevated far above the utilitarian view of deliverance from physical ills and uncertainties of this life or the security of going to Heaven for its own sake, to the heights of the positive view and experience of fellowship with God.

The manner of celebrating the Eucharist in Ukambani churches is so simplified that it lacks the type of appeal we are advocating. Traditional objects and ideas could be used to enrich the service without unnecessary expense. Music, tunes, instruments, and ritual which make sense to the people, can create both solemnity and joy at the service. It would also be meaningful for the congregation to sit in a semicircle or full circle, with the Eucharist Table at the centre. The people have lived for years in circular houses, and obviously a circular or oval church building may give a more familiar atmosphere of community and fellowship than do the now common rectangular church buildings. When people sit to eat together, they do so generally in circles with their dishes in the middle. Similarly at public gatherings they sit in circles (or three-quarter circles). Why not, therefore, capture these aspects of African background and use them in constructing churches and in celebrating the Eucharist? They are the people's external form of expressing community life and fellowship. But when the Eucharist Table is placed at the far end of a rectangular building, or at a distant altar, the set-up creates a separation which seriously disrupts the meaning of eucharistic worship. The liturgical life of the Christian community must shape the church building where it is to be staged. Round church buildings are nearer than rectangular ones, to African expression of community activities, fellowship and unity.[1]

The problem of feeling 'unworthy' and therefore refraining from the Eucharist is both genuine and serious, both pastoral and theological. It requires pastoral care, instruction on self-examination and preparation, guidance on the practice of repentance and confession, in addition to sound teaching on the whole subject of the Sacraments. All these aids to spiritual problems and life seem to be virtually unknown in the churches of Ukambani, apart from the Roman Catholic Church, and most believers have neither books nor persons that can help them cultivate a deeper Christian life, or find ways to overcome problems of their conscience. One of the outstanding assets of the East African Revival is its emphasis on public (and private) confession of personal sins.[2] Similar practices have a high priority in the so-called Independent Churches. But the East African Revival is not well represented in Ukambani, both the A.I.M. and A.I.C. being rather unfavourable though not antagonistic to it. As Telfer has shown, the problem of sin crept into the Early Church at the very beginning, and became the most serious hurdle to jump over.[3]

To the Akamba, Christianity brought with it a legion of sins and unearthed many more locally. But seemingly it only exposed the people

[1] P. Hammond, *Liturgy and Architecture* (1960), in which he discusses the important link between these two themes.
[2] Cf. M. A. C. Warren, *Revival: an Enquiry* (1954); and N. Langford-Smith, 'Revival in East Africa', in *The International Review of Missions*, Vol. XLIII, No. 169 (Jan. 1954), pp. 77–81.
[3] W. Telfer, *The Forgiveness of Sins* (1959), 22 ff. *et passim*. Cf. C. N. Moody, *The Mind of the Early Converts* (n.d., prefaced 1920), esp. Chap. II.

to these thorns of conscience without satisfactorily showing th
to fight the battle. Moreover, at the present time of rapid
and great perplexities, their hearts yearn for something t
give them comfort and assurance, that can fill them with hope and
courage as they face the problems of their total life situation. Has the
Church nothing more than a gentle pietistic voice to offer? The strong
Akamba (and African) interest in a Futurist Eschatology may
partially be an unconscious attempt to find a spiritual homeland
beginning here and now in this life, but not knowing how to find it
they revert to a largely mythical future which may be no more than a
shallow veneer of escapism.

Would not the greater part of the answer to this problem come
ultimately from a fuller understanding and practice of sacramental
living? It is only at the Sacraments that Christians come to the
focal point of their eschatological birth and nourishment, judgement
and renewal, worship and communion, appropriation and anticipation of the heavenly benefits, 'until He comes'. Then, and only then,
must they expect the imperfect to pass away. The Sacraments form
the nexus between the physical and the spiritual worlds, and through
the concrete and material realities, eschatological realities become
evident and available in the temporal and physical realm.

We have in this chapter considered the Eschatology of the Sacraments as one of the methods used in the New Testament to convey
eschatological realities. This liturgical method uses not only the
materialistic language but also concrete material elements which
sacramentally are made vehicles of grace and eschatological realities.
It is at the Sacraments of Baptism and the Eucharist that the Church
comes to its fullest point of self-realization and awareness as an
eschatological community. Both Sacraments are christological
and eschatological, and therefore epitomize the whole Gospel.
Their liturgical and theological importance rightly deserves full
attention. For it is through them that we catch glimpses and acquire
experiences of the realm of the eternal. But in all their intensities,
these glimpses and experiences are incomplete. As an appetizer they
fulfil the promises of God in Christ Jesus, and as eschatological
realities they promise those riches of God in Christ which neither
the eye of man can see nor his tongue articulate.

We saw also that, although in their traditional life the Akamba
lack sacramental concepts and practices, it is not altogether impossible
for them to assimilate the meaning of Christian Sacraments and to

relate them to their life and understanding. The main drawback here is the type of Christian teaching they receive, which is anything but adequate. Apart from the Roman Catholic Church in Ukambani, the Churches there have missed a great deal of sacramental life. There are elements in Akamba traditions, such as the ceremony of naming and humanizing children, initiation rites and the practice of giving meaningful names which readily lend themselves to points of contact with Christian ideas and ceremonies, in connection with the Sacraments. While these Akamba practices have other purposes, both religious and social, they present themselves as starting points from which the theology of the Sacraments could be built. By 'baptizing' them, they can be converted to contain and convey Christian theological meaning, not so much in the actual vocabulary as such, but more so in the ceremony itself. The ceremony comes first, then a vocabulary grows around it, and if this principle is applied, Christian meaning will permeate into the words which in their Akamba (or African) setting have meanings different from those of their Christian counterparts. The Sacraments are, therefore, a key factor in the process of Christianization—for they contain and epitomize the whole Gospel, and in that capacity they are an effective method of conveying eschatological realities. They bridge together the material and the spiritual, the physical and the metaphysical, the temporal and the eternal. Apart from them, we cannot peer into the next realm and we cannot experience now what in Christ will be the ultimate norm for the faithful.

CHAPTER V

The Nearness of the Spirit World

In the foregoing chapter we saw how that at the Sacraments of Baptism and the Eucharist, the material and spiritual worlds converge. It is the intention of this chapter to explore further the nature of the spirit world, as conceived by the Akamba (and other African peoples) and the New Testament. The major dimension of Eschatology clearly takes us into the realm of the spiritual realities.

(a) Akamba Conception of the Spirit World

We start here by considering and analysing the Akamba terms about dying. In passing we shall draw attention to parallel ideas from the Old Testament, by alluding to biblical passages without indulging in a discussion of these parallelisms. The Akamba use many terms to describe the act of dying which, with their approximate English translations, we can list as follows:

(i) *Atiia aa-umau*—'follow the company of one's grandfathers.' Cf. 'going to one's fathers', in Gen. 15: 15, or being 'gathered to one's people', in Gen. 25: 8; 49: 29; Deut. 32: 50, etc.[1]

(ii) *Eka kung'ulya*—'stop saying "no" or snoring.' Death is the final 'YES' for everyone.

(iii) *Ina 'mutingwa'!*—'sing "catch me"!' The metaphor comes from the cry of a drowning person. Death is like a river with water, and the people, like timber, must float on the water and be taken elsewhere. Cf. Pss. 42: 7; (73: 19), Jon. 2: 3, 5, Rev. 12: 15.

(iv) *Inuka*—'go home'. Present life is like living in a foreign land, but the next world is the permanent home for everyone. Cf. Job 17: 13, Deut. 32: 50, etc.

(v) *Isiwa*—'be summoned, be fetched.' This may be done by God, His messenger 'death', or one of the spirits if God so instructs him (it). Cf. Ex. 11: 12 f., Lk. 16: 22.

---

[1] See further, Pedersen, *Israel*, I–II, pp. 327 f., 496; and III–IV, pp. 478 f.

(vi) *Ita mwoyo*—'empty out the "soul".' Cf. Is. 53: 12. *Mwoyo* is an onomatopoeic word from the sound made by dying cattle, when being slaughtered (cf. Ps. 44: 22 (23), II Cor. 4: 11).

(vii) *Koma vyu na vyu*—'sleep for ever and ever.' Cf. a similar metaphor in the Bible, Job 3: 13, 17 ff., Jer. 51: 39, 57, Dan. 12: 2, Acts 7: 60 etc. Relative to this life death is like sleep. Though the person is awake in the other world, those who are on this side of life cannot awake him.

(viii) *Kunyaa*—'to dry up, to wither, to evaporate.' The dying person 'withers' away from this world; his life 'evaporates' like vapour. Cf. Job 14: 2 (and the רְפָאִים in Job 26: 5 and Is. 14: 9).

(ix) *Kw'a*—'die, pass away.'

(x) *Kwitwa*—'to be called', and to die is to answer that call. Cf. *isiwa* number (v) above.

(xi) *Lea andu*—'reject the people.' At death a person leaves human beings and joins himself to the living-dead.

(xii) *Lea kandu*—'reject or refuse food.' A person normally stops eating before he dies; and even when he is one of the living-dead, he can no longer have a full share of meals with the survivors.

(xiii) *Nituveniwe mundu*—'we have been deprived of (our) man.' At death, human society is weakened by the departure of one member, unless he dies 'at a ripe old age' (cf. Pedersen's account of the Israelites).[1]

(xiv) *Oswa*—'be taken away, be received.' This implies that the Owner of the individual takes him away, as when parents take away their daughter from her new husband if the couple are not properly married. Cf. Elijah's translation, II Kin. 2: 3, 5, 9 ff.; Ps. 73: 24.

(xv) *Syoka*—'return, go back,' (cf. iv, *supra*). This implies going back to the place of origin. Cf. Gen. 3: 19; 49: 29, 33, Job 1: 21.

(xvi) *Taanisya*—'separate oneself, disintegrate, forsake.' A person bids goodbye to his body and to people, but he will meet the people in the next world when they die.

(xvii) *Tambaika*—'have a miscarriage.' This is used mainly in connection with death at a very early age. Cf. Job 3: 11, 16; *contra* 5: 26.

(xviii) *Thela*—'terminate, be finished, end.' This is particularly with reference to breathing and other activities of the body, but the person himself survives.

---

[1] Pedersen, op. cit., I–II, p. 206; III–IV, pp. 477 ff.

(xix) *Thela veva*—'have one's breath come to an end.' Cf. the phrase, 'breathe one's last', Gen. 25: 8; 35: 29, Jos. 20: 9, Job 14: 10, etc.

(xx) *Thi*—'depart, go.' Cf. Gen. 35: 18, Jn. 19: 30, Lk. 9: 31; going down to the grave, Pss. 16: 10; 30: 10 (9).

(xxi) *Thi kula andu ala angi maendie*—'go where the other people have gone.' The idea is that when a person dies, he joins the society of the departed. Cf. Gen. 25: 8, Jud. 2: 10, Job 30: 23, etc., and further discussion by Pedersen.[1]

(xxii) *Tia*—'leave, forsake, abandon.' The human world is forsaken at death (cf. I Tim. 6: 7, Job. 1: 21), and a person can return only as a visitor but not as a resident.

(xxiii) *Tumbuka*—'collapse, come to ruins,' used in a good sense, particularly in reference to the death of old people. Cf. the Hebrew idea of dying in 'a good old age', or 'full of days/years', Gen. 15: 15; 25: 8; 35: 29, Jud. 8: 32, Job 42: 17.

(xxiv) *Tw'ika wa Ngai (Mulungu)*—'become God's property.' A person living in this life belongs to human beings, but at death he is taken away (or claimed) as God's own property.

(xxv) *Veva nuendie*—'the breath (or spirit) has departed.' Cf. Job 14: 2b, Gen. 35: 18 f.

It is clear that for the Akamba, death means not annihilation but a departure to the spirit world. Formerly, in parts of Ukambani, only the bodies of adults were buried whilst those of younger people were thrown into the woods to be devoured by wild animals. The personality traits are not affected by what happens to one's body after death, and instead, they are continued in the spirit world. As we shall see in the next chapter, the Akamba have their own tribal notions of 'resurrection'.

Available information, though extremely scanty, on the ideas of dying in other African societies shows remarkable similarities. As an example, I list terms used by the Abaluyia (Kenya) and the Basoga (Uganda). Concerning dying the Abaluyia say: *dikoni* ('sleep', used of an old man who dies peacefully); *akhwohoka* ('fall by oneself', when a person commits suicide); *khung'oka* ('look for an exit') or *akuruhena esilenje* ('lift the leg') both for a hated person; *sennibulu-vara* ('step into the sheet', used because the corpse is wrapped in a

---

[1] Pedersen, op. cit., I–II, pp. 328, 460, 496; III–IV, pp. 477 f.

white sheet for burial); *khufwala isweta* ('wear a sweater'); *okhutsia emakombe* ('go to the place of the dead'); *uhuyi* ('go home').[1] Among the Basoga when a person has died, people say: he has breathed his last; he has kept quiet; he has gone; he has gone down to the grave; his life was snapped into two like a brittle stick. If people do not like a person, when he dies they say that death has beaten him, has made him finish food, has made him dry, has stiffened him, has made him quiet, has squeezed him, has made him go far away, has cut him down or has forced him down. Other expressions refer to the dead person that 'he is dry as if from yesterday', or 'our friend was told by *Walumbe* (death) to tie up his load and go'.[2] Other but not so detailed examples can be cited from elsewhere in Africa. The Herero (S.W. Africa) believe that God calls away old people when they die; the Bambuti Pygmies (in the Congo Kinshasa) believe that at death the soul of man is carried away by bees or flies; The Barotse (Zambia) hold that God calls back people at death and nobody can refuse. This same idea is expressed by the Ila (Zambia) metaphorically and vividly when they say that 'God snaps off His pumpkin!'. For the Yoruba (Nigeria), death is God's bailiff, and a debt which must be paid by all. The old people anticipate their death saying, ' "I am ready for home" ', or ' "I am going home" '.[3]

It is clear from these additional examples that Akamba concepts of death, on the whole, are very similar to those of other African peoples, with perhaps only differences in the details of the actual expressions.

Man (*Mundu*) is composed of the body (*mwii*), spirit or breath (*veva*), heart (*ngoo*), life (*thayu*), and mind or intellect (*kiliko, kililikano*). We need to bear in mind, however, that these are academic distinctions. The *spirit* is the 'life-principle', and its existence is manifested through breathing. But it cannot exist alone, i.e. it must have a *body*. The *heart* is the seat of the emotions; and the screen on which one's personality is displayed. It can be 'big' (i.e. furious), or 'soft' (i.e. kind and generous), 'hot' (i.e. cheerful and sociable), 'dead' (i.e. sorrowful, sad), etc. *Life* resides in one's body so long as the spirit is there, and departs with the latter. The *mind* has the

[1] S. Yokoo, *Death among the Abaluyia*, dissertation in the African Studies, Makerere University College (1966), 13 f.

[2] A. Bulima-Nabwiso, essay in the Department of Religious Studies, Makerere University College (1966).

[3] E. B. Idowu, *Olodumare: God in Yoruba Belief* (1962), 187 ff.

function of comprehending and discerning the world around and within a person.[1]

Death transposes the music of life from one key to another, switching it from the rhythm of the physical to the rhythm of the spiritual world. A person *has* a *veva* (spirit) but he *is not* a *veva* himself, and at death he does not turn into a *veva*. His whole being, except the physical body, moves into the spirit world. There it receives another body which is identical to the body left in the physical world. He becomes a living-dead, and begins to live in another mode of existence.

We may draw comparisons from a few other African societies, with regard to the concept of man's composition. The Abaluyia (Kenya) consider man to be in two main parts: *mbili* (body, material) and *mwoyo* (soul). At death the body is no longer *mbili* but corpse (*omukhuza*). The *mwoyo* (soul) has three characteristics: voice or sound, heart, and is alive (or lives). If a person is afraid, it is his *mwoyo*'s heart which fears; if he is happy, it is his *mwoyo*'s heart which rejoices. Thus, the *mwoyo* is the seat of emotions. The soul (*mwoyo*) distinguishes a living body (*mbili*) from a dead body (*omukhuza*). At death the *mwoyo* is transformed into existence in the hereafter. The dead continues to exist as a whole person. Yet, while a person is still alive, his *mwoyo* can depart from him and visit places (in dreams for example), and if the person is awakened while his *mwoyo* is thus away, he dies! The shadow represents the *mwoyo*, and for that reason the Abaluyia avoid stepping in the shadow of a widow who recently lost her husband.[2]

A number of other African societies regard man as body and soul. The Bachwa (Congo Kinshasa) think that the soul of man is small and visible in the pupil of the eye. At death the eye breaks, the soul departs and the body ceases to function. The Bambuti (Congo Kinshasa) hold that the soul leaves the body through the nose, at death.

The Lugbara (Uganda) conceive of three parts to man: body, 'guardian spirit' (*adro*) and 'personality' (*tali*). At death both the 'guardian spirit' and 'personality' forsake the body and return to God: the one to Him in the streams, in His immanent aspect; the other to Him in the sky, in His transcendent aspect.[3] The Lozi

---

[1] Cf. the Israelite ideas about the composition of man, as discussed by A. R. Johnson, *The Vitality of the Individual in the Thought of Ancient Israel* (1949).

[2] Yokoo, op. cit., 14 ff.

[3] J. Middleton, *Lugbara Religion* (1960), 193, 253 f.

(Zambia) on the other hand, think of man in four parts: *mubili* or *situpu* (envelope, presumably the body); *moyoo* (soul) which at death leaves the body and goes to God; *mulimu* (emanation or spirit) which survives and constitutes the living-dead; and *silumba* (ghost or double), of which there are three types: one of a man who has slain or worked evil against another, the other of the living-dead which may haunt people when offended or neglected, and another kind which serves diviners or sorcerers.[1]

Whatever technical divisions are used, it is clear that African peoples we have considered here see man in two main parts: the physical part which at death is put into the grave or otherwise disposed of, and the non-physical part which survives and bears the personality traits of the individual in the hereafter. Death may separate these two and destroy the first part but not the second. This is a universal belief among all African peoples as far as one's evidence shows. Obviously there are differences of emphasis and manner of looking at the belief, from people to people, and many of the traditional ideas are being changed by the presence of both Christianity and Islam, and to a less extent by modern science.

To appreciate more fully the Akamba (or African) concept of the spirit world, we need to put it into its ontological context. Akamba ontology can be classified into five modes of existence: (i) God, the Originator and Sustainer of all things, (ii) Aimu and the living-dead, (iii) Man, (iv) animals and plants, and (v) objects without the capacity to have life.[2] Abstract things like ethics, morals, customs, values, etc., have no separate existence of their own. These modes describe Man as he is: his origin, his destiny after death, and his present environment. This is an intensely anthropocentric ontology. It is a unity centred upon Man, in such a way that death cannot destroy him. To destroy Man would, in effect, mean destroying the whole coherence of being, including the destruction of the Creator.

---

[1] V. W. Turner, *The Lozi Peoples of North-Western Rhodesia* (1952), 51.

[2] Cf. J. Jahn who, following A. Kagame, divides the so-called African philosophy into four categories of: *Muntu* (human being), *Kintu* (thing), *Hantu* (place and time), and *Kuntu* (modality). He says that 'nothing can be conceived outside them', *Muntu* (ET 1961), 100 ff.

So also cf. P. Tempels, *Bantu Philosophy* (ET 1959) where he expounds what he calls the 'dynamic conception of being' in Bantu ontology (pp. 33 ff.), in which he isolates 'force' as the essence of being: 'Force is the nature of being, force is being, being is force' (p. 35). These two interpretations will not fit our Akamba ideas, and one questions their validity for other African societies.

But our enquiry has to deal with the second mode of existence. This is the spirit world, inhabited by beings whom, in Chapter I, we distinguished as the Aimu (spirits) and the living-dead, although the same Kikamba word refers to both.

At death, a person becomes a living-dead, and joins other members of his household who have preceded him in the spirit world. This is a cardinal belief in Akamba life. For several years, however, he will show keen interest in the welfare of those who survive him in this life, and may come occasionally to visit his former place of abode and see his relatives. He is still known to them by his name(s), but when they see him they do not accept his visit with warmth and enthusiasm. There is a sense of separation, a vague but real sense of barrier because they know that he has died. People cannot say to him, 'Here is a seat, sit down and let us prepare a meal for you.' He 'appears' only to one or two members of the family, particularly the older ones, and enquires about the welfare of the others. He cannot participate fully in their social activities, and he gives the impression of one who is in a great hurry. There is communication between him and his surviving relatives, but it is not full 'communion'. He gives no news of the spirit world: any may vanish out of sight at any moment. For all practical purposes, this living-dead is still a 'whole person', and those who see him do not get frightened since he is still a member of their larger family. His appearance strengthens family links between relatives in this life and those in the spirit world.

For the Akamba the spirit world is a complete copy of the physical, and it is not removed from the latter. It is a land of rivers, hills, animals, etc.; and the activities of its inhabitants resemble those of people in this life, such as working in the fields, keeping cattle, establishing families, and the like. Children who die young continue to grow and become adults, get married and raise families.

After three to five generations, when ordinary people can no longer recognize a living-dead by name, he becomes a spirit, *Iimu* (pl. *Aimu*). We pointed out in the previous chapter that names are extremely important in Akamba life, as they describe the personality of an individual. To lose one's several names is in effect to lose one's personality and 'human' existence. By this process, to become an Iimu is to become 'sub-human' (rather than 'super-human'). But, on the other hand, to raise a family with many children is to extend and more or less perpetuate one's names, one's humanity, one's personality. That is the way to become 'immortal' as far as the world of Man

10

is concerned. It is in this light that we should see and interpret Akamba marriage customs (polygamy, absence of spinsters and old bachelors, levirate marriages, etc.).[1]

The Aimu live much like the living-dead, but they are not regarded as intimate members of human families. They do not frequent their former places of abode in this life. These, together with the whole race of the Aimu, feature prominently in Akamba folklore. They are pictured as capable of doing extraordinary things like flying in the air, assuming any shapes they want, walking on one leg, walking or working extremely fast, and even dying several times. They are ubiquitous, although it is believed that they tend to congregate in certain spots like hills, rocks, and large ponds.

People in Ukambani feel that Aimu pervade the entire country, and consequently one's life is continuously being influenced by this belief about them. They live in the intermediate mode between God's and Man's modes of existence, and their world must not be allowed to get either too close or too far from the human world. People both dread them and paradoxically want them to exist. When the equilibrium is lost, then a sense of insecurity and uncertainty comes upon the people, and they offer sacrifices to restore the balance. Thus, the spirit world is controlled by Man to the extent that he brings it closer or drives it further, as the case may be, in order that the two worlds can coexist in an equilibrium beneficial to Man. We have already seen that Akamba sacrifices are not sacramental acts. When the Aimu are too far away then their contact with the human world is weakened and almost severed. They bring misfortune (so the people believe), and they are given food-drink offerings, thereby reviving the contact between the two worlds. If, however, they get too near to human beings, they interfere with people's lives by causing madness, possessing them, frightening them with frequent appearances. To prevent the spirit world getting so close, people make offerings to keep away the Aimu and the living-dead. Thus it is the living-dead and the spirits who actually define and constitute the spirit world, as far as the Akamba are concerned.

Cases of Aimu possession are frequent, and women are said to be more prone to possessions than men and children. One general Aimu possession swept through Ukambani from 1906 to 1908, and

---

[1] Cf. similar ideas among the (early) Israelites, for which see Pedersen, op. cit., I–II, pp. 77 ff., 91 ff., 254 f., 259, *et passim*.

people believed that the Aimu had come from Europe![1] Before a person becomes a medicine-man, he begins to receive vision-dreams from the Aimu while he is still young. Later they appear to him and instruct him concerning the diagnosis and cure of diseases. Medicine-men may also induce voluntary Aimu possession and act as mediums to establish communication between the human and spirit worlds. If a person is sick for a long time, the medicine-man may tell him that his departed grandparents (now the living-dead) need a goat or sheep or cow (cf. Deut. 26: 14). When the animal is slaughtered, the meat is eaten by everyone, but small pieces of it are placed on the ground, inside or outside the house, for the living-dead who have asked for that particular animal. The person is said to get cured afterwards.

It is also believed that women have Aimu husbands, and when God gives a child to a woman He sends an Iimu (presumably her 'spirit husband') to form the foetus in her uterus. The Aimu even announce in advance to the parents concerned that a child will be born, especially if the mother has been without a child for many years. Children may inherit the likeness or qualities of a particular Iimu or living-dead, but the Iimu is not re-born. The Akamba do not believe in the reincarnation of the departed as such. Only certain traits of character or physical appearance may be reproduced in a descendant, resembling those of the departed, but the two continue as separate individuals.

Some of the Aimu may be considered as 'guardians'.[2] They help people by giving them success in hunting, cattle-breeding, bee-keeping, etc. They may also speak through medicine-men, mediums or victims of their possession, to pass on information or give warning of impending danger. There are many incidents in folk stories in which friendship is established between human beings and Aimu.

[1] See Hobley, *Akamba* (1910), 10 ff.; and Lindblom, *Akamba* (1920), 239 f. The fact that it was called *Kiesu*, and that the people believed the Aimu to have come from Ulaya (Europe), shows that the Christian message was beginning to make an impact in the country. *Kiesu* is undoubtedly an adjectival-noun from 'Yesu' (Jesus), but Hobley refutes this, calling the accompanying dance a 'mania' (p. 12)—which judgement easily fits into the colonial mentality of the time.

[2] Anthropologists would call them 'familiar spirits' (as G. I. Jones tells me). Lindblom, op. cit., 214, limits the help of the Aimu only to their descendants. This is not the case, since they help those whom they choose to help, but it is easy for the people to assume or say that their particular Aimu 'guardians' are related to them (i.e. were once their ancestors or other relatives).

Those who receive information from Aimu concerning events affecting the nation or general public, are known as *athani* (seers, foretellers, 'prophets'). One such person, a woman called Syokimau, is reputed to have foretold the coming of Europeans and some of the changes they brought about in the country. But these people (athani) have no special religious functions in society.

At the same time there are Aimu who are hostile towards human beings. They possess people and cause them to slash their bodies with knives, to jump into fires, to run away into the forests, and to have epileptic fits (cf. Mk. 9: 20–2 pars.). Aimu from other races and tribes,[1] like Europeans, Maasai, Gikuyu, and Galla, get blamed for national calamities such as famines and epidemics.

The Akamba believe in metempsychosis, but the belief does not play a prominent role in their lives, nor is it developed as, for example, in Hinduism. Trees, rivers, hills, etc., do not have spirits of their own. The Aimu are thought to dwell there (or 'possess' them) temporarily (cf. Gen. 16: 14, Neh. 2: 13). For example, if a python, a frog, or a porcupine is seen near one's home, it is not killed because people believe that it belongs to the Aimu or that it is 'possessed' by them. When a domestic animal has biological abnormalities, it is also considered to belong to the Aimu, and will eventually be slaughtered on a sacrificial occasion. In folk stories, nearly every object is capable of being 'possessed' by the Aimu; and when plants are thus 'possessed' they produce fruits of enormously large sizes.

Some Akamba believe that the Aimu do not die,[2] but others believe that they do. In Akamba folklore, there are many stories about Aimu, some of whom are killed by people, while others are completely 'indestructible'. Most of those that die come back to life after another while. The Akamba are not, however, particularly concerned with the life span of the Aimu.

It is said that since the arrival of the Europeans, the Aimu do not appear as often as they used to.[3] Many of the places previously set

---

[1] For further description of the foreign Aimu, see Lindblom, op. cit., 229 ff. Hobley describes another type, 'Aimu ma Kitombo', who 'are evil spirits, and are supposed to be disembodied relics of people who have killed their neighbours by the help of black magic' (op. cit., 89). I have not otherwise heard of this group of Aimu.

[2] So also G. Kanig, *Dornige Pfade eines jungen Missionars in Ukamba* (1902), 17; and Lindblom, op. cit., 215.

[3] Lindblom pointed this out when he studied the Akamba in 1911–12, op. cit., 216.

aside for Aimu, have now been occupied by people, but both Christians and non-Christians still see Aimu and the living-dead.

The Akamba do not know where the world of the Aimu and the living-dead is situated. They only know that it is very close to the human world, and a person finds himself there immediately upon dying. Both G. Kanig in *Dornige Pfade eines jungen Missionars in Ukamba* (1902), and Lindblom in *Akamba* (1920),[1] say that the spirit world is in the nether region below. This is not altogether correct, and undoubtedly these authors were reading too much into whatever reports they obtained from the Akamba. When earthquakes occur, it is thought that the subterranean world is in turmoil and the Aimu assemble before God.[2] But on the other hand, thunder, lightning and hail are brought about by God through the Aimu who thus act as His messengers. The spirit world of the Akamba is neither below nor above the ground, but everywhere and close to the physical. It is thought to be good and fertile, otherwise people would return from there to this world.

After death, a person gets access to that mysterious 'force' of Nature, and in this respect he is, as Hofmann also observed, clothed with 'spiritual' power.[3] The living-dead and the Aimu are, in a sense, 'nearer' to God than are ordinary people, since they can assemble before Him or be sent by Him, which is something that people do not experience. But on the whole, their world is simply a continuation of present life, without either presents or punishment for deeds done in this world. The certainty of the continuation of life in the spirit world inspires no hope for the future, nor is it doubted by anyone. And this survival offers no opportunities for growth or progress in a 'spiritual' or 'ethical' direction. It is only a withdrawal from the visible world into the invisible.

---

[1] Kanig, ibid.; Lindblom, op. cit., 209; and likewise E. Brutzer, *Der Geisterglaube bei den Kamba* (1905), who speaks about the duties of the wife in the 'Underworld' being similar to what they are in this life (p. 4).

[2] J. Hofmann, *Gebert, Heirat und Tod bei den Wakamba* (1901), 24. I have not come across the belief as he asserts it, that the Aimu assemble before God.

[3] Hofmann, op. cit., 24. Brutzer goes as far as saying (according to his informants) that upon death people are known as 'gods' ('ngai'): 'Wenn der Mensch gestorben ist, so wird er Yimu, Ngoma oder Ngai gennant,' (op. cit., 3). This should not be taken literally, since it is the Kikamba way of saying that the dead person is 'like Ngai' (God), rather than that he is 'ngai'. The simile simply refers to the fact that the departed is in the invisible realm, like God. One of the phrases about dying describes the departed as joining God's 'household' or becoming His property (phrase xxiv, *supra*).

The living-dead and the Aimu are pictured as being 'geographically nearer' to God than men are. But to them He is still the Creator, the non-spirit (in the Akamba sense) and non-human OTHER, as He is to ordinary people, although He may send them occasionally to perform His will. God's mode of existence is outside that of the departed, and in this respect He is transcendent to them. But He neither punishes them nor rewards them for whatever they did in this life.[1] On their part they do not thirst for His holiness or righteousness; nor do they have spiritual 'communion' with Him. The people say in comparison that God dwells up in the 'heavens' (*matuni*) whereas the Aimu and the living-dead dwell below on the earth. This is not a geographical distinction only, it is also a theological distinction. Another distinction they draw is that God is better than the departed, since they do not remain with human beings whereas God is always helping men. So the Akamba say characteristically, that 'Mulungu does us no evil; so wherefore should we sacrifice to Him.'[2] The ontological 'distance' between God's mode of existence and that of human beings does not fluctuate, and hence there is no need to sacrifice to Him, except when national calamities strike.

Such then is the picture of the spirit world according to Akamba 'Eschatology'. It is inhabited by beings, part of whom were once people in the physical world. They have, through death, departed into the Time period which we called *TENE*. Their life is a mere continuation of human existence, even if procreation continues there. It is not a goal to which people can look forward. Rather, it is the inevitable lot of mankind, and for the Akamba the problem of immortality, or otherwise, does not arise. Their chief concern is with the way the living-dead and the Aimu may affect life in this world.

The world of the departed presses hard upon that of ordinary people. It pervades their whole life, their vocabulary, folklore, social relations, acts of sacrifice, etc. An outsider may judge some beliefs and ideas to be confused, others contradictory, and some illogical. But they are nevertheless present in the minds and hearts of

---

[1] In describing the 'Aimu ma Kitombo', Hobley says that they are banished by 'the Supreme Being . . . to the woods where they wander without anybody to care for them', because of killing their neighbours with black magic. This is completely foreign to Akamba ideas of the hereafter, and Hobley's description (op. cit., 89) is possibly influenced by Mt. 12: 43–5 par., which his informant had probably heard and 'corrupted'.

[2] Recorded by Lindblom, op. cit., p. 244.

the people, and they affect them in their daily life. The spirit world forms an integral part of the whole existence of the Akamba.

Even though the spirit world of the Akamba interpenetrates with the human world, it lacks direct relationship between God and Man, and God and the departed.

Death is a gradual removal of the individual, as a person without the body, from the mituki period to the tene period, from the moment of intense consciousness (of individuals and communities) to one of shadowy existence, from the mituki period of remembrance by personal names to one of being forgotten as a spirit (Iimu). For the Akamba death is only a final process of disintegration even if one is gathered to one's forefathers, the community of those who are gradually being forgotten, being lost from the intensity of living to the obscurity of the tene horizon. It is a departure for home, but relative to human beings that 'home' is one where the individual finally disappears, melts away into the existence without 'personal names' and hence without personality, deprived of the totality of being. God does not enter into the picture in this process of evaporation to reintegrate, recondense the vapour of human being into a new whole, a new 'persona', a new nameable being. Hence the spirit world is one in which the personified (through personal names and remembrance by the living) evades personification and can only be a portion of a collective sum—the spirits, made up of both the departed and those that belong to the race of spirits, in the intermediate mode of existence between God and man. Thus, for the Akamba, and indeed for many African peoples as far as evidence is available, the Eschatology of man takes him back to the remotest possible point in Time beyond his point of beginning to, in reality, a point of non-being, since it takes him beyond where he is createable. Or, to put it another way, God does not recreate what at death has begun to disintegrate. There is no teleology in African Eschatology; what there is might be called 'deteriology'—at least that is the theological and philosophical conclusion to which our analysis seems to drive us. In terms of Time, death ultimately deprives the individual of his participation in the mituki period, it removes him from the moment of intense living, from a two-dimension of Time to a one-dimension of Time—the tene, the past, even beyond the point of his start—and hence to the point of his non-being, complete disappearance, depersonification, and non-presence. Obviously the peoples concerned would not push the argument that far; their chief concern is, naturally, with the relations between the living-dead, the spirits and human beings. What actually happens in the distant tene-period (not future) is hardly their concern.

(b) The Spirit World in the New Testament

In His ministry, Jesus makes constant encounters with unseen powers in form of 'the devil' (Mt. 4: 1, 5, par.), 'demons' (Mt. 9: 33, Mk. 1: 34, etc.), 'evil' or 'unclean spirits' (Mk. 1: 23, 27; 3: 11, etc.). Every writer of the New Testament makes some reference to one or more of these spirit powers.

One current theory about their origin asserted that they were 'the offspring of fallen angels . . .'[1] (cf. II En. 18: 3–5, Jub. 5: 2, II Pet. 2: 4, Justin Apol. 5).[2] In Rabbinic literature it was also held that they were the offspring of Satan and Eve, and that their numbers were countless.[3] A 'prince', known by several names,[4] ruled over them. They possessed a 'spiritual' substance (I En. 15: 9, cf. Eph. 6: 12) and human passions (Tob. 3: 8; 8: 3), and could beget children.

From the Temptation to the Cross, Jesus is fighting against these powers of evil, Satan being the arch-enemy of the Gospel (Mt. 4:1–11 pars.; 16: 23 par., etc.). His healing of diseases and other infirmities, His casting out of the demons, and even His raising of the dead, are acts which constitute the eschatological overthrow of evil powers by the Messiah (Mk. 1: 23 ff.; 3: 10 f.; 5: 1 ff.; 9: 25, Lk. 13: 11–13, 16, etc.). These powers are, apparently, considered to be the cause of physical disorders of individuals (Mt. 17: 15 ff., Lk. 13: 16, cf. I En. 15: 11), as well as moral and spiritual sickness of the people (Mt. 12: 27, 39; 13: 38 f., Mk. 3: 23–7, Lk. 22: 53, Jn. 8: 44 ff.).[5] But throughout the Synoptic Gospels, the power of Jesus stands supreme

---

[1] T. W. Manson, *A Companion to the Bible* (1939), 341; G. B. Caird, *Principalities and Powers* (1956), 67.

[2] Cf. I En. 6–8; 15: 8, that the Nephilim (Gen. 6: 2 ff.) became 'evil spirits'.

[3] One Rabbi gives their numbers as seven and a half million, so notes Manson, op. cit., 343.

[4] The names include: Mastema (Zad. Work 20: 2), Satan (or Accuser, Job 1: 6 ff.; 2: 2 ff., Zech. 3: 1, Mk. 4: 15, Lk. 13: 16, I Cor. 7: 5, etc.), Sammael (II Bar. 4: 9, Mart. Is. 2: 1), the Angel of Death (Jer. Targum of Gen. 3: 6), Azazel (Lev. 16: 1–28, I En. 6; 8; 10), Beliar or Belial (II Sam. 22: 5, II Cor. 6: 15), Beelzebub (Mk. 3: 22–6 pars.), the Author of all Evil (Test. Sim. 5: 3, II Cor. 6: 14 f.), etc.

[5] T. Ling, *The Significance of Satan* (1961), 31, rightly notes that whereas there is no exorcism in the Fourth Gospel, the author does not deny the existence of demons.

above that of the unseen beings (Mk. 1: 27; 9: 25, etc.). Indeed, as M. Dibelius observes in *Die Geisterwelt im Glauben des Paulus* (1909), this authority of Jesus Christ over the demonic and other opponents of God pervades the whole of Paul's exposition of the meaning of the Cross.

The casting out of demons in the Synoptic Gospels shows that the eschatological hour has arrived, and the Kingdom of God has come (Mt. 12: 28 par.). The disciples are empowered to overthrow the demons in Christ's Name (Lk. 10: 17 ff., (Mk. 16: 17)).[1] This warfare is directed against Satan (or the devil, the evil one, the enemy, 'the strong man') and his work in the world (Mt. 4: 1–11 pars.; 13: 24–30, Mk. 3: 23 ff. pars., Jn. 12: 31; 16: 11, etc.). Christ's victory over him is realized already in His life (cf. Jn. 16: 11, Lk. 10: 18). Satan occupies a leading position in the New Testament demonology[2] and, therefore, to bind the 'strong man' first makes it possible for his house to be entered and his goods plundered (Mt. 12: 28 f. pars.). This is precisely what Jesus does in His ministry, and most effectively upon the Cross.

This great victory is repeatedly acknowledged in the life and teaching the expanding Church. The 'unclean spirits' come out of those who are possessed, when the Gospel is preached in Samaria (Acts 8: 7). Likewise Paul exorcises the 'spirit of divination' in the slave girl at Philippi (Acts 16: 16 ff.). At Ephesus, 'evil spirits' come out of people when handkerchiefs or aprons from Paul are taken to them (Acts 19: 11 f.), and in the same city the seven sons of Sceva attempt to exorcise evil spirits in the name of Jesus (19: 13 ff.). Paul warns the Church in Corinth very sternly to discern between 'the cup of the

---

[1] E. Langton, *Essentials of Demonology* (1949), points out that the current methods of banning evil spirits were: the use of amulets or charms and fetishes worn or placed on the arch of the doorway, the use of scriptural passages and Aaronic blessing (Num. 6: 22 ff.), the repetition of the Shema, or simply dropping off the syllables from the demon's name. One such example of dropping off the syllables, went like this: 'Thou N son of N, thy mother has warned thee, and said, "Guard thyself from Shabriri, Briri, Iri, Ri. I am thirsty in a white cup" ' (p. 23, the example is quoted from T. B. Abodah Zarah 12b).

[2] The subject of demonology has not received very much attention among N.T. scholars this century, but some of the outstanding works include: M. Dibelius, *Die Geisterwelt im Glauben des Paulus* (1909); B. Noack, *Satanas und Soteria* (1948); E. Langton, *Essentials of Demonology* (1949); S. Eitrem, *Some Notes on the Demonology of the New Testament* (1950); H. Thielicke, *Zwischen Gott und Satan* (1955); G. B. Caird, *Principalities and Powers* (1956); T. Ling, *The Significance of Satan* (1961).

Lord and the cup of the demons' and between 'the table of the Lord and the table of demons' (I Cor. 10: 21). Writing to the Ephesians, he tells the Christians that 'we are not contending against flesh and blood, but against the principalities, against the powers, against the world rulers of this present darkness, against the spiritual hosts of wickedness in the heavenly places,' (6: 12).

More than any other writer of the New Testament, it is Paul who repeatedly speaks about spirit beings of a wide variety. These include: Principalities (ἀρχαί, Eph. 6: 12, Col. 1: 16; 2: 15),[1] Rulers (ἄρχοντες, I Cor. 2: 6, 8, Eph. 2: 2), Powers (δυνάμεις, Rom. 8: 38, also I Pet. 3: 22),[2] Authorities (ἐξουσίαι, Eph. 3: 10, Col. 1: 16; 2: 15),[3] and Elemental spirits (στοιχεῖα, Gal. 4: 3, 9, Col. 2: 8, 20),[4] besides demons (I Cor. 10: 20 f.) and Satan (Rom. 16: 20, I Cor. 5: 5, II Cor. 11: 14). Most of these terms are used to mean both spirit beings and human authorities, rulers and principalities.

James asks his readers to 'resist the devil and he will flee from you' (4: 7b). A similar warning is given in I Peter 5: 8 f.: 'Your adversary the devil prowls around like a roaring lion . . . Resist him . . .'. In the same epistle the author says that Christ preached 'to the spirits in prison', and is exalted 'at the right hand of God, with angels, authorities, and powers subject to Him' (3: 19, 22). In II Peter and Jude we hear of fallen angels who were banished to the nether gloom.

Angels are among the innumerable beings of the spirit world, and mention of them is made in almost every book of the N.T., and especially in Revelation. They also play an important role in Jewish apocalyptic and extra-canonical literature. There is no need for us to go into the vast study of either angelology or demonology here, and

[1] 'Principalities' (ἀρχαί) are also considered to be 'angelic and demonic powers', Bauer's *Gk.-Eng. Lex.*, p. 112; and likewise in the *TWzNT*, Vol. I, pp. 481 ff. (article by G. Delling). Cf. Dibelius, op. cit., 99 ff., stressing that all these spirits will be subjected by Christ.

[2] Bauer, op. cit., p. 207, considers δυνάμεις to mean also personal supernatural spirits. Cf. W. Grundmann, in the *TWzNT*, Vol. II, pp. 308 f., pointing out that these demonic powers take on a new character when viewed from Christ's position.

[3] One of the meanings of ἐξουσίαι as beings of the spirit world is acknowledged by Bauer, op. cit., 278; and by W. Foerster in the *TWzNT*, Vol. II, pp. 564 f., 568 ff.; and by O. Cullmann in *The State in the New Testament* (1957), 95–114, *et passim*. Dibelius, op. cit., 99 f., pointed this out, but (according to Cullmann, *supra*) he later rejected the idea (after 1936).

[4] The word στοιχεῖα has given rise to much discussion. See, for example, C. F. D. Moule, *Colossians and Philemon* (1957), 91 f.; Bauer, op. cit., 776; Dibelius, op. cit., 227–30, *et passim*.

our attention must be focused on that aspect of the N.T. which is more relevant to our problem.

The prime N.T. emphasis on 'the nearness of the spirit world' is in the encounter between the Reign of God and the heart of Man. It is significant that the N.T. is silent on the spirits of the departed, apart from those who are in Christ. The Incarnation brings the spirit world into the physical, so that the person who becomes *in Christ* is enabled to live simultaneously in both worlds. He appropriates 'the powers of the age to come' (Heb. 6: 5) as he awaits the final revelation (Rom. 8: 19, II Thes. 1: 7, I Pet. 1: 13). This is totally different from the sheer fact of survival after death, which we encountered in Akamba ideas of the hereafter. The experience of the Christian produces in him an active hope of participating in eternal life, a hope resting not upon the impersonal rhythm of Nature, but upon God and what He has revealed through Jesus Christ. This is the anchor of present life and the light which radically illumines the meaning and hope of the future life.

For those who are *in Christ*, the gateway into the spirit world is no longer natural death, but the sacramental dying with Christ, at Baptism. The individual is thereby raised into a new existence and, as Taylor points out, he becomes 'so "sure of God", that he can also feel assured that he will himself "survive".'[1] As such, passive survival gives way to an active participation in the hope and substance of what will be hereafter. God, rather than survival itself, becomes the Object of this great hope. While on this side of life the soul grows by feeding upon 'the living bread which came down from heaven' (Jn. 6: 51). So Baillie reminds us that 'God must be sought and loved for His own sake, not merely as a Purveyor either of moral power or of endless life.'[2] Yet God does not exist for the sake of man. But since the Christian is living in the 'End Time', his goal is already a present experience, with the Holy Spirit as Witness (II Cor. 1: 22; 5: 5, Rom. 8: 16, cf. Heb. 10: 15).

This experience of sacramental death, resurrection, and growth of the individual, brings him into close intimacy with God. The Shekinah of God is beamed upon the individual, awakening him not only to God's existence but to his own being. He stands out as he is; he sees

---

[1] A. E., Taylor, *The Christian Hope of Immortality* (1938), 12.

[2] J. Baillie, *And the Life Everlasting* (1934), 159 f.; cf. Taylor, op. cit., 103; and the opening words of the Westminster (Shorter) Catechism: 'Man's chief end is to glorify God, and to enjoy Him for ever.'

Jesus Christ and in Him what he himself will be. The self is activated and pointed towards God first, then to IT-self, and to the world of which it is an integral part. The person is thereby reclaimed from being the property of death and the subject of passive survival, to being the precious possession of Jesus Christ, and one of God's own people (cf. I Pet. 2: 9 f., Heb. 10: 21, Eph. 2: 11 ff.).

It is only because of the Death and Resurrection of Jesus Christ, thereby tasting death for every one (Heb. 2: 9), that we can penetrate into the N.T. spirit world. The author of Hebrews urges believers to 'draw near with a true heart in full assurance of faith' (10: 22); and likewise James pleads with his readers to 'draw near to God and He will draw near to you' (4: 8). As Von Hügel rightly argues, Time is no longer a barrier between present life and the Age to Come, but instead it is 'the very stuff and means in and by which we vitally experience and apprehend that Life.'[1] But naturally, by being still in the Time rhythm, this experience is an incomplete process while we wait 'until the day dawns and the morning star rises' (II Pet. 1: 19, cf. Heb. 10: 25) and until the perfect arrives (I Cor. 13: 10).

To be incorporated into Christ is a paradoxical experience. It is to lose oneself as a physical entity and to find it anew as a spiritual entity, but with the imperishable 'Imago Dei' (cf. Mt. 10: 39 pars., Jn. 3: 16). This is the work of the Great Shepherd, viz., 'to seek and save what is lost' (Lk. 19: 10, *NEB*), even at the great cost of laying down His life for the sheep (Jn. 10: 11, 15). In His Resurrection the sheep can now 'go in and out and find pasture' (Jn. 10: 9), and He must seek even the one sheep which is still lost (Lk. 15: 3–7).

In this understanding of the true nature of the spirit world in the New Testament, the Eternal God on the one hand, and the true individuality of Man on the other, confront each other. It is in this relationship that for Man eternal life finds expression in the fellowship between him and God, between the recipient and the Giver. Without this fellowship, the whole essence of the Gospel hope would be reduced to a barren survival, a monotonous existence which lacks inspiration and meaning. But since this is an eschatological reality, the fellowship of which we may experience here and now, it fills us with the prospects of full appropriation in another dimension of Time and of existence. This is the warming effect which came upon Paul so that he could write: 'My desire is to depart and to be with Christ, for that is far better' (Phil. 1: 23).

[1] Baron F. Von Hügel, *Eternal Life* (1912), 386.

Christian fellowship operates on four planes: Communion with God, with one another on earth, with the departed saints and the heavenly company, and in Holy Things. The full scale of this multi-dimensional ocean of fellowship was inaugurated by the Incarnation of Jesus Christ and the coming of the Holy Spirit. As George observes, in the use of the phrase 'our Father', 'Jesus gave men a sense of kinship with God, and within this family relationship communion was more rich and intimate than the children of Israel had ever conceived to be possible.'[1] This communion is vertical and God-ward, horizontal and Man-ward, if this imagery of direction still has meaning in our scientific world.

We need not dwell at length upon the question of communion except to make brief observations. The profound intimacy, warmth of trust and confidence, combined with filial obedience to the Divine will, as exhibited in the life of Jesus Christ, form the pattern for our Christian communion with God. It is in this life that we see glimpses of the meaning of Communion with God, and hence the nature of the spirit world at its best, but it is not a pattern in a legalistic sense; it is made possible and available for the saint through his incorporation into the Body of Christ. The Father-Son relationship, as shown to the world in the life and teaching of Jesus, becomes the experience of the saint as he participates in 'the divine nature' (II Pet. 1: 4). It is the new vision which enables the saint to stare at the things eternal. As Kirk writes, this 'unbroken personal intercourse with the divine is the end for which man was created . . .'.[2] So now, he who is 'in Christ' has literally and absolutely *seen* the Father (Jn. 14: 9); to him is revealed what the wise and prudent may not see (Mt. 11: 25); and he beholds and hears what the O.T. saints had longed to see and hear (Mt. 13: 16 f. par., cf. I Pet. 1: 10 ff.). In Christ he is introduced to the mysteries of the Kingdom (Lk. 8: 10). The invisible God is openly portrayed in Jesus Christ (Jn. 1: 14; 14: 9, II Cor. 4: 6, Heb. 1: 3), and the spirit world thus breaks into the physical in a historical reality. But it would be absolute naïvety to imagine that this spirit world is exhausted by man who still is subject to the limits of Time. It is no more and no less than an eschatological preview of the spirit world.

---

[1] A. R. George, *Communion with God in the New Testament* (1953), 237. Cf. the discussion centred on *Abba*, to which we made reference in the previous chapter.
[2] K. E. Kirk, *The Vision of God* (2nd ed., 1932), 108.

The 'portrait' of fatherly love brought into our historical situation by Jesus Christ is illustrated in the infinite care, concern, and interest which God exercises over all His works. He clothes the lilies and grass (Mt. 6: 28 ff. par.), watches over the falling birds (Mt. 6: 26 par.), makes His sun to shine and rain to fall upon all (Mt. 5: 45); He responds to those who ask, seek or knock (Mt. 7: 7 f.), and welcomes the prodigal son (Lk. 15: 20 ff.). This is the Father with whom the saint has fellowship. He is called to 'live the Christian life in the setting of a fellowship, the fellowship of the new Israel, of which Christ was the Head, but from which in His lonely human life He could derive no fellowship,' as George tells us.[1]

Communion with God is expressed by Paul in terms of being 'in Christ'. George points out that it is not simply a 'unio-mysticism' in which the person is lost in the Divine, but an 'I-THOU' fellowship.[2] The Sacraments are the external expression of its reality (cf. Rom. 6: 3 ff., I Cor. 10: 16), which is centred upon Jesus Christ through whom the saints have full access to the Father (Eph. 2: 18, cf. Heb. 7: 25; 10: 19 ff., Rom. 5: 2).

In Johannine literature, the concept of 'abiding in' summarizes the idea of communion with God. The Father–Son relationship of mutual indwelling (Jn. 14: 10; 17: 21) is handed on to the believer (Jn. 15: 4–7; 6: 56, I Jn. 4: 13, 15, 16). God has been revealed in such an absolute and intense reality, that our physical senses have made material contact with the invisible and eternal God (Jn. 1: 14; 14: 7, 9; I Jn. 1: 1–3). The spirit world has therefore come so near that we can actually see God through seeing Jesus Christ. And consequently, our communion with God is so rich that 'the next life is conceived as a continuation of' the present, and Johannine writings 'are thus the climax of the New Testament teaching on this theme.'[3] Again Jesus Christ is the way to that fellowship (Jn. 14: 6; 10: 7, cf. 6: 35).

Communion with fellow Christians derives from communion with God (cf. I Jn. 1: 3). He who is *in Christ* finds not only his own real personality, but that of others who are similarly *in Christ*. In every sense he becomes a member of the Body of Christ, of which

---

[1] George, op. cit., 121.

[2] Cf. George, op. cit., 191 ff.; and an existential approach to the Man–God relationship in M. Buber's *I and Thou* (ET 1937). I would go further than George, and say that the relationship is so intimate that the individual is virtually 'dissolved' in God's own existence. See further discussion in the next chapter.

[3] George, op. cit., 214, 220.

Paul speaks so much. As Taylor tells us, the saint is one 'of a society of persons who see God, themselves and each other as all truly are.'[1] In that intimate society the spokes of fellowship are Christocentric, and the rim that binds them together is Jesus Christ Himself (cf. Eph. 4: 15 f., Col. 2: 19, I Cor. 10: 16 f.).

Since our communion with God and with one another is grounded on Jesus Christ, it follows that death can neither dissolve it nor weaken it. The powers of death have been disarmed by Christ through His Death-and-Resurrection event. Therefore, death cannot eclipse the relationship between members of the Body of Christ who have departed and those who survive. This is where we may properly speak of the *Communion of Saints*, and where fellowship between the living and departed Christians may rightly be encouraged and cultivated.

It is commonly accepted that the phrase *Sanctorum Communio* is a later insertion into the Apostles' Creed, and its notorious obscurity has given rise to many interpretations throughout the history of the Church.[2] Thus, for example, after a detailed and mainly linguistic discussion of the origin and meaning of the phrase, Badcock comes to the conclusion that ἡ κοινωνία τῶν ἁγίων 'cannot mean communion with the saints; it might mean either that communion which the saints enjoy, the genitive being a possessive genitive, or communion in the holy things; and . . . in all probability it would be the latter.'[3] But in tracing the historical interpretation of this phrase, Kelly comes to the contrary conclusion, namely that it stands 'for that ultimate fellowship with the holy persons of all ages, as well as with the whole company of heaven, which is anticipated and partly realized in the fellowship of the Catholic Church on earth'. Even after considering all the various interpretations, Kelly adds that 'the inescapable conclusion to which it points is that, so far as the creed is concerned, the dominant conception, at any rate between the fifth and eighth centuries, was "fellowship with holy persons". The

[1] Taylor, op. cit., 80 f.

[2] F. J. Badcock, 'Sanctorum Communio as an Article in the Creed', *JTS*, Vol. XXI (1919–20), p. 107, says that the article first appears in the Creed of St. Jerome, *c.* A.D. 378, being introduced into Christian circles not later than A.D. 350, and having arisen in a Greek-speaking country (p. 116). On the other hand, J. N. D. Kelly, *Early Christian Creeds* (1950), argues that the article originated most probably in Gaul, and was, therefore, not Greek in origin (pp. 389 f., 395).

[3] Badcock, op. cit., 121; see also his book, *The History of the Creeds* (2nd ed., 1938).

sacramental exegesis came later in time, and has all the air of being secondary'.[1]

Badcock's conclusion on linguistic basis is legitimate, but Kelly's seems to carry greater weight. We should look at the question of the communion between the living and departed saints (believers) in the light of the Scriptures, in addition to the historical and linguistic interpretations of *Sanctorum Communio*. It is remarkable, however, that the New Testament is largely silent on the issue, except perhaps Heb. 12: 22 ff., to which we shall return later. We have asserted that the centre of Christian communion is Jesus Christ, for both those who are on this side of life and those who have departed. As such, He forms the bridge and the common denominator of fellowship between the Church Triumphant with 'all the company of Heaven' and the Church Militant. Those who have died *in Christ* are still *in Him* though now they are in the state of being *with Christ* (Phil. 1: 23), but in a fuller experience than the sense in which Christ is with us until the consummation of the age (Mt. 28: 20). Their fellowship with Him and with one another derives from Him, just as our fellowship derives its origin, essence, and meaning from Him. Their experience of that fellowship after death may well be different from anything that we know in this life, but as far as our earthly experience is concerned, they share with us the common life of being *in Christ*. This is something that death cannot paralyse. Are we to suppose then that they have no interest in the Church on earth, that part of the one Body of Christ and of which they are members just as we are? Again the Scriptures seem silent, but with fear and trembling we might assert that in Him the 'Communion of Saints' cannot be dismissed. Beyond this assertion we dare not venture. But at least the great cloud of witnesses (Heb. 12: 1) cannot have perfect, complete or entire communion with the Lord without including us in that umbrella of communion. Death is only their 'apogee' in relation to the Church Militant, but it is their 'perigee' in relation to one another and to the angelic society (Heb. 12: 22 ff.).

But whereas death does not sever communion between the saints and the Lord, 'earthly relationships do not appear to be translated into Heaven', as Simon rightly observes.[2] The Genesis idea of death as a means of being gathered to one's people (25: 8; 35: 29; 49: 33)

---

[1] Kelly, op. cit., 391, 393 f.
[2] U. Simon, *Heaven in the Christian Tradition* (1958), 219.

is disregarded. Even the institution of marriage has no place in the Age to Come (Lk. 20: 35 pars.). Does it mean, therefore, that relations of parent-and-child, wife-and-husband, brother-and-sister, or rich-and-poor, are all abolished, as each saint inherits the full fellowship with God and with one another in Christ Jesus? So also physical property as we know and have it on earth is of no avail in Heaven (I Tim. 6: 7, cf. Job 1: 21, Lk. 12: 16 ff.). Only that which is planted in Christ, the relationship which begins here and now, between the saint and the Lord, is capable of surviving the cruelty and harshness of death, and the harshness of Time, presumably. This is the relationship which transcends the bonds of blood, sex and friendship (Gal. 3: 26 ff.), 'for you have one Teacher, and you are all brethren' of one Father (Mt. 23: 8 ff., cf. Eph. 4: 4). Earthly ties are destroyed by being dissolved and superseded in the more intimate relationship 'in Christ' in which the scope of brothers, sisters, etc., is deepened, heightened and broadened (cf. Mt. 10: 29 f.). For the individual, the nearness of the spirit world means that he is begotten into a vast spiritual community (cf. Eph. 2: 19 ff., I Pet. 2: 9 f.) founded not upon natural kinship but upon the will of God (Jn. 1: 12 f., cf. Mk. 3: 31–5 pars.). It even involves solemn farewells (Acts 20: 38, II Cor. 13: 11, I Thes. 4: 13, cf. II Tim. 4: 6 f., I Cor. 15: 29) on this side of life, without a hint about meeting one another across the barrier of death. Only Christ is seen after death (Jn. 20: 25, etc.) and, as the saint follows Him (Jn. 13: 36), he finds the existence of other saints, but only within the framework of being 'in Christ'.

The Corinthian practice of baptizing people 'on behalf of the dead' (I Cor. 15: 29) may perhaps be an indication that the believers were concerned about the welfare of their departed relatives and friends. If that was so, it poses the difficult problem whether surviving saints can exert some influence upon the departed, be they Christian or otherwise. The silence of the N.T. on the issue neither forbids nor enjoins communication between the saints on both sides of life, if it is done 'in Christ'. The rise and development of Christian diptychs show an attempt to meet a genuine concern in this direction.

The first mention of prayer for departed Christians appears in Cyprian's (Carthage) first epistle, about A.D. 240; and the practice seems to have spread widely by Augustine's time.[1] As Dix points

---

[1] Dom G. Dix, *The Shape of the Liturgy* (1943), 498 f.; Augustine, *De Civitate Dei*, XXII.10, Serm. CLIX, etc.

11

out, these diptychs illustrate 'the vividness of belief in the communion of saints and the unity in Christ of all Christians living and
dead.' They made their appearance in many liturgies.[1] But from
about A.D. 600 onwards, they also began to be abused, to the extent
that at their public recital 'the inclusion or exclusion of a name
was held to be a sign of communion or of excommunion.'[2]

The fourth plane on which Christian fellowship operates is in
Holy Things. We have seen that one of the possible interpretations
of *Sanctorum Communio* is 'communion in holy things', that is, the
Sacraments. There is ample evidence that this article of the Creeds
has been given sacramental interpretation by a number of theologians
from the fourth century through the middle ages, up to modern
times. But this does not contradict the stronger and earlier interpretation of fellowship among living and departed saints, of which we
spoke earlier. These two interpretations do in fact complement each
other, and one does not necessarily exclude the other. But apart
from this difficult phrase in the Creeds, as we saw in the previous
chapter, at the Sacraments the whole Church experiences the most
intimate form of fellowship. At Baptism, the new member enters
into the circle of that fellowship, and his experience of the fellowship
is renewed and heightened at the Eucharist. The Sacraments are not
only the glass through which we can dimly peep into the spirit
world, but they are also the points of contact betweeen the two
worlds. It is in the Sacraments that the Christian is most literally made
part of Christ's Body. Here the saint is carried proleptically into
the spirit world, into the mode of resurrection life given at Baptism,
and into the mysteries of eating the Flesh and drinking the Blood of
Jesus Christ (Jn. 6: 56). This is a form of communion *par excellence*
(I Cor. 10: 16). It is at the communion in Holy Things that all the
aspects of communion are summed up and experienced in one act.
Here, the faithful are immersed in fellowship with God, with one
another on earth, with the departed saints and the heavenly society.
For those who are on this side of life, communion in Holy Things is

---

[1] These liturgies included: the Liturgy of St. James (in which the diptychs
came after the consecration), the Liturgy of St. Mark in Egypt (coming in course
of the eucharistic prayer), the Alexandrian Rite (coming after the opening of the
eucharistic prayer), the Eastern Syrian Rite (coming at the offertory prayer,
with a list which included O.T. and N.T. saints, etc.), according to Dix, op. cit.,
505 f.

[2] F. L. Cross, ed., *The Oxford Dictionary of the Christian Church* (1957), 404.

in anticipation and hope, but for those who have departed it is in waiting till all should be incorporated and made perfect in Christ.

(c) The Teaching of the Africa Inland Mission Concerning the Spirit World

We have seen that the spirit world forms an integral part of Akamba ontology. It presses hard upon the physical, and the people are keenly aware of its nearness. We have also seen how, in a different context, the New Testament looks at the spirit world. We need now to examine how Christian teaching in Ukambani has handled this problem.

The teaching of the A.I.M. concerning the spirit world of the Akamba is very brief. It is contained in an addendum to the catechumen booklet, as follows:

VII: What are some of the things of past life which should be removed from one's life? . . .

8. The spirits of the dead. Lk. 16: 19–31.

(a) Can the spirits of our dead ones come to afflict us? No. The rich man came to know that there was no way of going back to the earth so that he could warn his own people (family), and Lazarus was not allowed to do that either. The spirits of people who died unsaved cannot leave their (place of) punishment. Lk. 16: 26.

(b) How are people deceived concerning the spirits of the dead? Satan has a large host of demons or evil spirits which imitate the spirits of the dead and speak like them, and do unusual things, and thereby deceive people. I Tim. 4: 1.

(c) Can evil spirits foretell what will happen? No; they can guesss, and often they might guess correctly, but they don't know.

There is also a short section on divination (*kwausya*) which is relevant for our discussion here:

7. Concerning divination. Deut. 18: 10, 11.

(a) God commanded that witches be destroyed. Ex. 22: 18.

(b) Magic (Sorcery) is of the flesh. Gal. 5: 20.

(c) To consult witches or evil spirits for divination purposes shows that a person's faith in Christ is incomplete.

(d) Many people die because of being treated by medicine-men (*awe*).

(e) The lot of all sorcerers is in the lake of fire. Rev. 21: 8.[1]

---

[1] The Kikamba Catechism (n.d.), 34–6. This section is omitted in the revised Swahili–English version (n.d., 1962?).

A few comments on this teaching will suffice. It is unfortunate that Lk. 16: 19–31 should be the proof text in the argument against the traditional communication between the living-dead and their surviving relatives. The passage is concerned primarily with unbelief and lack of response shown by the Jews even when God's Kingdom had appeared, whatever other interpretations we might give to it. Furthermore, the Akamba know of no place of punishment for the living-dead, as alluded to in the last sentence of 8 (a).

Demons are unknown in Ukambani, and the use of *ndaimoni* in the Kikamba Bible implies that these are beings other than what Akamba call *Aimu*. This conveys the idea that one may communicate with the Aimu but not with the demons (*ndaimoni*). To speak of the departed as 'spirits' (*maveva*) has no meaning to the people, since the Kikamba word, *maveva*, simply means 'big breaths', and the departed are never known by such a term. The use of words and phrases like: 'demons, spirits, spirits of the dead, evil spirits, Satan', all in one short section, must necessarily cause confusion to a people who are not familiar with such vocabulary. The Kikamba word, *Aimu*, is not used even once; and *ndaimoni* is simply the Greek-English word transcribed into Kikamba.

Surely Dives wants his brothers to be 'helped' and not 'afflicted' (Lk. 16: 28) by someone returning to them from the dead. He does not say that he himself wants to return to his brothers. The A.I.M. approach is on the assumption that the spirits of the departed (as the living-dead) return to 'afflict' the Akamba. But this is not the case, for in most cases they are friendly, and they depend on their human families to keep them in remembrance. It is also another false assumption to say that they 'foretell' the future. As we saw in Chapter II, the future plays no significant part in Akamba life. When it is necessary to know something in the future, the people go to diviners and not to the spirits of the dead.

The section on divination shows some confusion between divination and sorcery. These two arts are not practised by the same people in Ukambani. If we were to apply Ex. 22: 18, practically every woman in the country would be killed! The argument that 'many people die *because of* being treated by medicine-men' strikes a Mukamba as being nothing but nonsensical and absurd, and would never stop him from going to consult the medicine-man. Medicine-men have always been and are regarded as the greatest friends of their communities. They help the needy, treat the sick, give advice and help to solve all sorts of problems.

The most fruitful approach to the problem would have to be what the Mission refers to in section 7 (c), i.e. the idea of building 'complete' faith in Jesus Christ. This is positive and constructive, compared to the negative prohibitions laid down in the catechism. It is clearly noticeable that nothing is said here about the New Testament understanding of the subject, apart from bringing in spirits and demons.

(d) Akamba and New Testament Views of the Spirit World

Concerning the relation between the Akamba and New Testament views of the spirit world, the points of divergence are not hard to find. Thus, in the New Testament economy, the spirit world is both theocentric and Christocentric; and through the Sacraments those who are in Christ begin already to live the life of the next world. The experience is so real that physical death is not the first gateway through which a person is ushered into that other world. Sacramental death at Baptism is the doorway into the New Testament world of the spirit. The clearest intimation of the spirit world as given in the N.T. is that for the saint it is a world of communion with God and with the whole society of Heaven. It is this that gives meaning to the Christian view of immortality and the resurrection of the dead. In Jesus Christ the spirit world is brought so close to the physical that the two overlap until what is physical is eschatologically transformed into the spiritual. This is the truth that the Sacraments epitomize and anticipate. Here the Akamba view is blank, and as far as evidence is available other African societies are equally unaware of this New Testament scheme of things. On the other hand, however, the Akamba spirit world is filled with an active society of the living-dead and the spirits, Aimu, which maintains a close link with the human society. Perhaps it is in this direction that we may search for points of fruitful relation between the two views of the spirit world.

We saw that there are two main interpretations of *Sanctorum Communio* in the Apostles' Creed, namely: fellowship between living and departed saints, and fellowship in Holy Things. But we may be allowed to pursue the matter a little further. Our reference to Christian diptychs showed us that the Church of the early centuries did not abandon the problem at that point. Furthermore, the Catacombs in Rome, for example, show Christian affection which went deeper than the grave, as expressed in inscriptions such as 'Vivas in Christo, in Bono . . . Vivas in Christo, dulcis, semper vivas in Deo,' etc.[1]

The N.T. is not altogether silent about this problem. In Heb. 12: 22–4 we approach perhaps the most explicit unveiling of the state of the departed. They are already 'at home' in Mt. Zion and Jerusalem, and in the midst of angelic beings. They form the ecclesiastical community, together with the spirits of other 'just' men. So far the scene runs approximately parallel to Akamba ideas. But the Christian differentia enters in when God as Judge, Jesus Christ as the mediator, and a new covenant, come into the scene and occupy the centre. These transform the stage into a platform of worship and communion. Upon that platform, what in Akamba (or African?) thinking might be termed mechanical 'immortality' of the soul, is converted into a full-scale life of fellowship, unhampered by temporal circumstances, the strain and stress of this life, or by death itself. The saint who stands on that platform is described as being made perfect (v. 23), and a member of a consecrated community ('firstborn'). This is the height to which Jesus Christ elevates those who are *in Christ*, to the glory of the Father Who is 'not God of the dead, but of the living; for all live to Him' (Lk. 20: 38, cf. pars.). Indeed, on this platform stand also those 'other sheep' which are brought into the one flock under one Shepherd (Jn. 10: 16). There congregate likewise the angelic hosts so vividly portrayed in Revelation, offering their constant worship to God and the Lamb. There stand all those whose names are enrolled in Heaven (v. 23, cf. Rev. 3: 5; 13: 8; 17: 8, etc., Phil. 4: 3), i.e. in 'the books of life'.

Here then we can establish a link between Akamba conception of the spirit world and the N.T. view upon which we have focused our discussion. As the Akamba feel themselves surrounded by innumerable 'spirits' (the living-dead and the Aimu), so do the Christians with their great cloud of witnesses (Heb. 12: 1), angels, the Church of the firstborn, and the spirits of just men (12: 22 ff.). But whereas the spirit world of the Akamba is conceived physically and anthropocentrically, the N.T. view is 'spiritual' and Christocentric.

The Akamba share their meals and drinks with the living-dead. This is an act of fellowship, but it is the departed who are replenished

[1] Simon, op. cit., 219.

by the survivors while they give nothing in return on such occasions. The sharing of meals in this manner reveals the Akamba conception of community life, which extends vertically and invisibly to the in-inhabitants of the spirit world, as it also extends horizontally and visibly to those who are still on this side of death. This concept might be linked with the idea that in the Eucharist we declare our corporate existence in the Body of Christ, which includes both the departed and surviving saints.

It may well be that the strong interest which the Akamba (and other African societies) show in the living-dead could be translated into profitable purposes in the Church. For example, should the Christians altogether cease to pray for one another even when death intervenes and separates friend from friend, husband from wife, sister from brother, missionary from convert (cf. Christian diptychs, *supra*)? Is it not likely that the departed saints show active interest in the welfare of the Church on earth and, in ways unknown to us, continue to contribute to the extension of the Kingdom of God in the entire creation? These are conjectural questions, but they are not altogether illegitimate and irrelevant to our study. The act of embracing the Christian Faith need not mean a complete severing of mutual interest between the departed and the survivors. Rather, the final result of the Christian message in a society such as the Akamba is to transpose the tribal spirit world into the Christian one. Akamba life is so deeply rooted in the spirit world that, until Christianity can penetrate that far, it will for a long time remain on the surface, incapable of providing a radical and all-embracing meaning to the total *Weltanschauung* of the people. This applies as well to many African societies, since evidence shows great similarities between their concepts of the spirit world and those of the Akamba.

To the Akamba, the spirit world becomes dangerous if it gets 'too near' or 'too far', and sacrifice or offering must be given to restore the right equilibrium. But to the Christian, the two worlds overlap in Jesus Christ, and the goal is to transform the physical into the spiritual, a process which the Sacraments already epitomize. For the Akamba, death means entry into the period which we termed *TENE*, and the individual 'degenerates' from a living-dead whose name is remembered by the survivors, into an Iimu after three to five generations when his name is forgotten. As far as the mituki period is concerned, the individuality of such a person is blotted out. But the Christian discovers his personality more fully by being incorporated into Christ. Therefore in passing through physical death—an experience he has rehearsed in Baptism—his name is not only retained permanently in the book of life (Phil. 4: 3, Rev. 3: 5, etc.), but in addition he gains a 'new name' full of meaning and having a divine affinity (Rev. 2: 17; 3: 12). He is activated to an existence dominated by relationship with God which is so unique and firm that nothing can either erase or mar it (cf. Rom. 8: 28–39). He becomes immune to any forces of change which otherwise would diminish his being.

Here we land upon the extremely important point about Time. In the Akamba (or African) view as we have analysed it, the eventual destiny of the departed is to be cast into the dimension of tene, the distant past where, viewed anthropocentrically, the departed becomes virtually uncreateable and entirely lost. In this inevitable process, individual destiny is to be entirely removed from the mituki (present) dimension of Time, in effect to be removed from the area of complete intensity of living. The New Testament, however, sees the destiny of man as a concentration and consummation of existence in the mituki period, the present—which means the presence of God. The individual is intensely made to exist, for he is in the presence of God. This intensity of existence ignores or supersedes (I do not know which) the dimensions of Time except the present. It means that both the past and the future, if we consider the three dimensions, are dissolved or assimilated in the present, for it is the presence of God, and therefore completely irreducible. So then, in the New Testament scheme of things, the individual enters the spirit world, there to find more truly his existence, for it is an existence in God, and dependent upon Him. The individual in Christ is not removed (as in the case of African concepts) from the mituki period to either the future or the past: instead he is more deeply involved and rooted in the mituki period, the period of intense existence and being. It is in fact an experience of resurrection, for he is no longer subjected to a deprivation of being or personality which death or Time work upon all. The forces now at work are different: they are the forces of summation and not subtraction, of gathering and not dispersing, of bringing together what otherwise would be scattered by Time's dimensions and the powers of death. This is the very centre of the resurrection life, of re-being, re-existence, intensified and made absolutely final. This is the theme for our next chapter, for it is the final word in New Testament Eschatology.

CHAPTER VI

The Resurrection as Corporate Eschatology

(a) Akamba Ideas of Resurrection

WE saw that, according to Akamba beliefs, death does not immediately annihilate life. Only the process of gradual removal to the tene period eventually disintegrates individuality. The departed continue to live in the spirit world, together with other members of their household, and even domestic animals. As a whole, life beyond death is a copy of what it is in this world. In addition to the belief in the continuation of life, the Akamba believe also that people rise again from the dead. Their notions of resurrection or resuscitation are not highly developed, but they nevertheless colour people's understanding of Christian teaching on the doctrine of the Resurrection.

For the Akamba resurrection is not a future event to which they as a nation or as individuals look forward. It is something which occurs only in the tene period. It is also essentially a corporate and almost private phenomenon, involving households and relatives, as well as domestic animals. These are the two basic features of the traditional ideas about resurrection. God does not bring about this event. Instead, the agent is one or more of the Aimu, spirits, but not one of the living-dead. The living-dead are, on the other hand, the object of this kind of resurrection.

Ideas about resurrection come only from folk stories. Accordingly, when Aimu fight with human beings, nearly all the people in a particular area are killed. Whoever survives manages to kill the Aimu, and the last Iimu to die says to the human survivor(s):

> Cut my little finger,
> Grind it into powder,
> Toss the powder in the air,
> And you'll see all your dead relatives
> Come back to life.[1]

---

[1] In some stories it is the blood of the Iimu, instead of powder made from the little finger (or toes), which is thrown in the air. See stories of this kind in my book, *Akamba Stories* (Oxford, 1966).

When this is done, all the departed relatives, together with their domestic animals, return to life. There is great rejoicing among the people. Those who died having physical blemishes return to life without them, and the young come back as adults (depending on how much time has elapsed since they died). Children born in the spirit world do not, apparently, accompany their families when these return to what is intended to be earthly life. There are no other changes, and the people so restored to life begin to lead a normal way of life until they die once more.

There is also an 'individual resurrection'. This is brought about by an Iimu who deliberately touches the body or bones of a dead person and causes him to come back to life. Other relatives or their animals do not accompany him. If he should die again, the Iimu brings him back to life as many times as he might die. But the person is not completely like ordinary people: he is transformed into an Iimu, and if he tries to return to his human family, the Iimu that restored him to life comes and takes him away to join the company of other Aimu.

There is also another area where notions of resurrection are held by both Akamba and other African peoples. This is in the field of mythology in which, practically all over Africa, we have myths concerning the first men and the coming of death. These have three main strains. In one set of myths, man was originally endowed with the gift of immortality so that he would never die. In another set it is told that man was to rise again even if he did die. The third strain, which is not as widespread in Africa as the first two, tells that the first man received (from God) the gift of rejuvenation, if and when he did become old. There are many accounts of these myths and we need not go into a detailed documentation of them here.[1] They indicate, among other things, that African peoples have, at least in a mythological deposit, notions about human resurrection and rejuvenation. The trouble, however, is that the first men lost this original gift, and African mythology and wisdom for all their richness, have nothing to offer to remedy the situation or repair the loss. African myths look only 'backwards', to the tene period, and therefore all they can offer is an explanation of, but not the remedy for, the loss of immortality, resurrection and rejuvenation. Only by looking 'future-

[1] See, for example, H. Baumann, *Schöpfung und Urzeit des Menschen im Mythus der afrikanischen Völker* (Berlin, 2nd ed., 1964); H. Abrahamsson, *The Origin of Death* (Uppsala, 1951); J. S. Mbiti, *Concepts of God in Africa* (London, 1970).

wards' could they possibly reach at least a mythological remedy. But as we have argued all along, this is simply impossible since Time is traditionally conceived in primarily two dimensions of the *mituki* ('present') and *tene* ('past') periods. Therefore, the death of the individual only removes him towards what in fact has been lost; it cannot offer hope, since there can be no hope in what is lost. This contrasts very strongly with the biblical view that what was lost in Genesis, in the tene period, reappears in the eschatological scheme, placed no longer in the tene period but in an evidently distant future period (if we must use this three-dimensional view of Time). Therefore, with the resurrection (immortality and rejuvenation) placed 'in front' of it, biblical Eschatology *does* offer and provide a living hope. This is entirely absent in African religiosity, however rich and strong it might otherwise be.

At this point, we have to vary our method of approach, and discuss missionary teaching about the Resurrection before we come to the New Testament.

(b) *The Teaching of the Africa Inland Mission*

In Chapter II of our discussion we saw that the teaching of the Africa Inland Mission on Eschatology is exclusively futuristic. We gave a skeleton outline of what the A.I.M. and A.I.C. consider to be the 'Last Things'. One of the items in that teaching is a belief in 'the literal resurrection of the body' and 'the eternal blessedness of the saved, and the eternal punishment of the lost.'[1] On the subject of the Resurrection, the A.I.M. has this to say:

(Item 43): 'What is the Resurrection? The Resurrection is the raising up of the body of a person from the dead. Jn. 11: 44 . . .'
(44) 'Was Jesus Christ raised from the dead? Yes. He was buried and the third day He was raised, I Cor. 15: 4 . . .'
(45): 'What will be done to the bodies of the Christians who have died? They will be raised when Christ comes to receive His Church, and will be changed to become like His glorified body. I Cor. 15: 42 . . .'
(46): 'What will be done to the bodies of those who have died without having believed? They will be raised in order that they might be cast into the lake of fire. Rev. 20: 12–15 . . .'[2]

---

[1] A.I.C. Constitution, 5; the Kikamba Catechism, 20–4. See also the opening pages of Chapter II *supra*.
[2] Kikamba Catechism, 18 f. The wording and Scripture references are slightly altered in the newer Swahili–English version (1962) of the Catechism, pp. 18 and 39, which is not, however, used in Ukambani.

According to this approach there are four kinds of Resurrection: (a) of Lazarus and the like, (b) of our Lord, (c) of Christians, and (d) of unbelievers. The first two are past, and the other two are future. The emphasis is laid on the future, stress being laid that belief in Christ leads on to a blessed resurrection, while unbelief leads on to damnation. But those who believe have no idea what is the meaning of their expected resurrection, nor how or why it will be there. This aspect of the resurrection is defined in the words of Jn. 11: 44, and left at that! The passage quoted in support of item 45 is inappropriate and misinterpreted; obviously other passages would be better, such as I Thes. 4: 16b and Phil. 3: 20.[1] The Resurrection of our Lord is presented as being defined by the raising of Lazarus, and others, and there is no explicit connection made between it and that of the saints. But surely it is our Lord's Resurrection which must define and give meaning to all other types of resurrection. Unless the Resurrection of Jesus is made central it fails to give full meaning to the Christian Faith, and hence that Faith becomes a complete weakling.

Much of the A.I.M. teaching on resurrection is found in the Kikamba hymns. It is primarily futuristic and individualistic in emphasis. A few examples will suffice:

'I'll be caused to sit down by Jesus at His home' (hymn 30);
'Where we shall see those who arrived earlier' (hymn 41);
'The elect dead will be raised that morning
And we who are alive here will be changed' (hymn 61);
'We shall see our people,
Only those who have been saved . . .' (hymn 85);
'Now we shall rise again because of Jesus,
If we believe in Jesus Christ' (hymn 111);
'And when the journey is over we shall forget the troubles
And I shall see Him always, yea, and will always rest' (hymn 166);
'And when this night is over, my Lord,
Thou wilt take me to come to Heaven Thy home' (hymn 178).

This teaching is not always consistent. According to some of the hymns, the believer hopes to find himself in Heaven if he dies before the Parousia (Nos. 30, 55, 78, 85, 107, 178, chorus 21); and he expects to meet fellow friends and relatives who died as believers (Nos. 41,

---

[1] The Swahili–English Catechism includes, for this item, the following references: Phil. 3: 20, 21, I Cor. 15: 51, 52 and I Thes. 4: 16 in the Swahili section (p. 18), and Phil. 3: 20, 21, I Cor. 15: 51, and Rom. 8: 17, 18 in the English section (p. 39).

85). In other hymns, the believer who dies before the Parousia must wait for his resurrection (Nos. 61, 111); and in some it is said that he is raised (resurrected) immediately after death and made to appear before the Lord (Nos. 78, 85, 107, 193, 206), or to inhabit his 'house' (chorus 21) and rest (No. 166).

This teaching causes some confusion and, as we shall see, omits many important elements of the Resurrection according to the New Testament. For example, some of the hymns mention Christ's Death on the Cross for our sins, but they leave Him there dying or dead, and His Resurrection is not mentioned at all. Such Death is insufficient and ineffective for our redemption unless it is followed by the Resurrection. Indeed, much of the religious art in and from western Church tradition gives the impression that Jesus simply ended His ministry upon the Cross. But a dead Christ cannot be an efficient pioneer of a dynamic Faith. Men who are dead in sin do not need the picture of a dead Christ. They need one of the Christ who died-and-rose again. Only such a Saviour can inspire faith in this life, and hope in the life to come. Only such a Christus Victor can uphold and sustain life in the Resurrection mode of existence. This is the true portrait of Jesus Christ in the New Testament, and it is along these lines that we shall approach and seek to understand the Resurrection.

(c) *The Resurrection of Jesus Christ*

This is the most decisive issue in the Christian Faith, and without it the Faith, the Church, and the New Testament would be non-existent. Quite rightly there is more literature on this than on any other topic of New Testament Eschatology. It is the focal point for Christianity and the very kernel of the Kerygma. Good Friday is flooded with meaning only in the light of Easter Sunday, and the event whose termini are these two days is a unity containing the one Salvation phenomenon.

In His ministry, Jesus speaks repeatedly about His Death and Resurrection: Jn. 2: 19, Mk. 8: 31 pars.; 9: 31 pars.; 10: 34 pars., Mt. 26: 2.[1] At the Last Supper, there is a disturbing approach to the climax, as Jesus assures His disciples of His return to them in spite of the imminent death, Jn. 14: 18 f.; 16: 16. Accordingly, when He rises

[1] Lk. 9: 44, omits mention of Jesus being killed and raised the third day; and no reference is made to the Resurrection in Mt. 26: 2.

again He manifests Himself to the disciples, and the Church is visibly born.

If death drives Him in bitter humiliation to the lowest stage of creation (Eph. 4: 9, Phil. 2: 8),[1] the Resurrection elevates Him. It is through His Resurrection that He is 'highly exalted' (Phil. 2: 9), and granted Lordship (Phil. 2: 11) and honour on the right hand of God (Acts 2: 33; 5: 31; 7: 55 f.; 8: 34, Eph. 1: 20, Col. 3: 1, cf. Heb. 1: 3; 8: 1; 10: 12, I Pet. 3: 22). A new beginning comes into effect, grounded on this historical apex but immediately acquiring cosmic dimensions.

So the risen Lord confronts the world anew. He breathes upon the disheartened disciples (Jn. 20: 22), giving them the ἀρραβών (II Cor. 1: 22; 5: 5, Eph. 1: 14) of the new creation and new life.[2] His Resurrection stands as the dividing line between the death-working principle of the first man, Adam, and the life-giving principle of the eschatological Man, Christ (I Cor. 15: 45; Rom. 5: 12, 18). Only the power of this Resurrection could have transformed His cowardly and downhearted followers into a dynamic and mighty eschatological community after the experience at Pentecost. They are now able and have the right to live in the eschatological era inaugurated by His Resurrection.

The Church was then constructed upon the basis of the Resurrection, which became also the content of the Message she was committed to tell to the world. It was the cardinal tradition (παράδοσις) (I Cor. 15: 3 f., cf. II Thes. 2: 15; 3: 6) of the New Age replacing the archaic traditions of Jewish patriarchs (Gal. 1: 14). This was the whole truth of the Gospel (cf. Acts 26: 25, 19) by which men must either stand or stumble (cf. Acts 17: 3 f., I Cor. 1: 18 ff.).

[1] In Eph. 4: 9, some MSS omit μέρη (p46, D, G. etc.), while others add πρῶτον (B, Tex. Rec., etc.).

[2] Like everybody else I am aware of the difficulties of the Resurrection of Jesus, and some of the problems presented in the accounts of this event. I do not wish to indulge in what has almost become an exhausted field of research, comment and conjecture. Although there is great value in discussing the meaning and interpretation of the Resurrection of Jesus for us today, obviously this is not one's intention here.

See, among many others: H. Waldenfels, 'Ostern und wir Christen heute', in *Geist und Leben* (Munich), Vol. 40, No. 1 (1967), pp. 22–43; S. H. Hooke, *The Resurrection of Christ as History and Experience* (1967); W. Künneth, *The Theology of the Resurrection* (ET 1966); J. McLeman, *Resurrection Then and Now* (1965); I. T. Ramsey, and others, *The Miracles and the Resurrection: Some Recent Studies* (1964); C. F. D. Moule, ed., *The Significance of the Message of the Resurrection for Faith in Jesus* (1968), and a host of monographs and articles.

The early Church rightly celebrated Easter as 'the Queen of Days and the Festival of Festivals.'

As Dodd points out in *Apostolic Preaching*, the Resurrection of Jesus is central to 'the Common Gospel', both in the Jerusalem and the Greek Church. The fundamentals of the Gospel tradition current shortly after the earthly life of our Lord are contained in the locus classicus of I Cor. 15: 1 ff. (and briefly in Rom. 1: 1–4). Since the Church originates in the Resurrection of Jesus, to evangelize means to proclaim the theme of the Resurrection. This is the Message to which the whole corpus of the O.T., with a unanimous consent, bears witness, that the Resurrection happened *according to the Scriptures* (I Cor. 15: 4). It is also not only the consensus of the New Testament, but is at the centre of its message. Even when they doubted the fact of the Resurrection, the followers of Jesus who did so encountered the Resurrection as a historical reality. Whether or not they understood or could explain it, was and is another matter.

Just as the Resurrection of Jesus is the foundation of the Christian Faith and the Church, so it is also the phenomenon which illumines Christology. It unveils the so-called 'Messianic Secret' (cf. Mk. 9: 9). It is after the Resurrection that 'the son of Joseph (or Mary)' is highly exalted to the position of being called by the very name of God, Adonai (*O KYPIOΣ*: LXX),[1] cf. Heb. 1: 8 ff., Phil. 2: 9 ff. The great Christological passage of Col. 1: 15–23 presupposes the Resurrection, as do also Christ's exaltation (Col. 3: 1), and victory over the demonic powers (Col. 2: 15, cf. Rev. 20: 14, I Cor. 15: 26).

So the Resurrection of Jesus confronts us at every point of our Faith, and even of our doubt and uncertainty. It is the heart of the New Age, pumping the Blood of the New Covenant into all the arteries and veins of the Body of Christ. A Gospel based on the Resurrection must triumph. Ramsey rightly reminds us that 'it was the news of Jesus and the Resurrection that first won the ancient world.'[2] If the Church today is to expect similar victory where the Gospel is proclaimed, the Resurrection must be given its central place. Beginning with the Resurrection of Jesus Christ, there is a marked movement in the New Testament, and in the life of the Church, towards a crescendo at the Parousia. Paul puts more weight upon the Resurrection

---

[1] For further discussion see, for example, O. Cullmann, *Christology of the New Testament* (ET 1959), especially pp. 195–237; and V. Taylor, *The Names of Jesus* (1953), 38–51.

[2] A. M. Ramsey, *The Resurrection of Christ* (1945), 116.

than upon all the other eschatological realities. The doctrine and belief in it vividly colour the life, expansion, and thinking of the early Church. It is only in the light of the Lord's Resurrection that we can understand our own resurrection, and can hope for it with great anticipation and certainty (cf. Acts 23: 6, Rom. 6: 4 f., I Cor. 6: 14, 17; 15: 20 ff., etc.). It is the Resurrection of Jesus Christ which validates that of His followers; it is also His Resurrection which promises and guarantees the realization of human and cosmic resurrection.

(d) Corporate Resurrection

The Resurrection of Jesus makes the entire existence of the faithful absolutely Christocentric (cf. Jn. 3: 14 f.; 12: 32, Eph. 4: 16, Col. 1: 18, I Pet. 1: 18 f.). There is no distance of time or space which is not affected and embraced by His Resurrection.

Yet, we need to recognize that the belief in resurrection does not originate in Christianity. It was already current among the Jews at the time of our Lord. In his *Eschatology—Hebrew, Jewish and Christian* (1899), R. H. Charles traces the development of the doctrine from about the end of the fourth century or early third century B.C. to the N.T. period, and it is unnecessary to go over the ground so adequately covered by him and others.[1] It is also possible, though there is not enough evidence, as Glasson tries to show, that Greek ideas exerted some influence upon Jewish thought on the doctrine of resurrection.[2] In the O.T. we have the three stories of raising the dead: I Kin. 17: 17–24, II Kin. 4: 18–37; and 13: 21. There are other references to resurrection ideas, like Is. 24–27, Ezek. 37, Dan. 12: 2 f., Hos. 6: 2, and many more in the extra-canonical literature (see Charles, op. cit., *passim*). In the Gospels, belief in the resurrection is one of the strong dogmas of the Pharisees, while

---

[1] R. H. Charles, *Eschatology—Hebrew, Jewish and Christian* (1899, another title is: *A Critical History of a Future Life in Israel, in Judaism, and in Christianity*), 77 ff., 125 ff., *et passim*. See also J. McLeman and S. H. Hooke, both cited in note 2, p.1 62; K. Schubert, 'Die Entwicklung der Auferstehungslehre von der nach-exilischen bis zur frührabbinischen Zeit', in *Biblische Zeitschrift*, Vol. 6 (1962), pp. 177–214; J. Comblin, *The Resurrection in the Plan of Salvation* (ET 1965); etc.

[2] T. F. Glasson, *Greek Influence in Jewish Eschatology* (1961), especially pp. 26–32. There is, however, as he shows, a diversity between the basic Jewish and Greek ideas. Cf. K. Schubert, cited in the previous note, arguing that the concept of a resurrection body arose out of a combination of Hebrew and oriental life–death dualism with the Greek soul–body dualism.

the Sadducees are sceptical about it (Mk. 12: 18 pars.,[1] cf. Acts 23: 7 f.); and the common people seem to take it for granted (cf. Jn. 11: 24), as does also our Lord (cf. Mk. 12: 18–27, Jn. 6: 39 f., 44, 54).

In the earthly life and ministry of Jesus the resurrection hope acquires a fuller meaning and a much wider scope. One of the clearest Messianic signs is the raising of the dead, which He performs on several occasions (Mt. 11: 4 f. par.). For Him this is nothing extra-ordinary; it is a purely normal act belonging to His messianic functions. In the Fourth Gospel the resurrection is treated as universal and intensely Christocentric (Jn. 5: 21; 6: 39 f., 44, 54; 11: 25). It is only in relation to Jesus Christ that eschatological resurrection can make sense and become effective in the world. The author links it up with the Sacraments, so that 'he who eats my flesh and drinks my blood has eternal life, and I will raise him up (at the last day)' (6: 54). Jesus is the Author of the Resurrection (Jn. 11: 25), and His eternal origin entitles Him to that high office (Jn. 1: 2; 8: 58). Eternal life, which He gives, is none other than the very stuff and content of the resurrection life (Jn. 11: 25 f., cf. 4: 14) which knows neither decay nor end. What in Judaism was strictly a future event is here in the Person of Jesus Christ, realized in the present. It breaks into history on 'the third day'. So then in Him the Last Day has dawned and His voice sets the resurrection machinery in motion: 'for the hour is coming when all who are in the tombs will hear His voice and come forth, . . . to the resurrection of life, and . . . to the resurrection of judgement' (Jn. 5: 28 f.; cf. 11: 43 f., Mk. 5: 41 f. pars., Lk. 7: 14 f.). His quickening power scans the entire dimension of time and space (cf. Jn. 10: 18).

The three stories of raising the dead in the Gospels (Mk. 5: 35 ff. pars., Lk. 7: 11 ff., Jn. 11), together with those of the O.T., make sense only when viewed in the light of Christ's own Resurrection. They are proleptical, anticipating the eschatological resurrection of which the Easter event is the central and starting-point. In the phenomenon of the Resurrection at Easter, mankind as represented by Jesus Christ participates empirically in His experience (cf. II Cor. 5: 14 f., Gal. 2: 20). Henceforth Man can live in the mystical relationship centred upon the concept of being *in Christ*. This it is that makes it a corporate phenomenon.

[1] The Lucan parallel, 20: 27, implies 'some', though this cannot be argued conclusively.

12

But corporate resurrection rests upon and presupposes a corporate death—a concept that Paul excels in developing (Rom. 5: 6; 6: 3 f., Gal. 6: 14b, Eph. 2: 1, 5, Col. 2: 12 f.; 3: 3). So the human race and the cosmos die on Good Friday and rise again on Easter Sunday. Those who are incorporated into Christ are automatically thrust into an extremely intimate bodily relationship with Christ and one another. They participate corporately in the whole 'Christ-event', for they are His Body. What has happened to the Head of that Body must inevitably happen empirically and eschatologically to its members as well.[1]

Since members of Christ's Body are therefore involved in all that happened to the Head, they live in His Life (Gal. 2: 20c), suffer with Him (Rom. 8: 17, Col. 1: 24, I Pet. 4: 13), rise in His Resurrection (Col. 2: 12, etc.), and are to reign and be glorified with Him (Rom. 8: 17, 30, II Tim. 2: 12). The benefits of Christ's Resurrection are being conveyed constantly to the saints and to the world through the Holy Spirit (cf. II Cor. 3: 18). But because this is an eschatological phenomenon, it is experienced in the form of the tension between fulfilment and 'not yet'. It is already realized, but it is yet to be consummated at the Parousia. The N.T. clearly bears witness to this paradox (Rom. 6: 22 ff.; 8: 14 ff., I Cor. 6: 14; 15: 12–23, II Cor. 5: 14 f., Gal. 2: 19 f., Eph. 2: 1–7, Heb. 2: 9; 6: 19 f., I Pet. 3: 18, 21, I Jn. 3: 2, 14, etc.).

We saw previously that through Baptism the individual is incorporated into Christ's Body. From that moment on, his existence is in a corporate solidarity expressed in terms like 'the Body of Christ', 'the New Man', 'the New Creation', 'the Temple of God', etc.[2] He appropriates sacramentally the Resurrection of Christ which begins, guarantees and anticipates the final resurrection for all mankind and creation, since the Easter event, as Bultmann tells us, was 'lifted out of all temporal limitation.'[3] It was right, therefore, that from the early days of the Church

---

[1] The theme of the Body is under constant discussion, as exemplified by, among others, E. Mersch, *The Whole Christ* (ET 1938); L. S. Thornton, *The Common Life in the Body of Christ* (1941); J. A. T. Robinson, *The Body* (1952); J. Levie, ed., *La Théologie du Corps Mystique* (1946); E. Best, *One Body in Christ* (1955); articles in the *TWzNT*, etc.

[2] For further discussion see E. E. Ellis, 'II Corinthians V: 1–10 in Pauline Eschatology', in *NTS*, Vol. 6 No. 3 (April 1960), pp. 211–24; cf. G. W. H. Lampe, *I Believe* (1960), 132 f.

[3] Bultmann, op. cit., 303.

the Sacrament of Baptism was interpreted in terms of death-and-resurrection.

The Resurrection of Jesus inaugurated eschatological resurrection for mankind and creation. There remains only the future consummation of what is already appropriated sacramentally as a result of the historical event on the first Easter Sunday. It is with this that the Church has generally been concerned.

Ideas about a future resurrection were already current in Palestine in the N.T. times (cf. Mk. 12: 18–27 pars., Jn. 5: 29; 6: 39, 40, 44, 54; 11: 24). The main Christian differentia came with Jesus who as the Resurrection (Jn. 11: 25) was also the One who made it realized in the historical framework of the End-Time. What hitherto was to be a future event became a reality in History which nothing can erase. But to say that the Resurrection was realized in Jesus does not rule out its future dimension and implications for mankind, as some supposed (cf. II Tim. 2: 17 f., Poly. Phil. 7: 1, II Clem. 9: 1). Paul was quick to combat such tendencies, in his great chapter on the Resurrection (I Cor. 15). We need not enter here into a discussion[1] of I Cor. 15, except to underline the argument that without a resurrection hope all the fundamental items of the Christian Faith would disintegrate into nothingness and nonsense (15: 13, 14, 17, 18). As Barth comments, 'the resurrection of Jesus consists in this, that the resurrection is the divine horizon also of our existence.'[2] The end product of the individual who is 'in Christ' is the irreversible putting off entirely of 'the man of dust', and the putting on of 'the man of heaven' (I Cor. 15: 48 f., cf. Rom. 6: 9 ff., II Tim. 1: 10, Heb. 2: 9 f., I Pet. 5: 1, I Jn. 3: 2). This is a mode of existence entirely other, and the self-consciousness of participation in it begins at the point when the individual is sacramentally and eschatologically thrust into the baptism of death and resurrection. But the process is destined to reach its climax only in the full manifestation of the Age to Come. Our hope then looks forward only to the completion of the Resurrection-event which began in the past. Jesus Christ, as raised from the dead,

---

[1] See further discussions by K. Barth, *The Resurrection of the Dead* (ET 1933); M. E., Dahl, *The Resurrection of the Body—A Study of I Cor. 15* (1962), and literature in the latter book; C. F. D. Moule, 'St. Paul and Dualism: the Pauline Conception of Resurrection', in *NTS*, Vol. 12, No. 2 (1966), pp. 106–23; C. K. Barrett, 'Immortality and Resurrection' in *LQHR*, Vol. 34, No. 2 (1965), pp. 91–102.

[2] Barth, op. cit., 174; cf. V. Lossky, *The Mystical Theology of the Eastern Church* (ET 1957), 171, 196.

is therefore the true and only Way to the Father (Jn. 14: 6), and the mode of existence which is the norm in His presence. He leads mankind to this goal via the Valley of the Resurrection (Jn. 12: 32). The individual does not come to this destiny alone, but only corporately with those who are 'in Christ'. It is an intensely corporate process from its inauguration on 'the third day', in its appropriation through Baptism, up to its completion at the Parousia.

In terms of time, Christian resurrection means that the individual is rescued from the fate of being lost in the tene period. The Resurrection claims him for permanence in the dimension of the present. It is the Resurrection which claims and restores the individual from that which in his being has both been 'lost' in the oblivion of the past, tene, and what otherwise he anticipates in this life as his future in Christ. Thus, the Resurrection ensures that the individual is not deprived of his being, by being worn out, washed away, dragged off, drained of being by the force of Time's backward dimension. It is only the resurrection of those in Christ which protects them from the subtracting effects of the tene period which, as we saw and as we all experience, drags the individual towards oblivion and obliteration, and robs him of his being. Now the Resurrection puts a halt to this process and reverses the whole momentum of Time. Instead of Time depriving one of one's being, the Resurrection not only restores one's being but adds to the stature of that being. Instead of Time promising (in the future) what the person will be (cf. I Jn. 3: 2), the Resurrection in fact gives it to him in its entirety. The Resurrection restores what the past dimension of Time has removed, and realizes what the future dimension of Time promises now. Thus, the future dimension of Time is paralysed and neutralized by the Resurrection; the past dimension of Time is negated and reversed. These temporal implications mean that the Resurrection mode of existence cannot be defined in terms of Time dimensions, except, perhaps, to say that the Resurrection is a *presentization* of Time dimensions—a bringing together into the present of both the past and the future.

But what makes this uniquely Christian is that the Resurrection is an intensely christological phenomenon, bringing everything into the present before God and in Christ. For individuals it is the union between creatures and their Creator. Thus, the Resurrection is a personal experience, flooding mankind and the cosmos with the dimension of the present, in the presence of God, clothing them with immortality, incorruptibility, unchangeableness and lifeness. It is a resurrection into a consciousness of and participation in the very presence of God. What other dimensions this resurrection might or will have defies our capacity to imagine and articulate.

We must insist that this Resurrection-event involves not mankind alone, but the whole creation. Just as Christ's work of creation was cosmic, so also is His redemptive work (Col. 1: 16–20). The works of creation and redemption cannot be separated, for they are only two temini of a single but comprehensive transaction of God in Christ. Man's participation in the Resurrection-event would be incomplete as long as the rest of creation remains groaning in travail. This is the theme of Galloway's book, *The Cosmic Christ*, in which he tells us rightly that 'the destiny of creation was that it should return to the paradisiac state from which it had fallen so that the distinction between the things of heaven and the things of earth would be overcome.'[1] But this process has already been inaugurated by the Death and Resurrection of Christ. Just as in His Baptism on the Cross the whole creation was baptized, so also in His Resurrection on 'the third day' the new creation came into being, but only proleptically. The writers of the N.T. interpret this truth differently. Only when the past and future dimensions of Time are summed up into one dimension, in the presence of God, would the new creation really become evident, for that is truly the end of Time, not by its elimination but by its consummation.

Paul sees the reconciliation of all things as having been accomplished on the Cross (Col. 1: 20). But between the Cross and the Parousia he considers the whole creation to be groaning as it longs for its full liberation (Rom. 8: 19 ff.). It is a struggle to be freed from the subtracting effects of Time and its unending futurity. At the Parousia, which is the *consummation* of Time dimensions, the universe will be 'brought into a unity in Christ' (Eph. 1: 9, f., *NEB*). Thus, Man and Creation together must participate in the 'Heilsgeschichte' —the only legitimate form of history.[2] Therefore this phenomenon is

---

[1] A. D. Galloway, *The Cosmic Christ* (1951), 34. The author is rather weak in his argument in trying to deal with the impersonal element of Nature and the purpose of redeeming an otherwise non-living universe. For him, the encounter with God in Christ means a necessary encounter with God in all things (pp. 240, 250). The substance of his conclusions is that 'the ultimate destiny of the Church is to become the whole cosmos, so that there shall be no more Church' (p. 259). These assertions seem to go beyond the indication of the N.T.

[2] See further discussion of Heilsgeschichte in the context of Eschatology, in J. Comblin, *The Resurrection in the Plan of Salvation* (ET 1965); H. Greeven,

undatable; it can only be regarded as delayed and yet imminent and near.

The author of I Peter presents Christ's Redemption as the Gospel proclaimed not only to the living, but also to the dead and the spirits in prison (3: 19 f.; 4: 6). The author of II Peter sees in the future a terrific incineration of the whole universe. But it will be burnt up only to be replaced by the new (3: 10 ff.). In Revelation, we hear that the old creation will be swallowed up by the new Heaven and Earth (21: 1), symbolized by the new Jerusalem (21: 2 ff.) full of harmony and fellowship. In the Johannine literature, 'the world' and 'darkness' are presented as passing away now, so that their place is being taken by 'the will of God' and 'the true light' (I Jn. 2: 8, 17 cf. Jn. 1: 4 f., 12 ff.; 2: 19, 21 f.; 3: 1–15; etc.).

Outside the N.T., Irenaeus (c. 130–200) is the earliest exponent of the subject, in his doctrine of the 'recapitulation' (ἀνακεφαλαίωσις). Irenaeus says that the 'creation will be restored to its first condition and made subject to the righteous without hindrance'.[1] Creation must also be freed from its pastness and its futurity, and be brought into a conscious present, the presence of God in Christ.

We must consider further, what happens to the individual and his body, in connection with the Resurrection. At his Baptism the baptisand participates sacramentally in the Resurrection. It is an event which anticipates and guarantees the future and final resurrection both for him and the whole creation. The Resurrection is realized in him by virtue of his becoming incorporated into Christ, but he still hopes and repeats the 'I believe . . . in the resurrection of the body (the dead, the flesh)', which appear in all the major creeds of Christendom. The Resurrection as a future event has captured the attention and interest of many writers throughout the history of the Church.

The early Fathers who dealt with the subject include Clement of Rome on I Cor. 24–6, Irenaeus in *Adversus omnes Haereses*, V. 31 f., Tertullian in *De Anima* (58) and *De Resurrectione Carnis*, Origen in *De Principiis* (*passim*)[2] and others. But it was Augustine

'Kirche und Parusie Christi' in *Kerygma und Dogma*, Vol. 10. No. 2 (1964), pp. 113–35.

[1] Irenaeus, *Adversus omnes Haereses*, V. 32.1, in the translation by H. Bettenson, *The Early Christian Fathers* (1956), 134 ff.

[2] Origen argued for a spiritual rather than a materialistic interpretation of the Resurrection body. But he was a voice crying in the wilderness, and his voice was not heard by many.

more than anyone else who 'immortalized' the ideas of a material
Resurrection body, expounded in his *De Civitate Dei* (XX–XXII).[1]
Augustine's views became the orthodox interpretation of the doctrine
of the Resurrection. Thomas Aquinas did not depart from Augustine,
in spite of his attempt to distinguish between the 'accidents' and the
'substance' of the body.[2] The Roman Church has held the view of a
materialistic Resurrection since the Fourth Lateran Council in
1215.[3] Likewise it appears variously in Luther's writings,[4] and in
Calvin's *Institutes* (III. 25. 6–8).[5] There are obvious difficulties in

[1] Augustine says, for example, that a literal and materialistic fire will punish
the wicked (XXI. 2, 9, 10, 16); all people will be of equal stature (XXII. 15);
infants will rise full grown (XXII. 14, including abortions, XXII. 13); sex will be
retained (XXII. 17), no parts of the body will be lost, not even nails or hair (XXII.
19); etc. But he compensates some of these extravagant utterances with his
spiritual insight and vivid expression, as when he says that God 'shall be the end
of our desires Who shall be seen without end, loved without cloy, praised without
weariness' (XXII. 30). He also makes briefer statements on the Resurrection in his
Enchiridion ad Laurentium (chaps. 88–92). The translation I have followed here
is by M. Dods, 1871.
This approach compares with the sensuous views of the hereafter and the
Resurrection as expounded by some teachers of Judaism, for which see, among
other works, Charles, op. cit., *passim*, and R. A. Stewart, *Rabbinic Theology*
(1961).

[2] M. E. Dahl, *The Resurrection of the Body* (1962), examines briefly the views
of Thomas Aquinas, pp. 48 ff. He also warns us rightly that to an ancient writer
the notion of 'matter' was different from our notions today, if he had any such
conception at all (p. 48).

[3] For example, in the Catechism (*The Explanatory Catechism of Christian
Doctrine*, Imprim. F. C. Bourne, 1921), question 129 reads: 'What do you mean
by "The resurrection of the body"? A. By "The resurrection of the body" I mean
that we shall all rise again with the same bodies at the day of judgment,' (p. 15).
So also R. Guardini, *The Last Things* (ET 1954), 69.

[4] Luther does not make a long systematic exposition of the doctrine of the
Resurrection. His views appear briefly in the 'Larger Catechism', and in his
comments on I Cor. 15 and I Thes. 4: 13–18 (Erlangen and Frankfurt Edition:
51, 192 f.; 20 II, 92; 17, 216 f.; etc.; or the Weimar Edition: 36, 605; 49, 429 f.;
17, 219; etc.) His belief in the Resurrection of the Flesh comes out clearly in the
sermon on I Cor. 15: 39–44, which he preached on 25 May, 1544, in the Wittenberg
Parish Church (Weimar, 49, 429 f., Erlangen 20 II, 92)—according to *What
Luther Says*, ed. E. M. Plass (1959), Vol. II, pp. 1215 f.

[5] Calvin reaches the conclusion that 'since God has all the elements ready at
His bidding, no difficulty will hinder His commanding earth, waters, and fire
to restore what they seem to have consumed' (III. 25. 8, in the translation by F. L.
Battles, in the 'Library of Christian Classics', Vols. XX and XXI, p. 1003). Cf. a
fuller discussion of Calvin's views on Eschatology by H. Quistorp, *Calvin's
Doctrine of the Last Things* (ET 1955).
Cf. the Westminster Confession (Chap. XXXII); and, in a different context,
the Anglican 'Articles of Religion' (Article IV, see E. J. Bicknell, *The Thirty Nine
Articles* (3rd ed. 1955), 103 f.).

this traditional view, into a discussion of which we need not enter here.[1]

In spite of this long tradition, however, there is no explicit scriptural warrant to support a materialistic view of the Resurrection body. All that we are positive about is that it will be 'spiritual' and not 'physical', heavenly and not of dust (I Cor. 15: 44, 46–9). It will not be the old rags cleaned and bleached, but a new wedding garment (Mt. 22: 11) adorning the bride of the Lord (Rev. 21: 2). It will be the Body of glory (Jn. 17: 22, Rom. 2: 7, 10; 8: 18, 21; 9: 23, I Cor. 2: 7; 15: 43, II Cor. 3: 11; 4: 17, Col. 3: 4, Heb. 2: 10, I Pet. 5: 4) which is already being mystically and spiritually imparted to those who are 'in Christ' (II Cor. 3: 18).[2] The body will be incapable of becoming 'naked' again (II Cor. 5: 3, 4),[3] a true house and not a tent any more (II Cor. 5: 1, 4, cf. Jn. 2: 19, 21). It will be without limitations (I Cor. 13: 10, 12), fully at home with the Lord (Jn. 14: 3, II Cor. 5: 5, 8, Phil. 1: 23), permanent and not transient (II Cor. 3: 11; 4: 18), and like the Lord's in every respect (Jn. 17: 24, Rom. 5: 2, II Cor. 3: 18, Phil. 3: 21, I Pet. 5: 1, 10, II Pet. 1: 3 f., I Jn. 3: 2, Rev. 21: 11). If the 'fulness' ($\tau\grave{o}$ $\pi\lambda\acute{\eta}\rho\omega\mu\alpha$) of Christ (Col. 1: 19) is to be the ultimate heritage of those who are 'in Christ', the entire realization of this destiny can only be possible on a corporate basis and at the Resurrection of all. That is also the destiny of creation, of which Man is but a particle (cf. Rom. 8: 21, 23). It is almost unthinkable that at the final Resurrection there should be portions of God's creation not involved in the process of *presentization*, not brought into the conscious presence of God.

[1] See, among recent contributions to this discussion: Dahl, op. cit., 51–8; H. Cornelis and others, *The Resurrection of the Body* (ET 1964); J. A. Schep, *The Nature of the Resurrection Body: A Study of the Biblical Data* (1964); C. K. Barrett, 'Immortality and Resurrection', in *LQHR*, Vol. 34, No. 2 (1965), pp. 91–102; C. F. D. Moule, 'St. Paul and Dualism: the Pauline Conception of Resurrection', in *NTS*, Vol. 12, No. 2 (1966), pp. 106–23; B. Mitchell, 'What Philosophical Problems arise from Belief in the Resurrection?', in *Theology*, Vol. 70, No. 561 (1967), pp. 110–14.

[2] See, for further discussion, B. Ramm, *Them He Glorified: a Systematic Study of the Doctrine of Glorification* (1963).

[3] For the varied interpretations of this difficult passage, II Cor. 5: 1 ff., see J. N. Sevenster and W. C. van Unnik, *Studia Paulina* (1953, article by Sevenster: 'Some Remarks on the ΓΥΜΝΟΣ, II Cor. 5: 3'), 202–14; R. F. Hettlinger, '2 Cor. 5: 1–10', in *SJT*, Vol. 10, No. 2 (June 1957), pp. 174–94; E. E. Ellis, 'II Cor. V. 1–10 in Pauline Eschatology', in *NTS*, Vol. 6, No. 3 (April 1960), pp. 211–24; M. Brändle, 'Musste das Grab leer sein?', in *Orientierung*, Vol. 31 (15 May, 1967), pp. 108–12; and others.

But what of the individual and his identity? Is he to be 'merged' and 'lost' in the vast and intensely corporate New Man? The general consensus of (Western) theologians is that he retains his identity even in eternity.[1] Some writers also maintain that this individuality will be such that we shall be able to recognize acquaintances, friends and members of our families.[2] In his book, *A Critical History of the Doctrine of a Future Life* (10th edn. 1878), W. R. Alger argues for the certainty of recognizing friends in the next life, but admits that such expectations may not be fulfilled. A materialistic view of the Resurrection would lead to such a conclusion, without great difficulties. But if we admit that the Scriptures emphasize a spiritual rather than a physical Resurrection body, can we then wholly accommodate the idea that the individual retains his identity indefinitely? If such identity is retained, certainly it is not determinable on a physical or materialistic basis.

In the Bible stories of restoring people to life, the personality of the individual is not noticeably affected by death. But these incidents relate to people who are restored to life in their original physical bodies, and after only a few hours or days following their death. They do not receive the 'body of glory', and eventually they die once more. In the case of our Lord, the same body was raised but He was not recognized even by His closest followers (Lk. 24: 16, 31, 36, Jn. 20: 14, 15; 21: 5, 6), except when He removed the curtain of their inability (Lk. 24: 31, Jn. 20: 16; 21: 6). He passed through physical barriers (Jn. 20: 19, 26), yet He ate physical food (Lk. 24: 41–3, possibly Jn. 21: 13, 15 and Acts 1: 4).[3] He could appear to and

---

[1] See, for example, W. Milligan, *The Resurrection of our Lord* (3rd ed. 1890), 193, that in our future life we will live 'in our present compound being, with our individual personal lives, recognisable by others and recognising them'; Lampe, op. cit., 200, that each personality will receive a concrete expression enabling 'it to be so while retaining its individuality within the community of Christ's Body'; H. A. A. Kennedy, *St. Paul's Conception of the Last Things* (1904), 247 f., that 'the individuality which has been exhibited by the $\sigma\hat{\omega}\mu\alpha$ $\sigma\alpha\rho\kappa\iota\kappa\acute{o}\nu$ will by no means disappear . . .'; J. F. Bethune-Baker, *The Faith of the Apostles* (1918), p. 175; A. M. Ramsey, *The Gospel and the Catholic Church* (1936), 38; and others.

[2] Milligan, ibid.; and full volumes on the subject, by T. Gisborne, *Essays on the Recollections Which are to Subsist Between Earthly Friends, United in the World to Come* (1822, with 354 pages); C. R. Muston, *Recognition in the World to Come* (1830, with viii, 424 pages); and H. Barbaugh, *The Heavenly Recognition* (1859, with 288 pages).

[3] In Acts 1: 4, $\sigma\nu\nu\alpha\lambda\acute{\iota}\zeta\omega$ may also mean 'eat with', so W. Bauer, *Gk.-Eng. Lex.* The possibility of $\sigma\nu\nu\alpha\nu\lambda\iota\zeta\acute{o}\mu\epsilon\nu\sigma$ as contained in a large number of MSS, is remote but cannot altogether be dismissed.

disappear from human sight (Lk. 24: 15, 31 (51), Jn. 20: 19, 26, Acts 1: 9). These incidents indicate clearly that there is a transformation of personality between death and the Resurrection. If the change is noticeable in the One who knew no sin, is it not likely to be much more pronounced in those who are sinners and need a complete transformation from Adam's solidarity to that of Christ? All are destined to be changed (I Cor. 15: 51), and that can rightly be expected to be a radical change.

If we follow the temporal implications of the Resurrection we would assert that, through His Resurrection, Jesus was placed in the dimensionless present, the presence of God. Being a partaker of God's contemporaneity, He was no longer confined within the identities of the pastness of Time to which His puzzled followers tried to subject Him. He eluded the limitations, delineations and dimensions of Time. Because His followers were the victims of these dimensions of Time, they could not accommodate His Resurrection mode within the context of their temporal horizon. Therefore they could not recognize Him within so few days after His crucifixion, when He appeared to them. Only through momentary unveiling of this temporal blindness could they 'recognize' Him, and then He disappeared. The disappearance was perhaps for their benefit, otherwise they would not sustain for long this vision of the contemporaneity of God. Only when the faithful are raised in the spiritual body will they be able to 'see God' (cf. Mt. 5: 8; Jn. 1: 18), to accommodate and assimilate that mode of existence which is permissible in the very presence of God. Only a spiritual body can be impervious to the dimensions of time. A physical body would necessarily remain subject to time since time itself is a dimension of the physical universe. But whereas a physical body has no place in the Resurrection mode, the spiritual body of that mode of existence is not subject to limitations of the physical realm. For that reason we see the resurrected Lord passing through physical objects, eating physical food and even communicating audibly and visibly with His followers. If there is still a physical realm after the final Resurrection, the saints will not be barred from participating in that physicalness even if essentially they will be in the irreversible mode of spiritualness.

The individual who dies before the Parousia must 'wait', until the final 'place' of habitation is ready (Jn. 14: 2 f.), until the 'building from God' (II Cor. 5: 1) is completed. He waits also for the full incorporation of mankind into Christ. But the soul is not simply asleep, as some Christians believe. The interim period is not one of inactivity and potential death (cf. Rev. 6: 9 ff.). The soul waits in worshipful service and not in idleness. It waits in the presence of God, but waits until all things come to that goal, the Parousia or Presence of our Lord. All things must be summed up in Christ—subjected to God's presence in and through Christ. And that is the true meaning of the teleological End.

In that waiting, there is almost certainly a spiritual transformation (or 'improvement'), a process of 'perfecting' the souls before the Parousia. Admittedly, here we are in the realm of speculation, but a few passages indicate the possibility of some 'improvement'. The souls under the altar are 'each given a white robe' (Rev. 6: 11, cf. 20: 4), which is something that happens to them after the believers have been martyred. In Lk. 16: 24 f., 27 f., Lazarus is said to be 'comforted here'; and Dives shows sufficient spiritual concern about his brothers to ask that they be warned 'lest they also come into this place of torment'. The thief is to 'be with (Jesus) in Paradise' (Lk. 23: 43), and that experience should certainly bring a change for the better in his life, even if he probably undergoes initial conversion before dying. The O.T. saints can only be 'made perfect' together with 'us' (Heb. 11: 39 f.). If there was no prospect of such 'perfecting' it would not be necessary to speak of it in this passage. The author of I Peter tells us that Christ 'went and preached to the spirits in prison' (3: 19 f., cf. 4: 6). It would be utterly useless to preach to these spirits if no change could possibly come upon them. In all these passages the argument for a spiritual transformation after death is, admittedly, very slight, but we cannot dismiss it altogether.

Death is still 'the last enemy', according to the New Testament (I Cor. 15: 26). But in all seriousness, the N.T. is silent on whether or not physical death closes the door for the salvation of those who die *without or apart from Christ* (χωρὶς Χριστοῦ). We venture to speculate that the opportunity to hear or assimilate the effects of the Gospel is continued in the life beyond the grave (cf. I Pet. 3: 19 f.), and that death is not a barrier to incorporation into Christ, since nothing can separate 'us' from the love of God (cf. Rom. 8: 38 f.). This assertion does not diminish the urgency of the Gospel Message that 'now is the acceptable time; behold, now is the day of salvation' (II Cor. 6: 2). But if there is progress after death, we dare not say that death pronounces the final destiny of the individual. Jesus Christ, and not death, is the Judge and has the final say.

Cullmann is possibly right in saying that in the interim period the time rhythm of the dead is probably different from, and perhaps shorter than, ours.[1] The saints are not fully clothed with glory (cf. Rev. 6: 11),[2] because their eternal dwelling is to be inhabited corporately. It will be the one place (Jn. 14: 3), for the one flock, under the one Shepherd (Jn. 10: 16, Rev. 21: 7, cf. I QH 4: 21). This oneness is a mathematical symbol of co-existence, co-presence, contemporaneity; all things are pictured as being placed in the very *now* or presence of God.

It seems probable that individuality continues for a 'period', in the life beyond the grave, while the souls are still 'waiting', before everything has been summed up in Christ—things past, present and to come. During that 'period' the individuals discover, more fully than now, their true personality as it is found in Jesus Christ. They see what they have not been and what they are destined to be. But it is hard to believe that this individuality will persist beyond the final Resurrection and the Parousia. The ultimate end of Man is to be made like Jesus Christ, for 'when He appears we shall be like Him' (I Jn. 3: 2), and shall be fully conformed to His image to which we were originally predestined (Rom. 8: 29). At that 'time', in the now or presence of God, when all things are summed up in Him (Eph. 1: 10) and put under Him, and God is *all in all* ($\pi\acute{\alpha}\nu\tau\alpha$ $\grave{\epsilon}\nu$ $\pi\hat{\alpha}\sigma\iota\nu$ I Cor. 15: 28), then the 'many' will be absorbed into the 'One'. That is, they will give up their individual presence for the greater presence of God among them. The individual will relinquish his individuality but gain his perfect and corporate oneness. As such, there can be no marriage for the individual in the 'Resurrection mode' of existence, since those who participate in it 'are equal to angels and are sons of God' (Lk. 20: 35 f.). The intimacy of that existence, between the consummated 'many' and the indivisible 'one', will be more intense and real than any intimacy that marriage can bring to individuals on earth. It will be the life of true 'inter-existence', in which there are no barriers of individuality to mark off one person 'from' another. Each will be conscious of his own existence only 'in Christ' and in terms of the existence of 'himself-in-others-and-others-in-him'. It will be one multi-presence of all things in the presence of God in Christ.

---

[1] O. Cullmann, *Immortality of the Soul or Resurrection of the Dead?* (1958), 57.

[2] Is this 'white robe' simply their spiritual 'underwear', so to speak? Cf. C. S. Lewis, *Transposition and Other Addresses* (1949, the second essay, 'Weight of Glory').

In the Resurrection mode, the individual will be known only to God, by 'a new name' (Rev. 2: 17). It will be the Name of God, the Lord's 'own new Name' (Rev. 3: 12), imparted upon everyone in the consummated solidarity which has the 'name of the city of my God, the New Jerusalem' (Rev. 3: 12). The 'one new man' (Eph. 2: 15) is to exist by only one new name. By then the soul which is identifiable at the hour of death will have been changed from glory to glory (II Cor. 3: 18), until at the Parousia (Presence) it is wearing the same glory as that of the Lord Himself (Jn. 17: 22, Rom. 2: 7, 10; 8: 18, 21; 9: 23, I Cor. 2: 7; 15: 43, etc.). That means it will not be capable of departure since there will be no free dimension into which departure is possible. The 'many' will fully and equally partake of the Lord's divine nature (II Pet. 1: 4) which at present they only 'put on' (Eph. 4: 24, Rom. 13: 14, Gal. 3: 27) in anticipation.

Beyond the Resurrection, it will not be necessary, then, that friends should recognize one another as separate individuals. Our relationship will be grounded upon the Lord with such immovable tenacity that the only possible and natural dialogue will be absolutely 'face to face' (I Cor. 13: 12). The 'many-in-one' will gaze and gaze upon God and the Lamb (Rev. 22: 3 f., Mt. 5: 8) without weariness, in perfect worship and adoration, with hearts full of wonder and lips bursting in endless praise. The 'many-in-one' will have 'put on our heavenly dwelling' (II Cor. 5: 2), the same dwelling, the same imperishable nature, the same immortality (I Cor. 15: 53 f.), for child and parent, for wife and husband, for slave and master, for Greek and Jew, since all are one in Christ Jesus our Lord (cf. Gal. 3: 26 ff.). The 'many-in-one' will become perfect kings and priests unto our Lord and God (I Pet. 2: 5, Rev. 1: 6; 5: 10; (20: 6); 21: 5). This intimacy between God and His people will be so close that in that symbolic city there will be no temple, 'for its temple is the Lord God the Almighty and the Lamb' (Rev. 21: 22).[1] They will share ONE Name, the Lord's Name inscribed upon their foreheads (Rev. 22: 4). The new Name (Rev. 2: 17; 3: 12; 22: 4) means in effect a new 'personality', the personality of the 'many-in-one', which is the very personality of God (Rev. 22: 4).

It is in order to acquire fully this new 'Name' or 'Personality' that our individual personalities must be surrendered, for the gain

---

[1] Cf. the Qumran ideas, 4Q Flor. 1: 1–7, CD 3: 19 f., I QH 4: 25 ff.

is infinitely superior to anything that we can lose or give up. Only in this new capacity of wearing God's Name on our foreheads shall we, the 'many-in-one', be most able to worship God and the Lamb (Rev. 22: 3), with one accord and in the company of the entire creation. It will be perfected worship offered in the one endless day (Rev. 21: 25), in one unison of praise (cf. Rev. 4: 8), which nothing can drown or diminish.

At that point, the 'many-in-one' will have entered fully their eternal sabbath rest ($\sigma\alpha\beta\beta\alpha\tau\iota\sigma\mu\acute{o}s$) (Heb. 4: 3) which, together with other eschatological experiences, they taste now but only in anticipation. This will be the ultimate, $\tau\grave{o}$ $\tau\acute{e}\lambda os$, of our life, of our entire being, of our Resurrection, not simply as individuals but as the 'many-in-one', incorporate in the Summum Corpus Christi. And when we reach it, in Augustine's beautiful words, 'there we shall rest and see, see and love, love and praise. This is what shall be in the end without end,' (*De Civitate Dei*, XXII. 30).

That is the destiny of the Resurrection life, but through the Holy Spirit our eschatological guarantee ('$A\rho\rho\alpha\beta\acute{\omega}\nu$ II Cor. 1: 22; 5: 5, Eph. 1: 13 f.), we have already begun to inherit and appropriate the eternal realities of this Resurrection life (Heb. 6: 4 f.). Nothing can halt that process (Rom. 8: 32, 35–9) 'until we acquire possession of it (our inheritance), to the praise of His glory' (Eph. 1: 14). God has begun this good work in us here and now, and will 'bring it to completion at the day of Jesus Christ' (Phil. 1: 6). Until then, for those who are still alive, and those who die before the Parousia, the experience of being 'in Christ' is one of 'tasting' (cf. Heb. 6: 5), of 'longing', of 'waiting', of 'expecting'. The Spirit reveals to us now (I Cor. 2: 9 f.) what is hidden from our imagination, and what in the nature of eternal realities can only be expressed in mythical terms: ' "Behold, I make all things new" ' (Rev. 21: 5). We who are 'in Christ' see this great truth being actualized and realized in our feeble selves (cf. II Cor. 5: 17). But in the eschatological tension in which we exist, the realization simply points to the consummation (cf. Rom. 8: 21 ff., I Cor. 13: 10). In this tension we live by faith, we feed on the first fruits; and when the tension is replaced by the consummation, when our pastness converges with our futurity in the presence of God, then we shall walk and live by sight, we shall participate fully in the Messianic banquet, as the 'many-in-one', in perfect 'inter-existence', freed from the dimensions of Time and Space.

But amidst this wonder and marvel, this hope and anticipation, the Scriptures solemnly and definitely give a warning that there is a possibility of persons being disqualified, indeed, even after preaching to others (I Cor. 9: 27). The individual who is found without the wedding garment may consequently be cast into 'outer darkness' (Mt. 8: 12; 22: 13; 25: 30), or consigned to 'the eternal fire prepared for the devil and his angels' (Mt. 25: 41, or Gehenna, Mt. 5: 22, 29 f., Mk. 9: 43, etc.). It is possible for a soul to 'perish' (Jn. 3: 16), if that soul remains χωρὶς Χριστοῦ (Eph. 2: 12) and not ἐν Χριστῷ in spite of being exposed to the Gospel and after God's long waiting for its repentance (II Pet. 3: 9). This soul can pass into 'the second death' (Rev. 20: 6, 14; 21: 8), so that God may not resurrect such a soul. It is incapable of accepting the free 'gift of God' (Rom. 6: 23, Jn. 3: 16 f., etc.), and rejects God's love and grace (Jn. 1: 16; 15: 13, Rom. 5: 6–10, 21, I Pet. 3: 18, I Jn. 3: 16; 4: 9 f.). This means exclusion from the presence of God, since only those in Christ can be brought into the Resurrection mode of existence.

This leads us to consider briefly the duration of the punishment or state of exclusion for such souls, but it is an extremely difficult problem. One finds it almost impossible to imagine that their punishment will last for all eternity in the same way that Redemption is for eternity. For only the presence of God has this quality of eternity. But the one day during which the soul might remain 'apart from Christ' is sufficiently tormenting to make the experience of the non-presence of God 'everlasting'. But if at the end of that day the prodigal son returns home with a penitent heart (cf. Lk. 15: 17 ff.), the gates of his Father's home are never shut by day (Rev. 21: 25). Such love of the Father must ultimately win over even the most 'hopeless case' of sinners, and bring home the lost sheep to join the one great fold (Lk. 15: 4–6, Jn. 10: 16). There is not a single soul, however debased or even unrepentant, which can successfully 'flee' from the Spirit of God (Ps. 139: 1–18). God's patient waiting for the soul's repentance must in the end be surely more potent than the soul's reluctance to repent and turn to Him (cf. II Pet. 3: 9). The harmony of the heavenly worship would be impaired if, out of the one hundred in the sheepfold, there is one soul which continues to languish in Sheol or 'the lake of fire'. As Jesus Christ conquered death through His Resurrection, as He put His living presence where death had reigned in non-being and non-presence (or absence of being), so at His Parousia He will conquer even that which is 'the second death' (cf. I Cor. 15: 25 f., 53 ff.). And once 'death is swallowed up in victory' (Is. 25: 8, I Cor. 15: 54), what then can hold captive that soul which has hitherto suffered 'everlasting' punishment? God's love and presence will freely invade that soul (cf. Rom. 8: 35, 39) until—let us hope—the soul responds to the Father's embrace and kiss (Lk. 15: 20). This will in effect be the soul's Resurrection (cf. Lk. 15: 24, 32), even if it means going through the fires of Hell (cf. I Cor. 3: 15). Such is the love of God by which He accomplished a 'miracle' in us, through reconciling us to Himself, even 'while we were yet helpless' sinners and enemies of God (Rom. 5: 6, 8, 10, II Cor. 5: 18 f.). Yes, it happened exactly 'at the right time' when we were $\chi\omega\rho\grave{\iota}s$ $X\rho\iota\sigma\tau o\tilde{\upsilon}$ (Eph. 2: 12), and no condition of the soul could be worse than that. We may, therefore, venture to say that, even for the soul which is undergoing 'everlasting punishment', an apparent non-presence of God, this 'right time' may yet come. So, then, that soul would ultimately be 'saved' through the Death-and-Resurrection of Jesus Christ. At that point, it will enter the Resurrection-mode, and participate fully in the corporate life of the 'many-in-one'. 'Second death', pain, mourning, and the like, cannot therefore be absolute realities. They are doomed to complete annihilation and obliteration, by the Resurrection life brought about by Jesus Christ (I Cor. 15: 24–6, 53–7, Rev. 21: 4). The very being of God will so flood our separate beings that we will be resurrected into His own corporate and eternal being. That is what in Christ is assured us, and although we may not understand it we have no cause to feel modest or embarrassed about it.

This is as far as the New Testament takes us, and we cannot speculate beyond that point. It must only be 'with fear and trembling' that we may dare even go that far. We may, however, trust that in His exercise of love and justice God is competent enough to deal adequately with this extremely difficult area of theology. For our part, we are certain that God's Salvation, made historically manifest and available in Christ, surely demands human response within the framework of History. Therefore, the New Testament speaks of human History as 'the day of Salvation' (II Cor. 6: 2). That means that today, this historical moment of our consciousness, is a moment of urgent call to respond. The details of what happens beyond the historical plane of human existence are neither for you nor for me to dogmatize about. But for those who, even amidst flares of doubt and perplexity, may accommodate in their faith and life the reality of the risen Lord, it is to their advantage to hold that in Him is the end and the ultimate realization of their hope beyond this historical existence. And that applies equally whether or not they are mistaken. The New Testament, however, is absolutely certain that One has died and risen again, and in Him are both the origin and destiny of all things.

CHAPTER VII

Conclusion

THE Resurrection ought to be the last word in this study, but one may venture a few more thoughts in the way of a conclusion. We have made a study of New Testament Eschatology against a given African background which in certain ways reflects the African situation in general. Significant points of difference as well as contact have emerged, mutually throwing light on either area. Of these, the notions of Time and History are the most fundamental. The three dimensions of Time are taken for granted in much of Christian Theology, as if the linear concept of Time were the only one in the Scriptures. Obviously we cannot get away from this threefold dimension, but the New Testament does not subject itself exclusively to a linear three-dimensional concept of Time. From the Akamba (or African) side we have seen that a two-dimensional concept of Time is equally valid; and that many of the traditional concepts and religious practices are governed by that twofold dimension. What then becomes of Christian Eschatology?

In the New Testament Eschatology, there is in fact emphasis on two of the dimensions of Time, viz. what has been realized in the historical present of the Church, and what is to be consummated at the Parousia. What in the Jewish eschatological scheme was relegated to the Age to Come now becomes a present reality according to the New Testament, and its unrealized dimension takes on a different perspective in the light of the Incarnation. Christian Eschatology becomes a christological phenomenon which, *ipso facto*, must be impervious to temporal limitations, whatever understanding of Eschatology we might derive from linear and other concepts of Time. The Akamba two-dimensional concept of Time lays emphasis on a dynamic present and an ever-increasing past—giving History a backward momentum, moving from the present to the past. As such, there cannot be a teleology in Akamba (or African) concepts of 'Eschatology'. Both linguistically and mythologically there is no notion in traditional African thoughts that the world will ever come to an end. The rhythm of nature ensures an endless continuity of human life and the world. What comes to an end is really what is eventually removed from the present (mituki) period of Time to the past (tene). As such it simply disappears beyond the horizon of Time; it does not head towards a goal. Christian Eschatology is here radically different, for in its scheme all things are to be taken up in the Resurrection mode, in the very presence of God, partaking of newness and (at least for man) the divine nature. Newness is the word in Christian Eschatology, and it is a newness in Christ.

The conceptual background of African peoples is invaded by the New Testament message as soon as evangelization begins to take place. From some of the examples cited in this study, one finds a number of interesting parallels between traditional African societies and early Hebrew society. This gives a promising and fruitful area of comparative studies between African and early Old Testament cultural and religious background. But the New Testament is an entirely different world with major themes for which there are no parallels in the African religious background. Is it, therefore, possible for African languages to sustain theological concepts from the New Testament? This has been one of the issues to which we addressed ourselves in this study. The answer to the problem is both 'yes' and 'no'. On the conceptual level we have seen that, at least, eschatological concepts are not easily assimilated, apart from the literal understanding of the eschatological symbols. These eschatological symbols are certainly a vivid and rich method of conveying what otherwise is beyond physical realities. But the symbols are vehicles of theological meaning, and this is what the Akamba have failed to grasp on the conceptual level. Instead, they have come out with a purely materialistic image of eschatological realities, which in turn create a false spirituality in their Christian living.

There is, however, the liturgical level centred on the two Sacraments of Baptism and the Eucharist. While sacramental life in Ukambani is practically unknown, it is nevertheless here that a real theological breakthrough could be made. There are traditional practices and concepts, such as the ceremony of 'humanizing' a child and the initiation rites, which form an important background against which the theology of the Sacraments could be built. We discussed it some length in Chapter IV how this could be done in practical terms, and we need not repeat the discussion here. One feels strongly that in the area of the Sacraments many items of New Testament

Eschatology can begin to make sense in an African background. Indeed the whole curriculum of Christian teaching could profitably be built around the Theology of the Sacraments. Even where African languages may lack the vocabulary to sustain theological concepts, people would participate in or be exposed to a liturgical confrontation which is deeply rich in theological content. It was in the sacramental context that the Early Church became conscious of its own existence; and it was from that consciousness that it began to expand both evangelistically and theologically. Can we not expect the same principle to function at other times and in other places?

In the area of the spirit world, we noticed similarities of content but differences of emphasis. In the Akamba (and other African) understanding of the spirit world, the departed, together with the race of the spirits, populate the spirit world. There is contact between human beings and the departed, but there is hardly any relationship between the spirits and God. The New Testament is aware of spirit beings in form of angels, demons and unclean spirits. Apart from the angels who are on the good side, the spirit beings in the New Testament are malicious and opposed to the Kingdom of God. Yet the work of Jesus Christ involves the spirit beings, so that, for example, an overthrow of Satan and his legions is one of the eschatological and Messianic duties of Jesus. But there are spirits of the departed to whom the Gospel is preached (cf. I Peter 3), some of whom are the faithful (Heb. 12: 1, 23). These are the object of redemption in Christ both before and after the Cross. The use of Christian diptychs also shows that the Early Church did maintain a link between the living and the departed in Christ. But the explicitly strong emphasis in the New Testament regarding the concept of the spirit world is on the fellowship between the faithful and God; a fellowship which commences in this present life and reaches maturation in the hereafter when the faithful scale the Beatific Vision. We see here a radical difference in the two understandings of the spirit world, and obviously the New Testament has a new area to offer. But official Christian practice has lost the place of 'the Communion of Saints' in terms of fellowship between the departed and the living in Christ. It is here that the African background could be a source of revival for this otherwise legitimate (?) aspect of Christian Theology and living.

In terms of Time the Resurrection means a conscious awareness of being in the present dimension of Time, which in the Resurrection mode is tantamount to the presence of God. Thus the past gives up its contents of History, and the future brings its promises into a realization. This is a process activated in and by Jesus Christ, starting with the Easter Event. It is to be completed or consummated at the Parousia—the presence—of Christ, in a phenomenon which supersedes the dimensions of Time and Space. We saw nothing in African religiosity to parallel this, and in this or any other religious background the Resurrection must constitute the uniqueness of the Christian hope of the hereafter. It is a Resurrection to full participation in the divine nature, the ultimate stage of being incorporated into Christ. The details of that Resurrection life evade even theological discussion, let alone scientific description. The End is a teleological End according to New Testament Theology, which means a corporate and conscious participation in the presence and nature of God, 'when' (or 'where') man and the cosmos in Christ are freed from deprivation of being and expectation, from death and promise, from corruption (destruction) and creation. For that is the mode of existence in which we in Christ will have received and attained to all that summarily has been promised us in Him: the mode in Christ in which there is absolutely no beyond for us to become. The Resurrection, therefore, sums up all things in Christ as both the Alpha and the Omega.

One of the intentions of this study was to raise the question regarding Christian Theology in Africa. African Theology, as it now begins to be called, is increasingly being discussed, and one might be allowed to make a few observations here, though obviously this is a topic which deserves a separate, fuller and more detailed treatment. It is all too easy to use the phrase 'African Theology', but to state exactly what that means, or even to show its real nature, is an entirely different issue. And certainly it cannot be expected that such a Theology would be uniform throughout the continent of Africa. Theological systems and schools of thought will, let us hope, emerge, and it is these, rather than a single static system, which together may constitute *Theologia Africana*. What it will be, when it is, cannot be mapped out in advance like the path of an earth satellite.

Sundkler sees this Theology as an engagement in the fact of Christ: 'theology in Africa has to interpret this Christ in terms that are relevant and essential to African existence . . . In Africa the same Christ, the King, proves Himself to be the Life and the Fulness with power to liberate from sickness and death and devil'. He tells us that such a Theology 'must needs start with the fundamental facts of the

African interpretation of existence and the universe'. So he goes on to discuss what he calls 'the links with the beginning' and 'the links with the living and the dead', the worshipping community, and 'the pastor' as the 'mid-man'.[1] Sundkler certainly touches upon important points, but it seems rather contradictory that, having advocated the fact of the Christ, he departs in favour of mythical beginnings and links with the departed. He concentrates, in fact, on man both in his mythological origins and his present social structure. Is not this, then, an anthropological Theology? Strictly speaking, *Theo-logy* has to do primarily with God, and all other things must spring from that. If African Theology starts with, or even concentrates upon, anthropology, it loses its perspectives and can no longer be regarded as Theology.

Barrett sees the movement of the Independent Churches as bringing into being an area of African Theology. One might call this the Theology of Ecclesiastical Protest. According to him, these Independent Churches constitute an African Reformation and it is out of this that 'an African Theology emerges'. We may seriously question the term 'African Reformation', but Barrett makes a contribution in pin-pointing for us areas of African Churchmanship where, primarily unconsciously, theological activities are at work. These take on the form or sense of the Church (the Independent group) as a community relatively small for the members to cultivate and maintain a knowledge of one another, 'a warm philadelphia' among themselves and a face-to-face relationship. Barrett observes that these Independent Churches 'have patterned themselves after the existing social structure of contemporary tribes and societies . . . Their communities, therefore, resemble the familiar patterns of present-day African society far more than the larger Europeanized mission churches'. It is in this way that they accommodate men in their different situations of life. These communities allow for the laity to play their full part. They are also outward-looking. These then are the main insights of 'this emerging African theology [which] is still to a large extent inarticulate', as Barrett sees them.[2] But we can hardly regard this as anything more than a Theology of Churchmanship as lived and experienced by Independent Churches which are, nevertheless, a significant aspect of modern Christianity in Africa.

[1] B. G. M. Sundkler, *The Christian Ministry in Africa* (1960), 281 ff.
[2] D. B. Barrett, *Schism and Renewal in Africa* (1968), 169 ff.

H. Bürkle is keen to see an indigenous Theology arising out of the situation in Africa. He believes that Africa has sufficient heritage to get this Theology off the ground. He demonstrates this by the wide range of subjects covered in the book he has edited, with contributions from both Africans and expatriates. Half of the book, *Theologie und Kirche in Afrika* (1968), is devoted to African heritage in terms of culture, concepts of God, sacrifice, *rites de passage*, magic and witchcraft. The second part covers what he calls theological issues like Church and culture, history and community, ethics, African soul and Church services (worship), and the problem of the so-called 'brideprice'. It is hard to consider some of these themes as theological; the wide variety of themes and contributors makes it even harder for one to see a theological whole. The editor's introduction is all too brief, though we take note of his observation that the Church and Theology must belong together and that there is much scope for interdisciplinary work. But to what extent an interdisciplinary pursuit can bear theological character and fruit waits to be seen.

The first African theologian of our time to publish a substantial study in the area of indigenous Theology to my knowledge is H. Sawyerr, in *Creative Evangelism: Towards a New Christian Encounter with Africa* (1968). In this relatively short book, Sawyerr searches for theological understanding of Christian truths viewed from an African background. Perhaps the book is too ambitious in its wide coverage, but it is nevertheless a serious attempt to see Christianity accommodated in the traditional African framework of religion and thought. He finds points of contact between biblical and African understanding of themes like God and Creation, Jesus and the great family of the Church and immortality. Of special importance is the chapter on liturgy, in which (though not very successfully) he tries to show how, with regard to the ideas of God, spirits and worship, African background could be transformed into Christian understanding and practice. He puts the Eucharist in the centre of all this. Certainly not everyone will go along with Sawyerr all the way, and indeed some of his suggestions sound more theoretical or academic than practical, but he is saying something and is exploring an area which ought to have been explored long before now. He is here advocating what I would term Contact Theology, a Theology built upon areas of apparent similarities and contact between Christianity and traditional African concepts and practices. I am not convinced that there is a specifically African Theology in this book, but the author genuinely pleads for it even if he does not let it germinate in this conscious attempt.

A second African theologian who needs to be mentioned here is E. B. Idowu who, in his little book, *Towards an Indigenous Church* (1965), attempts to show his theological ideas of the Church on African soil (Nigeria, in this case). Of particular significance are his ideas of the meaning of 'Indigenization', which is one of the theological problems facing the Church in Africa. He expounds this in terms of the Bible, the language of Evangelism, Theology and Liturgy. He rightly bewails the fact that, after more than a hundred years of Christianity in Nigeria, the Church there 'has not developed a theology which bears the distinctive stamp of Nigerian thinking and meditation. Theologically she has been spoonfed by Europeans all along' (p. 22). And surely this is the lament which could be applied everywhere in African countries where Christianity has come via Europe or America.

And so the search goes on for an African Theology, but whatever its results they will not descend on a plate from the sky. Most embarrassingly, the very Church which has produced the majority of present-day African leaders and thinkers has itself hardly any theologians whether African or expatriate. The tragedy goes further back, in that, with only a few exceptions, missionaries who established Christianity in the past one hundred to two hundred years have not been theologians. The Church has now come into existence evangelistically but not theologically. At this date, 1968, we cannot count more than about half a dozen African theologians engaged in theological output (teaching, preaching and writing). This grim picture, however, now begins to take on a different and more hopeful look. Theological seminaries and colleges are being established all over the continent, with their academic standards similarly being raised; in several leading African universities, departments of Religious Studies have been or are being established, in which research and the study of Religion and Philosophy can be undertaken. But unlike many such departments in Europe or America, in these African universities at least three religious traditions are studied side by side, namely: Christianity, Islam, and African Traditional Religions. Each of these can rightly claim to be 'indigenous' in Africa, and certainly each makes its contribution to the life and thinking of the peoples of Africa. These departments of Religious Studies are clearly crucial places for a serious academic engagement, and no doubt any so-called African Theology must come through them.

What, then, might constitute this *Theologia Africana*? I see four areas which variously have to make their contributions towards an evolution of Theology in Africa.

(a) Biblical Theology must be the basis of any theological reflection, otherwise we shall lose our perspectives and may not claim the outcome to be Christian Theology. Here we have a rich heritage of scholarship handed down through the ages and by many Christian traditions. But such Biblical Theology will have to reflect the African situation and understanding if it is to be an original contribution to the Theology of the Church Universal.

(b) Christian Theology from the major traditions of Christendom will put us in the mainstream of ecumenical and apostolic heritage, so that we are not isolated from the Catholicity of the Church. Perhaps one drawback here is that theological seminaries and colleges in Africa are content to be fed with only this aspect of Theology, a factor that Idowu so rightly laments. Christian Theology, too, must be understood in and translated into the African milieu, if it is not to remain foreign and irrelevant to the Church in Africa.

(c) A study of African Religions and Philosophy must be taken more seriously than has hitherto been the case. It is here that we can expect a fruitful and living dialogue between Christianity and African religiosity. This is what Sawyerr has attempted to explore; and J. V. Taylor's book, *The Primal Vision* (1963), is addressed to the same problem. In a limited way I have also searched for this kind of dialogue in this work. It is here too that we must seriously ask ourselves to what extent the Christian Message as embodied in Christ Himself could be seen as a fulfilment of African religiosity. Similarly, how far can we, or should we, regard African religiosity as a *praeparatio evangelica?* It is not enough to answer these questions with one or two sentences. More study and research are obviously necessary, for the field is vast and excitingly promising. It is here (and in the next area) that we shall probably begin to discern a uniquely African contribution to Christian Theology at large. It is also probably here that the theological outcome will determine the most suitable structures of the Church and its Ministry in Africa.

In this section we must take note also of the presence of Islam in Africa, and its deep historical and cultural roots. A Christian dialogue with Islam is long overdue, and Africa perhaps more than any other continent, presents us with a unique opportunity for studying this dialogue and encounter. Already we see the two religious traditions being studied in departments of Religious Studies, but the actual encounter of the two Faiths has to be taken much further academically. Exactly whether or not such a study will contribute towards an African Theology it is too early to say; but it is a background which cannot be ignored.

Finally (d), there is the Theology of the living Church as it expands in its Life and Mission in African societies. This is what will test whether or not Theology is relevant to a given community and at a given time. It is here that we must appreciate the Church's concern for, and engagement in, the needs of its various communities. Here we see the Church in its six thousand Independent Churches and religious movements, so ably drawn to our attention by Barrett, and about which there is a vast literature. It is here, too, that we see the Church in areas of conflict, tension and revolution; the Church in industrial centres, in the slums, in the villages, in schools and hospitals, in refugee work; the Church ministering to the poor and the rich in our cities and towns, engaged in literature and radio and television work, in missionary and evangelistic work; the Church looking both inward and outward, being rejected, opposed and even persecuted; but as the Church, loving, forgiving, reconciling, worshipping and living. Thus, the Church as the Body of Christ must be its own major theological theme, in all situations, in all places and at all times, otherwise it ceases to exist, it ceases to make its presence and message relevant, and it runs aground in the stream of human History.

These then are areas of theological reflection for and in the Church in Africa. The carrying out of this task has hardly begun, but pointing it out at least makes the challenge urgent and stimulating. So long as the Church in Africa is unaware of its theological task, that task will remain undone. Prayer and piety alone will not do the task, which rightly belongs to the realm of Theology. And this task is sufficiently vast for theologians of every calibre to attempt it. Whether the resulting outcome will be African Theology, or African schools of Theology, is immaterial at this stage. In any case, the final test for the validity and usefulness of any theological contribution is Jesus Christ. Since His Incarnation, Christian Theology ought properly to be Christology, for Theology falls or stands on how it understands, translates and interprets Jesus Christ, at a given Time, Place and human situation.

What in this book I have attempted to do is no more than discuss New Testament Eschatology as an aspect of christological Theology. That, I believe, is where Christian Theology starts and where it ends. May the Lord have mercy on me and forgive me for engaging in this theological task so feebly and so inadequately.

Select Bibliography

NB. The bulk of bibliographical reference is given in the footnotes, and of the journals only a few are included here.

(a) *Akamba and Relevant African Studies*

A.I.M., *A Catechism of Christian teaching in the Kamba language* (Nairobi, n.d.); *Africa Inland Church: Constitution, rules and regulations* (Kijabe, 1954); *Kikamba–English dictionary* (Kijabe, 1939).

BAËTA, C. G., ed., *Christianity in tropical Africa* (Oxford/London, 1968).

BARRETT, D. B., *Schism and renewal in Africa* (Oxford/Nairobi, 1968); ed., *African initiatives in religion* (Nairobi, 1969).

BRUTZER, E., *Begegnungen mit Wakamba* (Leipzig, 1902); *Der Geisterglaube bei den Kamba* (Leipzig, 1905).

BÜRKLE, H., *Theologie und Kirche in Afrika* (Stuttgart, 1968).

BÜTTNER, C. G., 'Deutsch Ki-Kamba Wörterbuch,' *Zeitschrift für Afrikanische Sprachen* (1888).

DANQUAH, J. B., *The Akan doctrine of God* (London, 1944).

DUNDAS, C., 'History of Kitui', *JRAI*, Vol. XLIII (1913), pp. 480–549; 'The organizations and laws of some Bantu tribes in East Africa', *JRAI*, Vol. XLV (1915), pp. 234–306.

EVANS-PRITCHARD, E. E., *Nuer Religion* (Oxford/London, 1956).

FARNSWORTH, E. M., *A Kamba grammar* (Kijabe, 1954).

FORDE, D., ed., *African Worlds* (Oxford/London, 1954).

FORTES, M. and DIETERLEN, G., eds., *African systems of thought* (Oxford/London, 1965).

GOODY, J., *Death, property and the ancestors* (London, 1962).

HASTINGS, A., *Church and mission in modern Africa* (London, 1967).

HILDEBRANDT, J. M., 'Ethnographische Notizen über Wakamba und ihre Nachbarn', *Zeitschrift für Ethnologie*, X (1878), pp. 347–406.

HOBLEY, C. W., *Ethnology of the A-kamba and other East African tribes* (Cambridge, 1910); *Bantu beliefs and magic* (London, 1922).

HOFMANN, J., *Geburt, Heirat und Tod bei den Wakamba* (Leipzig, 1901); *Wörterbuch der Kambasprache, Kamba-Deutsch* (Leipzig, 1901).

HOLY GHOST FATHERS, *Catechism* (Kikamba) (Nairobi, 3rd ed., 1961).

IDOWU, E. B., *Olodumare: God in Yoruba belief* (London, 1962); *Towards an indigenous Church* (Oxford/London, 1965).

KANIG, G., *Dornige Pfade eines jungen Missionars in Ukamba* (Leipzig, 1902).

KENYATTA, J., *Facing Mount Kenya* (London, 1938).

KIMILU, D. N., *Mukamba Wa Wo* (Nairobi, 1962); 'The Separatist Churches', in *Dini na Mila: revealed religion and traditional custom* (Makerere), Vol. 3, No. 2/3 (Dec. 1967), pp. 11–61.

KRAPF, J. L., *Vocabulary of six East-African languages* (Tübingen, 1850); *Travels, researches and missionary labours* (London, 1860).

LARBY, N., *The Kamba* (Nairobi, 1944).

LIENHARDT, G., *Divinity and experience: the religion of the Dinka* (Oxford/London, 1961).

LINDBLOM, G., *The Akamba in British East Africa* (Uppsala, 1920); *Kamba folklore, I: Tales of animals* (Uppsala, 1928); *Kamba riddles, proverbs and songs* (Uppsala, 1934); *Kamba folklore, II: Tales of supernatural beings and adventures* (Uppsala, 1935).

MBITI, J. S., *English–Kamba vocabulary* (Nairobi, 1959); *Akamba stories* (Oxford/London, 1966); 'Afrikanische Verständnis der Geister im Lichte des Neuen Testamentes', in *Theologische Stimmen aus Asien, Afrika und Lateinamerika*, ed. G. Rosenkranz (München, 1967), Vol. II, pp. 130–47; 'Eschatologie und Jenseitsglaube', in H. Bürkle, ed., *Theologie und Kirche in Afrika* (Stuttgart, 1968), pp. 211–35; *African Religions and Philosophy* (London, 1969); *Concepts of God in Africa* (London, 1970).

MIDDLETON, J., *Lugbara religion* (Oxford/London, 1960).

MIDDLETON, J., and KERSHAW, G., *The Kikuyu and Kamba of Kenya* (London, 1965) (with full bibliography to date).

MIDDLETON, J., and WINTER, E. H., *Witchcraft and sorcery in East Africa* (London, 1963).

PARRINDER, E. G., *African traditional religion* (2nd ed., London, 1962); *West African Religion* (2nd ed., London, 1961).

PENWILL, D. J., *Kamba customary law* (London, 1950).

RUSSELL, J. K., *Men without God?* (London, 1966).

SAWYERR, H., *Creative evangelism: towards a new Christian encounter with Africa* (London, 1968).

SMITH, E. W., ed., *African ideas of God* (rev. ed., London, 1961).

SMITH, W. R., *The Religion of the Semites* (London, 1894).

SUNDKLER, B. G. M., *Bantu prophets in South Africa* (London, 1948); *The Christian Ministry in Africa* (London, 1960).

TANNER, R. E. S., *Transition in African belief* (Maryknoll, New York, 1967).

TAYLOR, J. V., *The growth of the Church in Buganda* (London, 1958); *The primal vision* (London, 1963).

TURNER, H. W., *Profile through preaching* (London, 1965).

WATT, S., *Vocabulary of the Ki-Kamba language* (Philadelphia, 1900).

WELBOURN, F. B., *East African rebels* (London, 1961).

WELBOURN, F. B., and OGOT, B. A., *A place to feel at home* (Oxford/London, 1966).

WHITELEY, W. H., and MULI, M. G., *Practical introduction to Kamba* (Oxford, 1962).

WILLIAMSON, S. G., *Akan religion and the Christian faith* (Accra, 1965).

(b) New Testament and Christian Eschatology

AUGUSTINE, ST. A., *De Civitate Dei*, and *Confessions*.

BAAR, H. de, *The Bible on the final coming* (ET Notre Dame, 1965).

BADCOCK, F. J., 'Sanctorum Communio as an article in the creed', in *JTS*, Vol. XXI (1919–20), pp. 106–26.

BAILLIE, D. M., *The theology of the sacraments and other papers* (London, 1957).

BAILLIE, J., *And the life everlasting* (Oxford, 1934); *The belief in progress* (Oxford, 1950).

BARCLAY, W., 'Eschatology and the individual', *LQHR* (July 1960), pp. 186–90.

BARR, J., *Biblical words for time* (London, 1962).

BARRETT, C. K., 'New Testament eschatology', *SJT*, Vol. 6, No. 2 (June 1953), pp. 136–55, and No. 3 (Sept. 1953), pp. 225–43; 'The Eschatology of the epistle to the Hebrews', in the *Dodd Festschrift* (Cambridge, 1956), pp. 363–93; 'Immortality and resurrection', *LQHR*, Vol. 34, No. 2 (1965), pp. 91–102.

BARTH, K., *The resurrection of the dead* (ET London, 1933); *Credo* (ET London, 1936).

BEASLEY-MURRAY, G. R., *Jesus and the future* (London, 1954); *Baptism in the New Testament* (London, 1962); *Baptism today and tomorrow* (London, 1966).

BERDYAEV, N., *The end of our time* (ET London, 1935).

BLACK, M., 'The Eschatology of the similitudes of Enoch', *JTS*, new series, III (1952), pp. 1–10.

BORNKAMM, G., *Jesus of Nazareth* (ET London, 1960).

BOWMAN, A. A., *A sacramental universe* (Oxford, 1939).

BRABANT, F. H., *Time and eternity in Christian thought* (London, 1937).

BRUNNER, E., *Eternal life* (ET London, 1954).

BRUNS, J. E., 'The use of time in the Fourth Gospel', *NTS*, Vol. XIII, No. 3 (1967), pp. 285–90.

BULTMANN, R., *Theology of the New Testament* (ET London, Vol. I, 1952; Vol. II, 1955); 'History and eschatology in the N.T.', *NTS*, Vol. I, No. 1 (Sept. 1954), pp. 5–16; *History and eschatology* (Edinburgh, 1957); *Geschichte und Eschatologie* (Tübingen, 1964) (updating above).

BUTTERFIELD, H., *Christianity and history* (London, 1949).

CADBURY, H. J., 'Acts and eschatology', in the *Dodd Festschrift* (Cambridge, 1956), pp. 300–21.

CADOUX, C. J., *The historic mission of Jesus* (London, 1941).

CAIRD, G. B., *Principalities and powers* (Oxford, 1956).

CAMPBELL, J. Y., 'The kingdom of God has come, *Ex T*, Vol. XLVIII, No. 2 (Nov. 1936), pp. 91–4.

CHARLES, R. H., *Eschatology: Hebrew, Jewish and Christian* (London, 1899).

CLARK, K. W., 'Realized eschatology, *JBL*, Vol. LIX (1940), pp. 367–83.

CLARK, N., *An approach to the theology of the sacraments* (London, 1956); *Interpreting the resurrection* (London, 1967).

CLAVIER, H., 'Breves Remarques sur la Notion de σῶμα πνευματικόν', in the *Dodd Festschrift* (Cambridge, 1956).

COMBLIN, J., *The resurrection in the plan of salvation* (ET Notre Dame, 1965).

CONZELMANN, H., *Die Mitte der Zeit* (Tübingen, 5th ed., 1964; ET *The theology of St. Luke*, London/New York, 1960).

CORNELIS, H., and others, *The resurrection of the body* (ET Notre Dame, 1964).

CULLMANN, O., *Baptism in the New Testament* (ET London, 1950); *Christ and time* (ET London, 1951); 'Eschatology and missions in the New Testament', in the *Dodd Festschrift* (Cambridge, 1956), pp. 409–21; *The State in the New Testament* (London, 1957); *Immortality of the soul or resurrection of the dead?* (London, 1958).

DAHL, M. E., *The resurrection of the body* (London, 1962).

DARRAGH, J. T., *The resurrection of the flesh* (London, 1921).

DAVIES, J. G., *He ascended into Heaven* (London, 1958).

DAVIES, W.D., and DAUBE, D., eds., *The background of the New Testament and its eschatology* (the *Dodd Festschrift* Cambridge, 1956).

DEWICK, E. C., *Primitive Christian eschatology* (Cambridge, 1912).

DIX, G., *The Shape of the Liturgy* (London, 1943).

DODD, C. H., 'The this-worldly kingdom of God in our Lord's teaching', *Theology*, Vol. XIV, No. 83 (May, 1927), pp. 258–60; *The Parables of the kingdom* (London, 1935); *The apostolic preaching and its developments* (London, 1936); 'The mind of Paul', *BJRL*, Vol. 20, No. 1 (Jan. 1936); *N.T. Studies* (Manchester, 1953) (with T. W. Manson).

EITREM, S., *Some notes on the demonology of the New Testament* (Oslo, 1950).

ELLIS, E. E., 'II Corinthians V: 1–10 in Pauline eschatology', *NTS*, Vol. VI, No. 3 (April, 1960), pp. 211–24; 'The present and future eschatology in Luke', *NTS*, Vol. XII, No. 1 (1965), pp. 27-41.

EVANS, P. W., *Sacraments in the New Testament* (London, 1947).

EVERY, G., *Lamb to the slaughter* (London, 1957); *The Baptismal sacrifice* (London, 1959).

FISON, J. E., *The Christian hope* (London, 1954).

FLEMINGTON, W. F., *The New Testament doctrine of Baptism* (London, 1948).

FORSYTH, P. T., *The Church and the sacraments* (London, 1917).

GALLOWAY, A. D., *The cosmic Christ* (London, 1951).

GEORGE, A. R., *Communion with God in the New Testament* (London, 1953).

GLASSON, T. F., *The Second Advent* (London, 1945); *His appearing and His kingdom* (London, 1953); *Greek influence in Jewish eschatology* (London, 1961).

GRÄSSER, E., *Das Problem der Perusieverzögerung in den Synoptischen Evangelien und in der Apostelgeschichte* (Berlin, 1960).

GUARDINI, R., *The Last Things* (ET London, 1954).

GUY, H. A., *The New Testament doctrine of the 'Last Things'—a study of eschatology* (Oxford, 1948).

HAMILTON, N. Q., *The Holy Spirit and eschatology in Paul* (Edinburgh, 1957).

HEITMÜLLER, W., *Taufe und Abendmahl bei Paulus* (Göttingen, 1903).

HETTLINGER, R. F., '2 Cor. 5: 1–10', *SJT*, Vol. 10, No. 2 (June, 1957), pp. 174–94.

HIGGINS, A. J. B., *The Lord's Supper in the New Testament* (London, 1952); 'The origins of the eucharist', *NTS*, Vol. I, No. 3 (Feb. 1955), pp. 200–9.

HOLMSTRÖM, F., *Das eschatologische Denken der Gegenwart* (Gütersloh, 1936).

HOOKE, S. H., *The resurrection of Christ as history and experience* (London, 1967).

JEREMIAS, J., *The parables of Jesus* (ET London, 1954); *The eucharistic words of Jesus* (ET Oxford, 1955); 'Flesh and blood cannot inherit the kingdom of God (I Cor. 15: 50)', *NTS*, Vol. II, No. 3 (Feb. 1956), pp. 151–9; *Infant baptism in the first four centuries* (ET London, 1960).

KENNEDY, H. A. A., *St. Paul's conception of the Last Things* (London, 1904).

KIRK, K. E., *The vision of God* (London, 1931).

KITTEL, G., ed. *Theologisches Wörterbuch zum Neuen Testament* (Tübingen, 1933 ff.) (continued under G. Friedrich).

KNOX, W. L., *St. Paul and the Church of the Gentiles* (Cambridge, 1939).

KÖRNER, J., *Eschatologie und Geschichte* (Hamburg, 1957).

KRECK, W., *Die Zukunft des Gekommenen: Grundprobleme der Eschatologie* (München, 1961).

KÜMMEL, W. G., *Promise and Fulfilment* (ET London, 1957); 'Futurische und Präsentische Eschatologie im Ältesten Urchristentum', *NTS*, Vol. V, No. 2 (Jan. 1959), pp. 113–26.

KÜNNETH, W., *The theology of the resurrection* (ET St. Louis, 1966).

LADD, G. E., *Jesus and the kingdom. The eschatology of biblical realism* (New York/London, 1964).

LAMPE, G. W. H., *The seal of the spirit* (London, 1951); 'Early patristic eschatology', in *SJT Occasional Papers*, No. 2 (Edinburgh and London, 1952), pp. 17–35; 'The place of confirmation in the baptismal mystery,

JTS, new series, Vol. VI (1955), pp. 110–16; *I Believe* (London, 1960); 'Eschatology' (editorial), *LQHR* (July, 1960), pp. 161–6.

LAMPE, G. W. H., and MACKINNON, D. M., *The Resurrection* (London, 1966).

LANGTON, E., *Good and evil spirits* (London, 1942); *Essentials of demonology* (London, 1949).

LEEMING, B., *Principles of sacramental theology* (London, 1956).

LING, T., *The significance of Satan* (London, 1961).

LOHSE, E., 'Wort und Sakrament in Johannesevangelium', *NTS*, Vol. VII, No. 2 (Jan., 1961), pp. 110–25.

LOSSKY, V., *The mystical theology of the eastern Church* (ET London, 1957).

MACCOWN, C. C., 'The eschatology of Jesus reconsidered', *JR*, Vol. XVI (1936), pp. 30–45.

MACGREGOR, G. H. C., 'Principalities and powers: the cosmic background of St. Paul's thought', *NTS*, Vol. I, No. 1 (Sept. 1954), pp. 17–28.

MACKINNON, D. M., 'Sacrament and common meal', essay in *Studies in the gospels* (in memory of R. H. Lightfoot, ed. D. E. Nineham) (Oxford, 1955), pp. 201–8.

MANSON, T. W., *The teaching of Jesus* (Cambridge, 1931); 'The sayings of Jesus' (in *The mission and message of Jesus*, with H. D. A. Major and C. J. Wright) (London, 1937); 'Realized eschatology and the Messianic secret', essay in *Studies in the gospels* (*supra*) (Oxford, 1955), pp. 209–22.

MANSON, W., 'Eschatology in the New Testament', in *SJT Occasional Papers*, No. 2 (Edinburgh and London, 1952), pp. 1–16.

MARSH, H. G., *The origin and significance of the New Testament baptism* (Manchester, 1941).

MARSH, J., *The Fulness of Time* (London, 1952).

MARSHALL, I. H., *Eschatology and the parables* (London, 1963).

MCLEMAN, J., *Resurrection then and now* (London, 1965).

MERSCH, E., *The Whole Christ* (ET Milwaukee, 1938).

MOLTMANN, J., *Theologie der Hoffnung* (München, 1965; ET, *Theology of hope*, London, 1967).

MOODY, D., *The Hope of Glory* (Grand Rapids, 1964).

MOORE, A. L., *The parousia in the New Testament* (Leiden, 1966).

MORRISON, C. D., *The powers that be* (London, 1960).

MOULE, C. F. D., 'The judgment theme in the sacraments', essay in the *Dodd Festschrift* (Cambridge, 1956), pp. 464–81; 'A reconsideration of the context of maranatha', *NTS*, Vol. VI, No. 4 (July, 1960), pp. 307–10; *Worship in the New Testament* (London, 1961); *The birth of the New Testament* (London, 1962); 'The influence of circumstances on the use of eschatological terms', *JTS*, Vol. XV, No. 1 (1964), pp. 1–15; (ed.) *The significance of the message of the resurrection for faith in Jesus* (London, 1968).

MUIRHEAD, L. A., *The Eschatology of Jesus* (London, 1904).

14

MUSSNER, F., *Christ and the end of the world* (Notre Dame, 1965).

NIEBUHR, R., *The nature and destiny of man*, Vol. II (New York, 1947).

NINEHAM, D. E., ed., *Studies in the gospels*, in memory of R. H. Lightfoot (Oxford, 1955).

NOCK, A. D., *Conversion* (Oxford, 1933).

OESTERLEY, W. O. E., *Immortality and the Unseen World* (London, 1921).

ORR, J., *The resurrection of Jesus* (Grand Rapids, 1965; rep. of 1908).

OTTO, R., *The kingdom of God and the Son of man* (ET London, 1938).

PEDERSEN, J., *Israel: its life and culture* (Copenhagen, Vols. I–II, 1926; III–IV, 1940).

PERRIN, N., *The kingdom of God in the teaching of Jesus* (London, 1963).

PIEPER, J., *Ober das Ende der Zeit* (1950).

PILCHER, C. V., *The hereafter in Jewish and Christian thought* (London, 1940).

QUICK, O. C., *The Christian Sacraments* (London, 1927).

QUISTORP, H., *Calvin's doctrine of the Last Things* (ET London, 1955).

RAMM, B., *Them He glorified. A systematic study of the Doctrine of Glorification* (Grand Rapids, 1963).

RAMSEY, A. M., *The resurrection of Christ* (London, 1945); *The Glory of God and the transfiguration of Christ* (London, 1949).

RAMSEY, I. T., and others, *The miracles and the resurrection: some recent studies* (London, 1964).

RICCA, P., *Die Eschatogie des Vierten Evangeliums* (Zürich/Frankfurt, 1966).

RICHARDSON, A., *An Introduction to the Theology of the New Testament* (London, 1958).

ROBINSON, J. A. T., *In the end, God . . .* (London, 1950); *The body* (London, 1952); *Jesus and His coming* (London, 1957); *Twelve New Testament studies* (London, 1962); 'Resurrection', article in *The Interpreter's Dictionary of the Bible*, ed. G. A. Buttrick, etc. (New York, 1962), Vol. IV, pp. 39–53.

ROBINSON, J. M., *A new quest of the historical Jesus* (London, 1959).

ROBINSON, W. C., *Der Weg des Herrn. Studien zur Geschichte und Eschatologie im Lukas-Evangelium. Ein Gespräch mit Hans Conzelmann* (Hamburg, 1964).

ROWLEY, H. H., *The relevance of apocalyptic* (London, 1944); 'The baptism of John and the Qumran Sect', essay in *New Testament essays*, ed. A. J. B. Higgins, in memory of T. W. Manson (Manchester, 1959).

SALMOND, S. D. F., *Christian doctrine of immortality* (Edinburgh, 1895).

SCHEP, J. A., *The nature of the resurrection body: a study of biblical data* (Grand Rapids, 1964).

SCHNACKENBURG, R., *God's rule and kingdom* (ET London, 1964).

SCHOEPS, H. J., *Paul: the theology of the apostle in the light of Jewish religious history* (ET, London 1961).

SCHUBERT, K., ed., *Vom Messias zum Christus. Die Fülle der Zeit in religionsgeschichtlicher und theologischer Sicht* (Wien/Freiburg, 1964).

SCHWEITZER, A., *The quest of the historical Jesus* (ET London, 1910); *The mystery of the kingdom of God* (ET London, 1925); *The mysticism of Paul the apostle* (ET London, 1931).

SCHWEIZER, E., *Erniedrigung und Erhöhung bei Jesus und seinen Nachfolgern* (Zürich, 1962).

SELWYN, E. G., 'Eschatology in I Peter,' essay in the *Dodd Festschrift* (Cambridge, 1956), pp. 394–401.

SEVENSTER, J. N., 'Some remarks on the ΓΥΜΝΟΣ, II Cor. 5: 3', essay in *Studia Paulina*, ed. Sevenster and W. C. van Unnik (Haarlem, 1953).

SHIRES, H. M., *The eschatology of Paul in the light of modern scholarship* (Philadelphia, 1966).

SIMON, U., *Heaven in the Christian tradition* (London, 1958); *The end is not yet* (London, 1964).

SMITH, C. R., *The Bible doctrine of the hereafter* (London, 1958).

STACEY, W. D., *The Pauline view of man* (London, 1957).

STANLEY, D. M., *Christ's resurrection in Pauline soteriology* (Rome, 1961).

STAUFFER, E., *New Testament Theology* (ET London, 1955).

STEWART, R. A., *Rabbinic Theology* (London, 1961).

STIBBS, A. M., *Sacrament, sacrifice and eucharist* (London, 1961).

STRAWSON, W., *Jesus and the future life* (Philadelphia, 1959).

Symposium on Eschatology, JBL, Vol. XLI (1922), pp. 1–204.

TAYLOR, A. E., *The Christian hope of immortality* (London, 1938).

THORNTON, L. S., *The common life in the body of Christ* (London, 1941).

THURIAN, M., *The eucharistic memorial* (ET London, Vol. I, 1960; Vol. II, 1961).

TORRANCE, T. F., 'The eschatology of the Reformation', in *SJT Occasional Papers*, No. 2 (London and Edinburgh, 1952), pp. 36–62; 'Proselyte baptism', *NTS*, Vol. I, No. 2 (Sept. 1954), pp. 150–4; *Conflict and Agreement in the Church*, Vol. II (London, 1960).

VON DOBSCHÜTZ, E., *The eschatology of the gospels* (London, 1910).

VON HÜGEL, F., *Eternal life* (Edinburgh, 1912).

VOS, G., *Pauline eschatology* (Michigan, 1952).

WESTCOTT, B. F., *The gospel of the resurrection* (London, 1874).

WILDER, A. N., *Eschatology and ethics in the teaching of Jesus* (London, 1950 rev.); 'Kerygma, eschatology and social ethics,' essay in the *Dodd Festschrift* (Cambridge, 1956); 'Eschatological imagery and earthly circumstance', *NTS*, Vol. V, No. 4 (July, 1959), pp. 229–45.

INDEX OF AUTHORS

INDEX OF SUBJECTS

INDEX OF BIBLICAL AND OTHER REFERENCES

For index of early Christian writers see under index of authors